THE
MUSTARD
SEED
CONSPIRACY

You Can Make
a Difference
in Tomorrow's
Troubled World

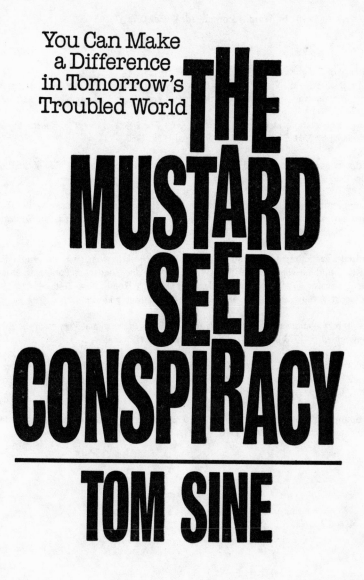

THE MUSTARD SEED CONSPIRACY

TOM SINE

WORD BOOKS
PUBLISHER
WACO, TEXAS

THE MUSTARD SEED CONSPIRACY

Dedication

This book is dedicated to Navie Sotr. Navie died on June 4, 1981, the same day this book was completed. He was a ten-year-old refugee from Cambodia who came to the U.S. with his parents to receive treatment for his leukemia (see chapter 9). The doctors at Children's Orthopedic Hospital successfully treated his leukemia, and it went into remission, but a virulent infection he brought with him from Thailand failed to respond to treatment or the most earnest prayers of Christians in the Seattle area.

Those of us who sponsored the family had come to love Navie very much . . . his flashing dark eyes, his quick smile, his eagerness for life. We had planned to do so many things with him and his parents when he got out of the hospital. It was extremely hard for us to let go of Navie, and even harder for his folks as we lived through this painful tragedy together. But we are thankful that Navie is now with the Father who loves him.

This book is dedicated to all the Navies of the world. The small ones, the voiceless ones whom we can neither see nor hear . . . who die silently and too often alone. This book is written with an earnest prayer that God's kingdom will come and his will be done among the small ones, the helpless and forgotten ones who have already suffered far more than anyone should.

Acknowledgments

This small book was the work of many hands and the consequence of many prayers. I particularly am grateful to those in my small community group who struggled through the entire process with me: Tim and Kerry Dearborn, Roger and Astrid Feldman, and Hal and Sheila Mischke. Lorraine and Arak Shakarian's generous editorial assistance helped me pull all the pieces together. I am also indebted to Karen Adams for her editorial help. Dozens of individuals all over the country graciously read all or part of the manuscript in process. Their input was invaluable in improving the focus and flow of the book; unfortunately, space doesn't allow me to list all their names. JoAnne Whitney patiently retyped the manuscript more times than either of us care to remember, and I am grateful to her for her willing assistance. CRISTA/ World Concern was gracious enough to allow me a leave of absence and a flexible work schedule so I could write the book.

My parents have constantly encouraged me, and the wise counsel and loving support of my two sons, Tom and Clint, has enabled me to complete this project. As I finished this book, I also realized I am more indebted to my grandparents and to the great circle of those who preceded me than I had ever imagined.

I have had a strong sense that the One who is faithful was with me through this entire process. I sincerely hope and pray that this book will reflect something of his loving intentions for the human future and enable readers to more fully discover how they can be much more a part of his Mustard Seed Conspiracy that is changing his world!

TOM SINE

Contents

Foreword by Mark O. Hatfield   9

Foreword by Foy Valentine   10

1. The Mustard Seed Conspiracy   11
2. Awakening from the Western Dream—A World in Trauma   22
3. Awakening from the American Dream—A Nation in
   Transition   45
4. Awakening to the Great Escape, The Secular Agenda, and
   the American Dream   69
5. Awakening to the Present and Coming Future of God   90
6. Seeking First the Future of God through Creative Lifestyles   111
7. Seeking First the Future of God through Creative Vocation   134
8. Seeking First the Future of God through Creative Community   157
9. Seeking First the Future of God through Creative Mission
   to the One-Third World   182
10. Seeking First the Future of God with the Two-Thirds World   209

Epilogue: The Beginning of the Conspiracy of the Insignificant   235
Notes   240

Foreword

Be prepared to be changed. Then be prepared for God to use you to change the world.

By first debunking the mentality of apathy and passivity towards the world around us, Tom Sine then lays out what the world can expect for the eighties and the biblical response to those conditions. He raises the church's collective vision to see that He wants to use "insignificant people" to institute His righteousness throughout the world.

The Mustard Seed Conspiracy is about faithful Christians who are willing to seek His kingdom above all else. Whether it be in Washington, D.C., Jackson, Mississippi, or Haiti, God wants to use Christians to change the world around them. All that is required is a little creativity, a little vision and faith.

Being a victim of The Mustard Seed Conspiracy through the faithfulness of a sophomore student at Willamette University where I was Dean of Students, I have seen what God can do through faithful people. The student at that time had faith to believe my life could be used by God to affect people throughout the State of Oregon. Little did he know that his life would affect people throughout the world. God has used Doug Coe in astounding ways to touch the lives of members of Congress, ambassadors, and Presidents, as well as others who aren't so well known.

I also believe that The Mustard Seed Conspiracy can affect our stewardship of resources in this nation, helping us to recognize that we are the most wasteful nation in the world and that God has given us these resources to be shared. It will affect our attitude towards the tremendous commitment to defense spending by helping us to see how these monies can be much better used turning "swords into plowshares." Lastly, it will cause us to get on our knees to seek God as to how He wishes us to be used in changing the world.

My prayer is that all who read this book would be encouraged and challenged to believe that God "is able to do exceeding abundantly beyond all that we are able to ask or think, according to the power that works within us."

MARK O. HATFIELD

9

Foreword

The kingdom of heaven, Jesus once explained to his disciples, is like wheat and tares growing together in a field until the harvest when the wheat will be gathered into the barn and the tares burned (Matt. 13:24–30, 36–43). Christians today sometimes seem to fear that the whole field has gone to tares. Tom Sine reminds us in *The Mustard Seed Conspiracy* that the wheat is alive and well. This book is a book of hope. It tells how the wheat is growing. Moreover, in most delightfully concise and specific ways, it tells where the wheat is growing and explains how compassionate and celebrative modern disciples are making it grow.

The author writes out of his own clearly authentic Christian experience. He writes, too, out of a genuinely profound sense of Christian calling. He takes Jesus seriously; and he wants all Christians to take Jesus seriously so that an almost terrible earnestness permeates the book. There are, however, plenty of light moments occasioned by flashes of humor, illustrations, and refreshing spiritual oases. There is occasionally even an appropriate note of irreverence for some of today's sacred cows.

With exceptional clarity and persuasiveness, the author combines his special expertise as a futurist with a fine sense of history, an excellent grasp of theology and a refreshingly hopeful overview of how God's Mustard Seed Conspiracy is growing.

The author's quotations are fresh and appropriate. His special interests related to the future give the book an unusual aura of relevance.

With a prophet's heart and soul and mind and voice, Tom Sine decries the cultural seduction of the church. He tells Christians to reject "The Religion of America," reminding us that Jesus Christ never calls his disciples to be mere survivors. The future, he rightly insists, will belong to those who have the highest level of commitment. He therefore makes this book a powerful call for Christians to move forward with such commitment to claim the future, secure and confident in the knowledge that "the kingdoms of this world are become the kingdoms of our Lord, and of his Christ" (Rev. 11:15).

FOY VALENTINE

1.

The Mustard Seed Conspiracy

This book is an invitation to a celebration and an adventure. You are invited to join a growing number of brothers and sisters all over this planet in celebrating the good news that the new age of God is literally transforming this present age. You are invited to join them in the unprecedented adventure of allowing God to use your life to change his world. Perhaps you are already a part of the adventure, but you would like to become more aware of how God is conspiring through your life and the lives of others to make a difference in his world.

THE CONSPIRACY OF THE INSIGNIFICANT

Jesus let us in on an astonishing secret. God has chosen to change the world through the lowly, the unassuming, and the imperceptible. Jesus said, "With what can we compare the kingdom of God, or what parable shall we use for it? It is like a grain of mustard seed, which when sown upon the ground, is the smallest of all the seeds on earth; yet when it is sown it grows up and becomes the greatest of all shrubs, and puts forth large branches, so that the birds of the air can make nests in its shade" (Mark 4:30–32).

That has always been God's strategy—changing the world through the conspiracy of the insignificant. He chose a ragged bunch of Semite slaves to become the insurgents of his new order. He sent a vast army to flight with three hundred men carrying lamps and blowing horns. He chose an undersized shepherd boy with a slingshot to lead his chosen people. And who would have ever dreamed that God would choose to work through a baby in a cow stall to turn this world right side up! "God chose the foolish things of the world to shame the wise; God chose the weak things of the world to shame the strong. He chose the lowly things of this world and the despised things—and the things that are not—to nullify the things that are, so that no one may boast before him" (1 Cor. 1:27–29, NIV).

11

It is still God's policy to work through the embarrassingly insignificant to change his world and create his future. He has chosen to work
through the foolishness of human instrumentality. And he wants to
use your life and mine to make a difference in his world. Just as Jesus
invited that first unlikely bunch of fishermen, he invites us to drop
our nets and abandon our boats and join him in the adventure of changing the world.

He invites us to join the Mustard Seed Conspiracy.

Thousands have already set aside lesser agendas and responded wholeheartedly to the invitation of Jesus. God's loving conspiracy is already
breaking through their lives and communities as they proclaim good
news to the poor, release to the captives, recovery of sight to the blind
and freedom for those who are oppressed (Luke 4:18).

Recently I visited a small group of Christians who have responded
affirmatively to Christ's invitation and have planted a small seed in a
multiracial community in Berkeley, California. They left suburban
homes, jobs, and lifestyles and started the Bartimaeus Community in
this transitional neighborhood. God is using their lives not only to
influence their immediate area but to have a powerful impact on the
larger Christian community in the East Bay. They model lifestyles of
creative simplicity in order to free up time and resources for ministry
to the poor. They sponsor a daily Vacation Bible School during the
summer for kids in their neighborhood. Their peace mission group is
actively working in the Bay area to promote disarmament. Discipleship
education is their primary vehicle for influencing Christians in their
area to take their faith more seriously. Almost imperceptibly, God is
working through this small beginning to change people's lives, to challenge structures, and to bring his future.

In an impoverished working class community in Rio de Janeiro a
small plant is growing relatively unnoticed. Three sisters—Mary, Louise,
and Sara—have moved into this slum. Mary works twelve hours a
day in a sewing factory with the other women of the neighborhood.
The working conditions can only be described as abominable, but she
wants to share in the life of her neighbors. With her barely adequate
income, she supports the other two sisters, who train the people of
their neighborhood in matters of community health and provide legal
assistance. Mary, Louise, and Sara are not really aware of the way
God is using their small seeds of love to change his world.

Hilda is one of God's special plants. She is a seventy-two-year-old
Jewish Christian who lives in West Germany. Her home has become
a center of loving reconciliation that seems somehow to draw people
from everywhere. On any given day one can find an unlikely assortment
of people there: a young Arab studying theology in Berlin to prepare

himself to pastor an Arab Christian church in a strongly Muslim village in Israel. A young woman from Lima, Peru, who found her way back to God in Hilda's home only weeks before. A disillusioned East German couple who also discovered Hilda's in their struggle to make a new beginning in the West.

Hilda's home—and the Bartimaeus Community, and the three sisters in Rio—are but small parts of the Mustard Seed Conspiracy that is turning the world right side up. We have the incredible opportunity to join these people and so many others in the celebration and the adventure of the inbreaking of God's new age. If we accept the invitation of Jesus, he will use our lives and churches to make a world of difference in a world of growing need.

But a surprising number of Christians no longer believe they can make any real difference in the face of a very uncertain future. When was the last time you heard a Christian talking about changing the world?

Many of God's people seem to have relinquished a major share of the responsibility and initiative for social change to secular institutions. They seem to have very limited expectations of what God can do through his people in these difficult days.

Other Christians have looked at our troubled present and our uncertain future and have concluded we are in the last days. Therefore they expect everything to go to wrack and ruin, and they believe it is absolutely impossible for anyone to make a difference. Our only hope for the future, they think, is to passively wait for our own escape.

I would challenge both these approaches. When we conclude, for whatever reason, that the people of God (the community of those who follow Jesus) can't make a difference, we take our lives, our gifts, and our resources out of the "ballgame" and wind up squandering them on ourselves. This tragic retreat not only has neutralized our ability to respond to the growing needs of others; it has also seriously undermined the ability of the church to fulfill its mission . . . to allow God to work through his people to change his world. Ironically, two authors who make no profession of being Christian have called to our attention the tremendous, largely untapped, potential of the church to become a major agent for social change and renewal. In their book, *The Emerging Order: God in an Age of Scarcity*,[1] Jeremy Rifkin and Ted Howard challenged the church to use our resources to change our society.

It is my hope that this book will convince you that God wants to use your life to make a difference in his world in direct response to the escalating challenges of our uncertain future. In order to achieve this goal, I will attempt to: (1) make you more aware of some of the challenges we are likely to face in tomorrow's world; (2) show you how we can

*derive a much clearer sense of direction in how to respond to these antici-
pated challenges through discovering God's intentions for the human
future; (3) explore with you creative ways you can respond to tomorrow's
challenges through seeking first the future intentions of God in your
discipleship, lifestyle, vocation, community, and mission today; (4) share
with you some imaginative, practical examples—some Mustard Seeds—
of how God is already working through his people to change his
world.*

There's a groundswell building. Christians from all different denominations and traditions are beginning to take their faith much more
seriously. They are beginning to realize they can make a difference.
Momentum is growing. New coalitions are forming. Christians are much
more fully investing their lives, talents, and resources in the initiative
of God. This book is about that movement. And God invites you to
join millions of others in working for the transformation of his world
today and tomorrow.

ANTICIPATING TOMORROW'S SURPRISES

We will begin our journey together in this book by looking at the
future—by asking, "What are the challenges that we are likely to confront in the last two decades of the twentieth century?" What will be
the urgent human needs and compelling opportunities to which we
must respond?

In the sixties and seventies, those of us in the church repeatedly
missed opportunities to make a difference in society because we were
surprised by change. In 1959 I am sure the church expected the decade
of the sixties to simply be an extension of the fifties. Of course it wasn't.
We suddenly found ourselves jammed into a vortex of change; Vietnam,
the civil rights movement, the student protests, the emergence of the
counterculture, the drug scene, the discovery of the American poor,
the challenging of American values, the Jesus People, and a host of
other unexpected developments swept over us in successive waves of
change and confusion. (Last week I was in a coffee shop when a young
man on crutches came in. I noticed his left leg was missing. And as
he passed my table I noticed the printing on his T-shirt: VIETNAM
WAR GAMES / PARTICIPANT / SECOND PLACE. As I read
those words I found myself plunged back into the profoundly painful
memory of that war and the brutal suffering so many experienced.)

The seventies provided no respite from the onslaught of change. They
were filled with the unexpected and the surprising: Watergate, the environmental movement, the energy crisis, the feminist movement, the
refugee crisis. And already in the eighties we have had a surprising

change of national leadership and direction, an assassination attempt on a pope and a president, and a renewal of urban unrest.

In the futures workshops I conduct for Christian organizations and churches, we look together at how effectively the church responded to the unexpected changes of the sixties, seventies, and early eighties. The conclusion is almost always the same: "We blew it! We reacted when we should have responded in love. We missed incredible opportunities to make a difference, simply because we didn't expect change."

Alvin Toffler has predicted we will experience as much change in the next ten years as we have in the past thirty years. If we are indeed in a period of escalating change, it is absolutely essential that we in the church learn to anticipate tomorrow's surprises before they blow up on our doorstep. If we are able to anticipate even a few of the human crises that may occur, we will have time to discern our biblical responsibility—and time to create new ministry responses before the crises arrive.

For example, had we anticipated the emergence of the drug culture in the sixties, we could have been on line years sooner with rehabilitational and educational programs. We could have made a difference in the lives of thousands of young people we failed to help because we simply didn't pay attention to what was going on. We ignored Timothy Leary's call to the young to drop out and turn on. We ignored the spread of drugs until it became a national epidemic. Then, in the eleventh hour, we finally came up with programs like Teen Challenge and began working with the late arrivals to the drug movement.

Granted, we couldn't have predicted all the changes of the last two decades, but we could have done a much better job than we did. The only options are to try to pay attention to the signals and anticipate change, or simply to let the future happen to us and be totally surprised again.

LEARNING TO PAY ATTENTION TO SIGNALS

My parents, who live in Burlingame, California, recently shared a true story about two of their friends. Henry and Rhoda are Scandinavian, and one of the things they brought with them from the old country was a love of gathering wild mushrooms. One weekend they went mushroom gathering in the foothills and came home carrying baskets overflowing with delectables.

Realizing they couldn't possibly consume all their bounty, they decided to throw a dinner party and invite a houseful of friends to help them devour the harvest. They fixed mushroom crepes, mushroom souffles, mushroom omelets, and they ate until they couldn't possibly consume another mushroom. They scraped the leftover mushrooms into the cat's dish.

Near midnight guests began to get their coats and excuse themselves. As people were beginning to leave, there suddenly came a scream from the kitchen: "The cat!" Everyone went running into the kitchen. There on the floor was the cat—thrashing, kicking, crying, her sides heaving— having what looked like a complete grand mal seizure.

Some exclaimed "Oh, oh!" and Henry called the doctor. The doctor told him "it was nothing to mess around with" and instructed them to meet him in Emergency in fifteen minutes. Everyone went piling into their cars and went dashing wildly to the hospital.

Picture the scene. It's one o'clock in the morning. The lovely dinner party has ended in the Emergency Room, with the guests stretched out on eight tables side by side by side—that's right—having their stomachs pumped. A dreadful, wretched experience. What a way to end a party.

They climbed down from the tables exhausted and trembling a little. One woman mumbled something about wishing she had never heard of mushrooms. They straggled to their cars and drove back to Rhoda and Henry's to get their coats and purses. Before leaving the house they thanked the hostess and slowly made their way to the front door. By now it was about one-thirty.

As they began to leave the second time, someone remembered the cat. What had happened to the poor cat? The group tiptoed toward the kitchen and quietly inched open the door. There on the floor was the poor cat, lying silently . . . with eight new kittens!

The message from the future is: check your signals! The church could have avoided a lot of unnecessary grief in the sixties and seventies and responded much more fully to the challenges of those decades had we paid more attention to the signals.

General Electric, Bank of America, and Westinghouse are three of some two hundred American corporations that have developed in-house systems for paying attention to the signals. An executive in one corporation told me that their goal was not only to anticipate changes that could compromise their growth, but also to identify possible changes on which they could capitalize, and which they could turn into profitable opportunities.

I was involved in redesigning a futures information system for the Weyerhaeuser Corporation to enable their new business research division to identify potential areas of corporate venturing. The Stanford Research Institute, the Center for Futures Research at the USC School of Business, and the Hudson Institute are but a few of a growing number of agencies which market forecasts to the corporate and governmental sectors.

However, none of these organizations is really designed to help the church pay attention to the broad spectrum of signals that relate to our unique mission. And there are no Christian organizations that provide this service. As a result, a few of us who are concerned that the church learn to anticipate emerging challenges and opportunities are designing a futures watch system. Hopefully, this information system will help Christian organizations anticipate areas of human crisis before they arrive and create innovative responses.

You see, the problem is that every church and Christian organization I have ever worked with does long-range planning. However, in their long-range planning they unconsciously assume a static view of the future. They plan as though the future is simply going to be more of the present . . . and of course it isn't.

Let me give you an example. A friend of mine named Ray is pastor of a thriving Methodist Church in California. Recently he told me he was having extreme difficulty raising money for an elaborate educational wing his church was building as a part of their long-range plan. As he was bemoaning his difficulty raising funds I interrupted him. "Ray, what are houses running in your area right now?" I asked. "Oh, it's ridiculous," he responded. "One hundred fifty thousand and up." "Who is buying those homes?" I questioned. "Mainly older couples." "Do they have children?" I asked. "Not as a rule . . . some kids in college occasionally." "Ray,"—I phrased my words slowly—"who is going to use your new educational building?" His face visibly blanched. In his long-range planning for the educational wing he had assumed a static view of the future and hadn't bothered to look at the demographic signals. As a result, he is constructing an expensive educational building in a community that will be essentially childless by the end of the decade.

Fortunately, a few Christian organizations are learning to pay attention to the signals. The Billy Graham Association has held two consultations on the future for evangelical leaders, to help them learn to anticipate and respond to tomorrow's challenges. At these consultations participants were given hands-on experience in both anticipating the new challenges and creating imaginative responses.

One of the most innovative uses of futures planning has been made by the Philippine Council of Evangelical Churches. What they have done, in essence, is forecast economic, social, and technological changes they expect in the Philippines in the next ten years, then created imaginative strategies to respond to those anticipated changes.

Let me give you one example. They project that the gap between real and actual incomes will continue to widen in the Philippines due to inflation, tax increases, and changes in wage structures. Families will be forced to augment their incomes. "Thus, more mothers will join the working force, leaving their children unsupervised. This will weaken family ties and thus the home. For pastors' wives opting to work, it will mean a decrease in involvement in the church and parsonage ministries."

In response to this anticipated economic and social challenge, the Philippine Council of Evangelical Churches is creating innovative economic programs through which women will be able to earn right in their own homes while continuing to supervise their growing children. The pastors' wives who need additional income will train the other women in their parish in these economic programs, while at the same time carrying on other ministries to the homes. These Philippine Christians have, through anticipatory planning, transformed a potential threat into a positive opportunity.[2]

If churches and Christian organizations could learn to pay attention to the signals and to anticipate challenges before they arrive, we could become pro-active instead of reactive; we could transform tomorrow's challenges into today's opportunities. And, in the process, the church could move much more decisively into a leadership position in society.

If we fail to pay attention to the signals, we will be right back where we were too often in the sixties and seventies—surprised by change, reacting instead of serving. If we are going to be the people of God in an age of rapid change we are going to have to develop the capability to: (1) anticipate tomorrow's challenges, and (2) create imaginative new biblical responses to those anticipated challenges.

OUR JOURNEY TOGETHER

For the reasons I have just mentioned I intend, especially in chapters two and three of this book, to deal very realistically with what I believe will be some of the urgent human challenges in the eighties and nineties. But this *is* a book of hope, and the last thing I want to do is lend aid and comfort to those who have already given up on the future. So I would urge you not to bog down in these chapters, but to read them hopefully, viewing the anticipated needs as emerging *opportunities* for the people of God to respond compassionately, creatively, and aggressively. You might keep a pencil and paper handy and listen for God's voice as you read, listing all the ideas you may come up with for ways you and your church might creatively respond to these emerging opportunities. Then press on into the second half of the book to discover dozens of ways Christians are already effectively responding to tomorrow's challenges today.

After attempting to answer the question, "What is humankind's likely future?" chapters four and five will struggle with the question, "What is God's intended future?", exploring common nonbiblical responses and the scriptural evidence. If we can discern God's intention for the human future as expressed through his Word, we can discern his intentions for society today. And we can gain a clearer vision of how he wants to work through our lives and churches to respond to the exploding needs of his world.

How do we carry the adventure and celebration of the future of God into our discipleship, our lifestyles, and our careers? It seems to be extremely difficult for most of us to translate biblical principles into our everyday life situations. Chapters six and seven will attempt to provide some roadmaps and creative examples of ways we might do this.

However, there is absolutely no way we can begin incarnating the future intentions of God into our everyday lives alone. Our only hope to realize significant change is to become a part of a Christian community of loving relationships. Only as we commit our lives to other brothers and sisters who share our sense of seriousness for the mission of God can we become different or make a difference. Pathways into Christian community are described in chapter eight.

Once we put the future intentions of God first in our discipleship, lifestyles and careers—through communities of shared life—we can join those all over the world whom God is using to carry out his conspiracy of loving change. In response to the escalating needs of tomorrow's world, God is raising up a people to seek first his future of righteousness, justice, peace, reconciliation, wholeness, and love . . . in anticipation of that day when Christ returns and his future comes in its fullness. The final two chapters outline specific ways and give a number of examples of how we can be the missioning people of God in a world of change.

The final question that we will ask is, "What would happen if sixty-nine million American Christians really sought first the kingdom of God in cooperation with brothers and sisters all over the world?" You will have to read this book right through the last page of the conclusion to find the answer to that question.

This book has a built-in study guide to make it as useful as possible for adult study groups, college and seminary classes, and Christian education programs. At the end of each chapter you will find a series of questions for discussion and action. But before we plunge further into the future, let me share my motivation for writing this book.

A WORD OF PERSONAL CONFESSION

An emaciated woman with a small baby came up to me begging for money. I didn't know what to do. It was my first visit to Port au Prince, Haiti, and I had just left the missionary's home for a brief shopping excursion. Suddenly I found myself plunged into a world of more deprivation, hunger, and pain than I had witnessed in my life. People kept asking me for help, and I was overwhelmed. I forgot about my shopping and rushed back to the missionary's house. I am still overwhelmed. I still haven't fully recovered from my first trip to Haiti. Increasingly I am becoming aware that through my lifestyle and my indifference I have unwittingly contributed to that suffering I witnessed in Haiti.

This book was born among the hovels of the back streets of Port au Prince. I write these pages as one very much aware that I am much more a part of the problem than of the solution. Even though I write with genuine conviction, I confess that my life is still one of struggle. I am struggling to authentically follow Jesus and to share his lifegiving love for the poor, unreached, and forgotten people with whom I share this finite earth. This book is offered as one small contribution to a growing dialogue on how we can more fully respond to the escalating challenges of today and tomorrow.

WELCOME TO A CELEBRATION AND AN ADVENTURE

God calls us to hope and to action. Our hope is based on the biblical reality that God is alive and well and is the Lord of history—that he is working to bring his new future into being. Our action is made possible by the power of God's Spirit working through our lives to change his world. The Mustard Seed Conspiracy will not fail. In the life, death, and resurrection of Jesus, the conspiracy has already conquered the world and is ushering in the new age of God.

So welcome to the conspiracy of the insignificant, invisible, and incomprehensible! God wants to use your small contribution to join others in transforming his world today and tomorrow. If together we can recover a vision of the future of God and realize how he would use our lives to manifest that future . . . if we can incarnate the celebrative future of God in our lives and communities of faith . . . if we can initiate a renaissance of Christian creativity and imagine wholly new ways to compassionately respond to tomorrow's challenges . . . God will make a greater difference through our lives than we can imagine. Ours is the celebration and the adventure of the inbreaking of the new age of God. Welcome to the Mustard Seed Conspiracy that is quietly changing the world!

For Discussion and Action

1. Who are some Christians you know who are making a difference? Share how God is using their lives to change his world.
2. What is likely to happen whenever Christians stop believing they can really be used through the church to change the world? What do they typically do with the lives, gifts, and resources God has entrusted to them if they don't think they can make a difference?
3. What is the Mustard Seed Conspiracy? What are some biblical examples of God's using the insignificant to change the world?
4. What are some examples from church history of God's working through the seemingly insignificant to make a difference?
5. What were some of the unexpected happenings of the sixties and the seventies? How did the church typically respond to those surprises?
6. Why does the corporate sector try to pay attention to the signals of the future and to anticipate change?
7. Why does long-range planning generally fail to enable Christian organizations to plan effectively for the future? Explain the difference between typical long-range planning and the anticipatory planning process used by the Philippine Council of Evangelical Churches.
8. Why is it especially crucial in the next two decades that the church learn to anticipate change?
9. Based on your knowledge of the neighborhood around your church, what predictions can you make for the next five years (i.e. property values, change in racial mix, increase in the number of seniors and single-parent families)? What specific implications do these changes have for your church in planning future programs and ministries?
10. What is the purpose of this book as presented under the heading, "An Invitation to a Conspiracy"?

2.

Awakening from the Western Dream—
A World in Trauma

The excited audience immediately pressed in from all directions as soon as the generously proportioned speaker finished sharing his global forecast. It was as though they were trying to touch the hem of his blue gabardine suit. You could almost smell incense in the air.

Herman Kahn, Futurist and Director of the Hudson Institute, a corporate think tank, had just regaled his audience with a dazzling forecast for our planetary future. At this first conference on the future in Washington D.C. in 1971, Kahn's optimistic presentation set the tone of the entire conference.

He painted a picture of a future of growing affluence, technological advance, and social progress. Kahn predicted that through increasing global production the rich would get richer, and that the wealth would "trickle down" to the poor throughout the entire earth. As we approached century twenty-one, not only would everyone have enough; growing numbers would experience affluence, with leisure time and opportunities for pleasure and growth beyond their wildest dreams.

We Americans have long believed in not only the supremacy of the Western dream, but also in the inevitability of bringing the entire planet to a better temporal future. Small wonder then that Herman Kahn's address met with such acclaim.

In fact, there wasn't a single presentation during the entire Futures Conference that challenged Kahn's heroic optimism—not a single negative forecast for the human future. In 1971, the future looked very bright. Remember, the first Earth Day had been celebrated only a year before, and the environmental movement was still in its infancy Most of us had no idea of the enormous hidden price we had been paying for the realization of the Western dream in terms of environmental degradation, health costs, and depletion of nonrenewable resources.

AWAKENING TO A FUTURE WITH LIMITS

No one was ready for the bombshell that dropped a year later, in 1972. A book called *The Limits to Growth*[1] rudely roused many of us from our sleep and violently shattered our dreams of a utopian future. Suddenly we were confronted with a new image of the future—a world with limits.

The Limits to Growth was the first report of an international group of scientists and industrialists called the Club of Rome. Using a computer system, they attempted to forecast the future of the planet, taking into account such factors as economic growth, depletion of nonrenewable resources, pollution, food production, and population growth—which are all growing at an exponential (doubling) rate. Their sobering conclusion was that, unless drastic changes are made, the earth will end not with a bang but a whimper by the year 2025.

The Club of Rome's forecast provoked a firestorm of controversy, and their prediction for the demise of planet Earth has been strongly challenged. However, no one has challenged the question their study has raised: "How much economic and technological growth can a finite planet sustain?"

In 1973, while the limits to growth debate still raged, a second bombshell hit. A message was received unexpectedly from the Middle East, almost as if on cue: "Go back to *Go* . . . do not advance until you pay the owners of the oil utility whatever they ask." In that one event we witnessed the end of growth as we had come to know and expect it. Some feel we are even more severely constrained by limits to our political and human ability to effectively manage growth.

Mankind at the Turning Point, the Club of Rome's follow-up to *The Limits of Growth,* was published in 1974. This book powerfully described our new human situation: "Suddenly—virtually overnight when measured on a historical scale—mankind finds itself confronted by a multitude of unprecedented crises: the population crisis, the environmental crisis, the raw materials crisis just to name a few. New crises appear while the old ones linger on with effects spreading to every corner of the earth until they appear in point of fact as global, worldwide crises. . . ."[2]

A procession of books published in the seventies, from Robert Heilbroner's *An Inquiry into the Human Prospect* in 1975 to William Irwin Thompson's *Darkness and Scattered Light*[3] in 1978, continued the struggle to describe our present predicament and our uncertain future. Their consensus was summarized in Jeremy Rifkin's and Ted Howard's book, *The Emerging Order: God in an Age of Scarcity,* which was published in 1979. Rifkin and Howard asserted that not only is the Western dream over, but we are entering an unprecedented period of global scarcity that will change all of our lives.

Almost ten years after his first presentation, Herman Kahn addressed the subsequent convocation on the future in Toronto on July 22, 1980. There were no utopian visions this time around. Even Kahn had made major revisions in his earlier forecasts to reflect the fact we are indeed running out of resources. And there was no mad rush to the podium this time, simply polite applause. Herman Kahn and even his modified, semioptimistic dream for the future were in clear eclipse.

The other speakers at the conference dealt openly with our global resource crisis and the traumatic period the world is entering. And this time the tone was set by keynote speaker Hazel Henderson when she insisted, "We can't grow on like this." She advocated a whole new image of the future and a new approach to economics that gives ascendancy to human good over unrestrained economic growth.

As we in the Western world reluctantly awaken from our dreams of unchecked growth and progress, it is important to realize that the future isn't over; we simply have to discover new dreams that are compatible with the realities of a finite world. We need to develop biblical responses to the new questions that have been raised:

How much growth and what kinds of growth can our planet sustain? What impact will a world of shrinking resources have on the burgeoning numbers of the poor with whom we share this planet? What can Christians do to insure the just use of shrinking resources for all peoples as economic competition increases? What is our biblical responsibility for the poor?

While a legion of books has now been written about the emergence of a new age of scarcity, Christian authors on the whole have not attempted to anticipate the specific human challenges that are likely to be a part of tomorrow's world. In this chapter I will outline a few of the specific new global challenges that we are likely to face in the last two decades of the twentieth century. Primary attention will be given to those forecasts that relate to the planetary poor. These emerging challenges are in reality emerging opportunities for the church to care, witness and serve this generation in the name of Christ. If we, the people of God, pay attention to the signals and create innovative ways to respond to these opportunities in advance of crisis, we really can make a world of difference in a world of growing need.

AWAKENING TO THE LAST FRONTIERS—STELLAR SPACE AND SEA SPACE

As we near the end of the twentieth century, we begin the conquest of the last frontiers—stellar space and sea space. We are at the threshold of a historic liftoff. All systems are go. The countdown has begun. The successful launching of Columbia has moved us into a whole new era.

"The space shuttle will be the clipper ship of tomorrow's world . . . moving us into a whole new age of exploration and discovery," predicts Ed Lindaman, futurist and former NASA spokesman. It is projected that permanent space colonies will be placed in orbit by 1995. Space planners speaking at the Futures Convocation in Toronto estimated that several thousand people could be living in space by the end of the century.

This exploration and colonization of the "high frontier" has the potential to stretch the human imagination beyond the confines of Mother Earth and provide whole new perspectives on our human existence. Millions of dollars of alloys and chemicals are likely to be produced in space by the end of the century.

But there is a negative side to this picture. In a world of dwindling resources, the development of space will directly compete with the development of poorer areas of the earth. In addition, much of the momentum for the development of the "high frontier" is coming from the Pentagon. They are developing the capability not only to zap "enemy" satellites but to launch nuclear missiles and fire laser weapons from space back towards the earth. Thus the exploration and development of outer space raise new ethical questions for Christians.

Since the first human footprint disturbed the silent soil of the moon the exploration of space has tended to overshadow all other frontiering activity. Most people are not aware that human society is on the brink of a major new conquest of ocean space. Not only is the ocean a rich source of food, but it is also a storehouse of cobalt, nickel, manganese and other minerals. The Law of the Sea Conference was nearing resolution as to how the resources on the ocean floor would be subdivided between rich and poor nations . . . until the United States scuttled the agreement, insisting on a bigger piece of the pie.

Undeniably, all nations need the resources to be found in the world's oceans, but there is serious question as to whether the resources can be mined justly and peacefully. Lynn H. Miller predicts we are likely to witness not only a new age of conquest of the "deep frontier," but also a new age of conflict at sea, on a scale we haven't witnessed for centuries.[4]

Herman Kahn and other technological optimists have pinned their hopes for the continuation and expansion of the Western dream in part on the exploitation of these last two frontiers. But estimates of dwindling global resources *include* estimates of minerals on the ocean floor. And while there are vast resources in stellar space, the costs of mining those resources is for the foreseeable future prohibitively expensive. Therefore, we can't count on the exploration and development of the last two frontiers to make possible a future of continued unrestrained growth.

AWAKENING TO A SHRINKING PIE

We have abruptly awakened to a new image of our planet as not only a finite but a shrinking pie. Unquestionably the major contributing cause to the shrinking of our pie has been the dramatic economic growth of countries in the Northern Hemisphere. Robert Heilbroner points out that the industrialized North has been growing at a rate of about 7 percent a year, or doubling about every ten years. If that rate continued for another fifty years we would require a volume of resource extraction thirty-two times larger than today's.[5]

Given the North's insatiable appetite for resources, it should surprise no one that we are running out. Of course the most prominent dwindling resource is oil. It is predicted that the supply will fail to meet demands between 1985 and 1995, even if costs rise 50 percent above present levels. In spite of this, our national demand for energy is actually projected to double by the year 2000.[6]

What are the consequences of our outrageous appetites in the industrialized North on those with whom we share the planet? Alvin Toffler, in his book, *The Third Wave,* has charged that we have treated the rest of the world as though it were our "gas pump, garden, mine, quarry, and cheap labor supply." [7] Our voracious appetite and our supreme sense of entitlement make us a very difficult dinner guest to share the table with. Few of us stop to think that we are consuming much more than our fair share of global resources to maintain our RV, neon-lit culture, and that our high consumption is driving up the cost of energy and other resources for the poorer nations.

Of course the industrialized North isn't solely responsible for the inequity and plight of the poor. Political systems and economic elites in the Third World often exploit their own people. Customs and culture within these regions as well as limitations of the land conspire to keep people poor. However, in an interdependent world there is abundant evidence that the planetary rich are making it at the expense of the planetary poor.

One of the discoveries I made in the past decade is that we are all in this together. I have learned that driving my 1972 Datsun more than necessary forces up the price of kerosene for my friends in Haiti. Every lifestyle decision we make in the North has an impact on everyone else in the lifeboat with us. And as a result of our lifestyles, we are a primary cause of global poverty today.

As the planetary population rushes toward 6.2 billion by the end of the century, we are not only running out of many of the resources we take out of the land; we are also running out of the land itself. The amount of land on which we can grow food is actually shrinking. In the poorer nations deforestation is a primary cause of disappearing croplands. The United Nations Food and Agricultural Organization estimates that 70 percent of the timber cut in these regions winds up under the cooking pot. In fact, the major energy crisis among many Third World peoples is the "firewood crisis." [8] For example, in Haiti many people are already cutting down their fruit trees to cook with.

In addition, the world is losing at least fourteen million acres of farm and pastoral land every year to encroaching desert. Between 1968 and 1973 the Sahel, a region in the Horn of Africa, became the most grim example of this phenomenon. The loss of farm and pastureland resulted in the death of two hundred fifty thousand persons. The incredible human suffering to the north in Somalia has been caused in part by desert encroachment on farmland.

Nearly two-thirds of the countries of the world are struggling against rapidly expanding deserts. A young man in Kenya reports, "I watched the first dust storm ever recorded in our farming area. I was shocked to tour the region and find that the land to the north of us was completely bare. Some African families were still living there, starved, bewildered, and refusing to leave their home territories. . . . In every case, the land deterioration followed human substitute of domestic stock for indigenous animals." [9] Desert encroachment is also caused by shifts in weather patterns, overgrazing, and inadequate soil conservation practices.

However, deforestation and desertification are not the only causes for the reduction of our total global cropland base. In the United States and other Western nations we are converting some of our best agricultural lands to nonagricultural uses. It is estimated that we have converted forty million acres to urban uses. We have converted thirty-two million acres to highways and roads. We convert about 153,000 acres a year for strip mining and we have tended to locate our cities right in the center of our very best farmlands. [10]

The future of U.S. farmland is not bright. Inadequate land-use policies are allowing vast areas of our best farmland to be transformed into shopping centers, parking lots, and suburban sprawl. I remember the sick feeling in the pit of my stomach as I watched bulldozers scrape down square miles of apricot orchards still laden with fruit in San Jose during the sixties. In less than a decade, San Jose was transformed from the fruit and nut center of California to a suburban wasteland.

As we approach the year 2000, the regions in California and Florida on which we have become dependent for our winter fruit and vegetables are slowly succumbing to the developers. Florida is projected to develop almost all of its prime farmland by the year 2000.[11]

When did you have your last franchise hamburger? Do you know where the beef for that hamburger came from? A number of franchises import their beef from Haiti, the Dominican Republic, and Costa Rica. Recently when I was in Haiti an elementary school teacher gave me a tour of school. (By the way, only 20 percent of the children in Haiti ever see the inside of a school.) I commented on the new blackboard at the front of the room. The teacher responded, "Oh, the children like Bernard and Marie sitting in the front never use the blackboard." "You have chalk and erasers," I responded. "Why don't the children use the blackboard?" "Because they fall down." "Fall down?" I questioned. "Yes," he explained. "Typically, the children haven't eaten in three or four days, and they can't work standing up . . . they are too weak."

I have discovered that one of the major contributing causes to malnutrition among kids in Haiti is protein deficiency. And one of the major causes of protein deficiency is the fact that some of the best pasture land in Haiti is leased by American hamburger franchises. This drives the cost of protein beyond the reach of the poor.

Alan Berg, in a Brookings Institute study of world nutrition, explained where the dramatic increase in Central American beef production is going. It is not ending up in the stomachs of malnourished kids in Costa Rica; instead, it winds up in the stomachs of Americans who eat in United States burger franchises.[12]

Until the mid–1950s, the United States was largely self-sufficient in beef production. Increasingly, however, corporate suppliers have looked for cheap beef grown on cheap land. And while some jobs have beeen created by Central America's $127 million annual beef export to the United States, Bread for the World concludes the net impact is negative: "Internally as well as internationally, the strong have gained at the expense of the weak; the rich at the expense of the poor. This is especially so if one considers people's ability to meet their basic food needs. Evidence indicates that the increase of beef exports from Central America has contributed to the growth of malnutrition and hunger." [13] Don't hungry children in Central America and the Caribbean "deserve a break today" too?

This problem is not unique to Central America. According to the United Nations, over half of the forty countries affected by the food crisis in the seventies depended on agricultural exports for at least 80 percent of their export income.[14] As we in the United States put millions of acres of our best agricultural land under shopping centers and parking lots, we are increasingly turning to the Southern Hemisphere for many of our agricultural products.

Increasingly, land in the Southern Hemisphere is being taken out of production for subsistence crops so we can have our between-meal snacks. Quite frankly, given our economic advantage, how can the poor effectively compete with us for the food grown on their own land?

If we the rich nations continue to expand our use and monopolization of the shrinking global cropland resource, we will push the poor to the very edge of famine. As we in the North continue to use a greater share of land on which the poor of the South grow their subsistence crops, they will become increasingly dependent on imported food. This is happening all over the Southern Hemisphere. For example, it is projected that nations in Southeast Asia will be twice as dependent on imported food by 1985 as they were in 1975.[15]

From where are the poor importing their food, and what inputs are required to grow that food? That's right, they import the food primarily from the United States and other Western nations. And that requires high energy inputs—fertilizer, pesticides, gasoline and oil—to grow food in the North. As the cost of energy continues to dramatically increase, a situation could well develop in which huge regions of poor could no longer afford the price of our energy-intensive food.

I am afraid many Americans join a well-known radio commentator in responding to this growing global crisis by demanding that "the backward nations . . . stop producing more babies and start producing more food." [16] Such a naïve attitude certainly takes the pressure off affluent Americans; we can blame the poor for the situation and feel no responsibility at all.

The problem is that such an approach doesn't square with the facts. Population is not the principle cause of our present crisis; it is largely a symptom. The basic cause is poverty, and our patterns of resource consumption contribute to that widespread poverty. The fact is that in virtually every country, from Taiwan to the Philippines, where poverty has been corrected, there has been an immediate and dramatic drop in population growth. When land reform and self-help projects help the poor get an economic stake against the future, they don't feel the need to have as many kids to provide for their security in old age.[17] It is certainly important to help the poor in family planning, but it is even more vital to aggressively attack the primary cause of population growth—poverty.

AWAKENING TO THE NEW REALITY . . . THE PARTY IS OVER!

The new reality of the eighties and nineties is that our spectacular consumer party is over! For the past two hundred years most of those in the industrialized West have been enjoying this party, and we in the United States have had the very best of it. But the new reality is a future in which over half the people on this planet will never get to come to the Western party. The party was made possible by vast quantities of inexpensive resources, not the least of which was oil. Now there are no vast quantities of inexpensive resources, and there is certainly no more cheap oil.

In futures workshops I conduct in Christian organizations I ask participants, "Where did we get the resources for the incredible party we are enjoying?" Someone invariably responds, "The land." I counter, "But where did we get the land from?" Light bulbs begin to click on, and someone replies, "The Indians."

The poor of the Third World have also helped pay for our party. During the period of colonization and even today we secure vast quantities of our natural resources from the countries of the south at far less than their fair market value. Enslaved and indentured peoples have been persuaded to "volunteer" their resources to make our party possible.

Of course our European culture, industry and "know how" contributed too, but my point remains: if we Americans had to pay anything like a fair market value for the land, timber, oil, minerals and other resources we appropriated from the Indians in the conquest of this continent, or if we paid anything like a fair price for the enormous quantities of resources we have secured from our poorer neighbors to the south, or if we paid the blacks and indentured peoples that helped build this land what their labor was worth, there is absolutely no way we would be enjoying the affluent lifestyles we have come to expect as our birthright. Some other folks helped pay for our party, and those folks never got to come.

When most of the Third World countries finally secured their political independence from their colonial past about 1955, I am convinced they believed their political independence would automatically mean economic independence as well, that they would finally get to come to the party.

But it didn't happen that way. Between 1955 and 1975 this planet experienced the greatest period of economic growth in the history of civilization. However, during this period of unprecedented economic growth the gap between rich and poor nations widened dramatically. Those of us who had been enjoying the party suddenly found ourselves inundated by more resources and consumer goodies than we knew what to do with. In the United States we used resources as though there were no tomorrow. And during this period of incredible growth the poorer nations remained outside with their noses pressed against the windows of the West.

Finally, in 1974, they decided they had had enough. The Group of Seventy-Seven (now comprised of more than a hundred countries) went before the United Nations and demanded economic justice. They demanded a New International Economic Order. They accurately charged that one of the reasons they had been unable to participate in the high-growth economic boom of the North was that the international economic system was rigged against them. Far from being governed by the "free market mechanism" in international trade, they are forced to sell their natural resources at a fixed price while buying Western manufactured products at an inflated price.

Predictably, the Western nations resisted granting any significant concessions in trade policies, loan repayment, or development assistance. In fact, then-Secretary of State Henry Kissinger refused to even talk with them. There is discussion now, but there is no indication that the United States, Western Europe, or Japan are prepared to make any significant concessions. In view of this fact, the only forecast that can be made for the future is that the gap between rich and poor nations will continue to widen as we approach the end of the century. This will not only place the party beyond the reach of the poor; it will also seriously undermine their ability to even survive.

This new reality brings us to a very serious theological question. Did God goof? Did he fail to place enough resources on spaceship earth for the growing number of passengers? The answer is no. God placed enough resources on this planet for everyone to live decently, but not for everyone to live like Americans . . . not even Americans. We are only 5 percent of the world's population, and yet we consume over 40 percent of the world's resources.

Pogo has said, "We have seen the enemy and he is us." Are we ready to face up to the reality that our lifestyles and our unconditional commitment to unlimited growth may quite literally be destroying people with whom we share this finite earth? This realization is not intended to make us feel guilty. We don't need more guilt to immobilize and paralyze us. But we could stand a little more responsibility.

One young married couple I know, Ted and Ann, came to grips with the reality that the way they lived had the potential of making life better or worse for the poor of the planet. They didn't wallow in guilt or self-flagellation for being affluent Americans. Instead, they sat down and prayerfully examined their lifestyle and their budget priorities.

And they found a number of ways they could creatively alter their lifestyle (such as using public transportation). They were able to free 32 percent of his monthly income as an engineer. This "extra" money was invested in a small Christian agricultural project in the Caribbean. Ted and Ann were surprised to learn that their investment paid the full-time salary of an agriculturalist who was working to enable a community of ten thousand people to become self-reliant in food production. One couple has found a way to be part of the solution, not part of the problem, for ten thousand people. What could God do with your mustard seed?

AWAKENING TO THE FUTURE OF THE GLOBAL POOR

Not only is there no party in the future of the poor; there is precious little hope. Most of the people in the Third World live in degrading situations beyond our comprehension—and often beyond the reach of our compassion. Seventy million people, including thousands of families in Somalia, at this moment are in imminent danger of starvation, according to Michael Harrington in his book the *Vast Majority*.[18] Four hundred million are chronically malnourished, and fully one billion don't get anything like enough to eat. Two billion, or almost half the world's people, make less than two hundred dollars per person per year. The brothers and sisters I work with in Southwest Haiti make less than one hundred fifty dollars per year, and pay four times the price you pay for tomato sauce.

Abraham sat on his haunches on a pile of rubble, his black eyes staring out at the ocean off the east coast of India from which a tidal wave had come and devastated his village only three days before. The entire region was a wasteland. Scarcely a tree was left standing. An American Christian relief worker, seeing Abraham sitting silently, approached him and tried to reassure him. "Don't worry; we will work with you to help you return to your life the way it was before." Abraham didn't reply at first. Then finally, without taking his eyes off the ocean, he responded, "How will you help me to return to my life as it was before when my father, wife, and three children are buried in this rubble that was my home?"

Many are assuming that the refugee crisis of the last few years is behind us, since there are no more pictures of boat people or immigrating Cubans on the evening news. The fact is that, even as we are beginning to close the door on refugees, the problem is likely to worsen. Refugees are a by-product of political destabilization. We are likely to see increasing political destabilization in the eighties; therefore we are likely to see wave after wave of refugees. Christian organizations need to act now in developing a global refugee strategy to deal with this anticipated challenge.

The children, the women, the elderly, and the handicapped bear much more than their fair share of suffering, deprivation, and death among the world's poor. In 1980, designated the Year of the Child by the United Nations, some deeply disturbing information was discovered regarding the treatment of the world's children. It was learned that children are intentionally maimed in India to make them more effective beggars.[19] A study by the International Labor Organization revealed that fifty-five million kids under fifteen are working in mines, farms, and factories at little more than subsistence wages. It was discovered that approximately twenty-eight thousand six- and seven-year-olds work in match factories from three in the morning to seven at night. Thousands of children work in oppressive working conditions throughout Asia to provide inexpensive consumer goods for American markets.[20]

Millions of other children are not victims of conscious exploitation; they are just victims. "Of every one hundred babies born in the world, forty will die before the age of six. Another forty risk permanent physical and mental damage because of malnutrition. Only three out of that hundred will get education and skills they need to perform creative and meaningful work." [21]

Four-year-old Niloy is such a child. Like thousands of other children in crowded Manila, he somehow got separated from his parents, and has no idea where they are. Niloy lives on the city garbage dump. He has become a child of the streets, begging, digging through garbage . . . struggling to survive.[22] World Concern, a Christian relief and development agency, is supporting a Christian ministry that has taken Niloy in and is helping him locate his parents.

Women suffer much more than men in the Third World. "They are considered less important, less intelligent, and less valuable than men. Legal, cultural, and religious discrimination have made women second-class citizens. Their almost universally low status is at the root of their suffering. Women's needs require a special emphasis if this long standing injustice is to be overcome." [23]

There are many more handicapped people in the poorer nations due to dietary deficiency and significantly higher accident rates. For example, the rate of blindness in the Southern Hemisphere is five times as high as in the North. And there are no programs of assistance for blind, handicapped, or elderly persons. Their survival is their own tedious affair.[24]

Well, what does all this mean for the future of the poor in the Third World? It doesn't look promising. The United States Office of Technology Assessment predicts that the projected levels of combined economic and population growth will seriously threaten the carrying capability of our finite planet through massive pollution of air and water, deforestation, creation of deserts, elimination of natural areas of wildlife habitats, depletion of fish stocks, progressive simplification and homogenization of nature. They concluded that these pressures on global systems will create escalating rates of inflation, which will take their greatest toll on the poorest of the poor.[25]

In early 1980, in view of this unprecedented human crisis, former West Berlin Chancellor Willy Brandt called on the nations of the world to hold a North-South summit. His report declares that not only are the world's poor jeopardized by the serious global inequity between the North and the South, but that world stability and peace are seriously threatened as well.[26] The growing economic inequity and the explosion in oil prices have caused the combined debt of the poor nations to grow from seventy billion dollars in 1970 to five hundred billion in 1980. " 'The Third World has overborrowed,' declares Thomas Balogh, an Oxford Economist. 'Any default could have a domino effect that could lead to catastrophe.' " [27]

The Global 2000 Report, published recently by the United States government, essentially states that the world's poor are in a growing state of jeopardy. "The world in the year 2000—more crowded, more polluted, and even less stable ecologically, and more vulnerable to disruption than the world we live in now, unless the nations of the world act quickly and decisively to change current policies." [28] Richard J. Barnet insists, "There are enough resources in the world to support a decent life for the predicted global population of the year 2000, but not to support lopsided opulence or continual ecological plunder." [29] In other words, it isn't a question of growth or no growth . . . we simply have to learn to grow responsibly on this planet. We have to pursue policies of planetary growth that enhance the future of all the world's peoples.

Some are predicting that, given present trends, we are likely to see twice as many hungry people on this planet by the year 2000 as there are today. Of course, there is always an outside chance that some breakthrough in plant genetics or the invention of an inexpensive food source could alter this scenario. But from where we stand now those possibilities don't seem likely.

Fortunately, there are Christians who are already paying attention to these signals and are acting. Bread for the World, the Christian anti-hunger lobbying group, won a long-sought victory in the dying days of the Carter administration. Congress voted the establishment of an emergency grain reserve. The government-owned reserve, containing four million tons of wheat, will be used to alleviate famine and other extreme food shortages around the world." [30] Indigenous Lutheran churches in East Africa have successfully launched a program in agriculture and evangelism. They are enabling thousands of rural farmers to become self-reliant in food production through better agricultural techniques, and to hear the good news at the same time. And Pope John Paul has become the leading international advocate of social justice for the poor.

As the United States seriously reduces foreign aid to needy nations (the likely trend of the future), it will become even more urgent for the church and voluntary agencies to significantly increase its assistance to the rural and urban poor. The dual tragedy of increasing need and decreasing government aid is really an opportunity for the church to act now to mobilize a major self-help thrust throughout the Southern Hemisphere.

AWAKENING TO AN URBAN BOOM

In spite of this overwhelming specter of need, most people in the Third World don't know the party is over, and many of them are still knocking themselves out trying to get to the party. Do you have any idea of where they try to go in their efforts to get to the party? That's right. They go to the city. And they are pressing into the cities in record numbers. Somehow they believe that if they can just get close enough to the urban consumer society, they can become a part of it. The city represents their last option.

Today there are six hundred million landless poor in Africa, Asia, and Latin America; by the end of the century, it is predicted that there will be a billion. These rural people are tenant farmers who own little more than their own bodies; when they can no longer work the land, they are thrown off it. Erik Eckholm forecasts that, "Conflict rooted in the inequality of land ownership is apt to become more acute in country after country." [31] The consequences of the dramatic growth of the numbers of landless poor and the resulting conflict will encourage even more people to flood into the urban centers of the Third World.

The cities of the Southern Hemisphere are facing an unprecedented boom. "By the end of the century, three quarters of all Latin Americans and one third of all Asians and Africans, will . . . be living in cities." [32] By the year 2000, Latin America will be more urbanized than Europe. The largest city in the world will be Mexico City, with over thirty-two million people. São Paulo, Brazil will be second, with twenty-five million. [33]

As the rural poor flood into Manila, Nairobi, Calcutta, Mexico City, and São Paulo, there will be no welcome wagons to greet them. In fact, the cities will not even be able to provide the most basic human services for this burgeoning human influx. When I was in Port au Prince, someone told me there was only one toilet for every two hundred people. Imagine an urban explosion made up of squatter communities—millions of moms, dads, kids, and grandparents with virtually no life-support systems of clean water, food, sanitation, or adequate shelter.

You can write your own scenario for the potential holocaust in these exploding urban centers. The greatest tragedy is that these people don't have to have their lives and futures jeopardized. Both the rural and urban areas in the Southern Hemisphere can be made into humane environments if we pay attention to the signals. We have the resources. What we need is Christians working aggressively together to avert widespread catastrophe.

A year or so ago, when World Concern was trying to raise money to alleviate widespread suffering in Cambodia, I was told by one layperson, "It's fine to send a little food to Cambodia, but we certainly shouldn't expect it to make any difference, because the Bible says in the last days there is going to be hunger and suffering, and 'the poor we have with us always.' There is nothing we can do about it."

Well, thank God, we discovered we *can* do something about it; we can by his power make a difference. Over twenty voluntary Christian and governmental relief agencies responded to the overwhelming tragedy in Cambodia. Hundreds of individual Christians worked in the distribution centers and refugee camps in Thailand. By January of 1981 a headline in the *Christian Science Monitor* announced, "SUCCESS. Cambodia Has Been Saved from a Holocaust by One of the Greatest International Aid Efforts in History."

> Cambodia, a nation which just one year ago faced what President Carter called "a tragedy of genocidal proportions," has walked out of holocaust's grip.
> Millions of Khmer (Cambodian) villagers who had been scattered around the country by famine or war have been returned home to rebuild their broken communities.
> Thanks to international aid, the Cambodians have been able to reopen their ports, get truck transport rolling, and revive basic agriculture.
> The specter of hunger—once so cruelly conspicuous in the countryside—has vanished.[34]

With the Vietnamese occupation of Cambodia, that country's problems are far from over. The Cambodian people need our continued support if they are to determine their own destiny in justice and peace. But thanks to the efforts of thousands of Christians working together, the Cambodians have been given a chance to rebuild their lives. If we pay attention to the urban explosion in the Southern Hemisphere, and if we work in concert with the churches of the South, we can be used by God again to avert an urban holocaust in the eighties and nineties. However, if we are to effectively respond to these urgent opportunities, the church will have to dramatically reprioritize its use of resources to free up as much as possible for a global self-help initiative among the urban and rural poor.

AWAKENING TO GLOBALIZATION OF PLANET EARTH

We are rapidly entering a transnational future in which different political, economic, and cultural forces are conspiring to create a single global society. There are those within the communist world who are interested in collectivizing us into a planetary political community based on their ideology and systems of dictatorial control. Soviet expansion is clearly a threat. But we are perhaps less aware that there are others who are also interested in collectivizing us.

Among the most powerful are those working for the economic collectivization of the planet. Richard Barnet charges that, "Global corporations exploit their superior bargaining power in weak, disorganized societies to carry out a series of activities which can offer exceptionally high profits for worldwide enterprise but which often promote economic and social backwardness in poor countries. . . . Because of their superior control over capital, technology, and marketing, global corporations can dominate local economics and preempt the power to plan for the society." [35]

Multinationals are not only involved in efforts to collectivize the planet; they sometimes pursue unjust economic means to achieve that goal. Some corporations participate in activities that are directly destructive of human life and dignity. The most visible example of this, of course, has been the Nestle's baby formula scandal; this company continues to market baby formula in rural areas among the poor where there is no clean water, no capability to sterilize bottles, and no ability to read formula instructions. [36] Amazingly, the United States was the only nation who voted against a recent United Nations resolution discouraging the marketing of infant formula among the Third World poor.

Perhaps less visible but no less destructive is the growing tendency to use the South as a dumping ground for the North. Some multinational corporations are unloading dangerous products on Third World markets with no apparent regard for the human consequences. When the Consumer Product Safety Commission banned the sale of children's garments treated with a fire retardant called Tris in the United States because it was found to be carcinogenic, the producers, not wanting to suffer a financial loss, shipped millions of children's garments overseas to consumers unaware of the risks.

In 1972, four hundred Iraqis died and five thousand were hospitalized after eating the by-products of eight thousand tons of wheat and barley, the sale of which had been banned in the United States because it was coated with an organic mercury fungicide.

The manufacturer of the Dalkon shield intrauterine device withdrew it from the United States market after seventeen women died from using it. The stock was subsequently sold overseas and is still in use in several countries. The list goes on to include hazardous pesticides, defective pacifiers, contaminated baby food, etc. As the list of banned products grows in the United States, we can reasonably expect corporations, with the continuing cooperation of government, to dump increasing amounts of dangerous products on the markets of our neighbors in the South.[37]

Ron Sider characterizes organizational structures of any kind that do violence to persons as "structural evil." Certainly our task as Christians in the eighties and nineties cannot be limited to fighting personal evil. We must find ways to strongly challenge this intolerable violence towards the unsuspecting poor on the part of organizations.

Now I am not suggesting for a moment that multinational corporations stop doing business in the Southern Hemisphere. But I strongly urge that all organizations who work in the South, including development agencies, churches, universities, and corporations, be responsible for their impact in the countries where they work. Fortunately, a few corporations are beginning to assume this responsibility. For example, as a result of the influence of Sister Marilyn Uline of the Adrian Dominicans, Ross Laboratories introduced a number of precautions against marketing abuses in the Southern Hemisphere, and they have instituted a nine-person task force to study Third World concerns.[38]

One of the most dismaying expressions of the new globalism is the massive armament of the planet. In 1976, world military expenditures exceeded $350 billion. In 1979, that figure soared to $425 billion. The major powers now have enough missiles to destroy one another fifteen times over. This balance of terror has appropriately been called "mutually assured destruction . . . MAD." [39] The stepped-up arms race is dramatically increasing the drain on global resources to create systems of violence, while seriously jeopardizing human survival.

To make matters worse, the longer it takes the United States to get back to the tables to secure a disarmament treaty with the Soviets, the more the megadeath weapons of the superpowers will proliferate to smaller and in some cases more unstable regimes.

Countries in the Southern Hemisphere purchased 9 percent of the total arms purchased in 1960. In 1976 their take had increased to 18 percent. Often they purchase advanced weapon systems not because they are under any threat but because of the status value of possessing sophisticated weapons. By the year 2000, over forty nations will have the capability to construct nuclear weapons, and chemical and bacterial weapons won't be far behind.[40] There's a high and growing probability that someone will use their nuclear weapons before we reach century twenty-one.

With the proliferation of sophisticated weapons systems and high impact explosives, terrorist activities will increase, and their powers of intimidation will increase as well. As more countries succumb to dictatorships of the right and left, human rights will be violated and institutional violence approved—increasingly, I fear, with the silent complicity of the United States government.

Perhaps one of the major areas of globalization that really threatens not only the people of the Southern Hemisphere, but all those who share this planet, is the collectivization of culture. One of the primary consequences of the era of Western growth has been that it has attracted many of the world's people to "the party"; people without an invitation or the price of admission have been trying to force their way in.

Someone has written that America has become the image of the better future for the Third World poor. Unfortunately, this seems to be true. They have been attracted by our conspicuous consumption, our idolatrous materialism, and our selfish individualism, and many have become convinced that the modern culture of consumerism and growth is superior to their own traditional cultures. As a result, we are witnessing nothing less than the homogenization of world cultures into a single grey blob—a global consumer society that listens to the same kind of music, drinks the same soda, and increasingly buys into the same Western values.

The collectivization of culture finds perhaps its greatest ally in the proliferation and power of global communication networks. A communication industrial complex is being formed in which Western interests are increasingly seeking to gain control of communication networks in the Third World. From satellite television to local radio, advanced communication systems are consciously being used to promote a new global culture.[41] And all too often, Christian missions have unwittingly been a part of what is in essence a worldwide promotion of Western culture and a Western image of the better future (we shall discuss this further in chapter ten).

There are those who are challenging the collectivization of culture under the domination of Western values. A resurgence of nationalism and an emphasis on indigenous culture are competing with the forces

of Westernization. Mahatma Ghandi was one of the first to challenge
the encroachment of Western values and the image of the better future
implicit in those values. "He challenged almost all of the western ideals
that had taken root in India. Science should not order human values,
he argued, technology should not order society, and civilization was
not the indefinite multiplication of human wants, but their limitation
so that essentials could be shared by all." [42]

Ghandi's image of the better future for his people was a decentralized
society in which persons became self-reliant in meeting basic human
needs. However, he was opposed to a society of growing affluence because he was convinced it led to moral bankruptcy. His vision for
the better future gave primacy not to economic development, but the
development of the inner spirit and the reinforcement of positive values
within traditional culture.

Fortunately, there is one major transnational trend that is likely to
challenge the collectivization of culture on this planet by either communist expansion or Western acculturation: the dramatic growth of the
church in the Third World. Buhlman, in his book, *The Coming of
the Third Church,* predicts that by the year 2000 over half of all the
Christians in the world will reside in the Southern Hemisphere. There
will be a shift in power and leadership in the international church.
The church in Africa, Asia, and Latin America, which is young and
dynamic, will continue to experience dramatic growth, while many
churches in Europe and the United States decline. Interestingly, the
greatest church growth outside the Southern Hemisphere is likely to
take place in Eastern Europe, China, and the U.S.S.R. [43]

AWAKENING TO A FUTURE OF CHRISTIAN OPPORTUNITY

In the face of the uncertain and frightening future that is predicted
for the world, where should we place our hope? There have been various
answers suggested by those who have studied present trends and future
possibilities.

Herman Kahn and a few others still haven't completely given up
hope for the ascendancy of the Western dream. While they may belatedly
concede that it is impossible to have unlimited growth in a finite system,
they look for scientific and technological breakthroughs, as well as the
exploitation of stellar space, to save us.

Alvin Toffler reflects another basis for hope. Like Willis Harmon
and Hazel Henderson, he places his confidence not in our technological
prowess, but in the human spirit. He believes humankind will find
within its inner resources the ability to transcend this traumatic period,

and that we will see "the eruption of a new civilization on the earth." [44] Harmon sees a new transformational society arising like a phoenix out of the ashes of a decaying age.

Even the doomsayers, who see the forces for global decline and entropy outstripping the forces for creative change, haven't given up all hope for the human situation. Even Dennis Meadows (the author of *The Limits to Growth*) on his darkest day counseled that radical action in dramatically increasing food production, while reducing pollution, depletion of nonrenewable resources, industrial growth, and population growth, could still derail our rapid plunge to global suicide.

In a joint presentation to the global futures conference in Toronto last summer, Graham Kerr (the former Galloping Gourmet) and I presented yet another basis for hope. We explained that we were examining the future from an entirely different premise than were Herman Kahn, Hazel Henderson, or Willis Harmon. Our premise is "that the human future is not ultimately in the hands of man, but in the hands of God. Therefore, we can't count on our technological know-how, the essential goodness of the human spirit, or even radical global correctives, to save us."

Our hope, instead, is in the confidence that God is alive and well. He is the Lord of history, as Francis Schaeffer has insisted, "He is the God who is there!" He and he alone is our hope. But this doesn't mean that we passively sit back and watch it all slide to doom and destruction on our color TV sets. It means we must actively cooperate with God in his initiative for the human future.

All of the challenges facing us in our uncertain future are at their core spiritual issues. From resource depletion to political destabilization, we are wrestling with principalities and powers that are diametrically opposed to the initiative of God in history.

Christians in the Third World are often much more aware than those of us in the "scientized" West of the way the spiritual struggle permeates all of life and human society. We are often blinded to the larger spiritual reality as we respond to the shadows of our materialistic culture; as William Irwin Thompson has said, "We are like flies crawling across the ceiling of the Sistine Chapel. We cannot see what angels and gods lie underneath the threshold of our perceptions."[45]

But ultimately all human culture and organization are involved in this cosmic struggle. "The structures of this world which were intended to be our servants have instead become our masters and oppressors," Jim Wallis asserts. "All of this is a consequence of the Fall in which the powers also participate. . . . no longer instruments of God's love, they are in diametric opposition and rebellion to God's will and purposes. In fact, they have made themselves into gods (Gal. 4:8) and demand worship and absolute allegiance as objects of ultimate worth and value." [46]

The escalating human tragedy discussed in this chapter quite simply is the consequence of sin. Individuals, organizations, and nations have entered into unwitting complicity with the powers of darkness. We have elevated self-interest above the common good and participated in structures that are oppressing, exploiting, and destroying those with whom we share this world. The resource crisis, the competition for economic growth, and the escalating deprivation of the poor are all by-products of our malignant self-interest and sin.

Fortunately, God in Jesus Christ has intervened in this darkened, selfish world and is changing it by the power of his love. "The people who sat in darkness have seen a great light, and for those who were sitting in the region of death a light had dawned" (Matt. 4:16, RSV). In Christ's life, death, and resurrection the light has come into the world, and the power of darkness has been destroyed. God's good future for all peoples has already arrived. But we in the West have failed to make clear that a life-changing encounter with Christ is not a private affair. It is intended to change the very fabric of all society. As we relinquish self-interest in devotion to God and in service to others, we become a part of an international insurgency that is turning the world right side up.

We have the opportunity to both proclaim and demonstrate the Good News that God wants to change our lives and our world. He longs to liberate all people from the tyranny of selfishness and sin and to bring into being a new age of wholeness and love.

As we seek to complete the task of global evangelism, it is important that we remember that most of those who are unevangelized are among the poor and suffering peoples of the world. We will have to do more than bring a word of hope, we will have to respond to their physical needs, seek to correct the systems that oppress them, and authentically incarnate in our lives the Good News of the future of God.

There are 2.7 billion unreached people who don't know that hope has come into the world. At present, however, 95 percent of our mission resources are concentrated in reaching only 17 percent of those who haven't heard the gospel. Ralph Winter has convincingly argued in light of projected population growth through the year 2000 that the church will not complete its mission to the unreached peoples of the world without dramatically increasing the mission emphasis of the church in both the North and the South.[47] World Vision's MARC system provides comprehensive information on where these unreached people are throughout the planet.

Over three quarters of those who are unreached are estimated to be beyond the range of traditional methods of evangelism. We need to create wholly new approaches to cross-cultural evangelism if we have any hope of completing this phase of our mission.[48] It is difficult to understand how some feel Christ's return is so imminent when we still have such an extraordinary responsibility to complete the task of global evangelism.

As we focus on evangelism of unreached peoples, it is time that we Christians in the United States realize the extent to which we also need to be "evangelized." Quite frankly, many born-again Latin American believers don't even believe we are Christians. They ask, how could we possibly be Christians when we live lifestyles of such evident greed and self-interest while Christians in other parts of the world don't have enough to eat? They ask how can we be Christians when we support economic and political systems that are crushing them? [49]

As we awaken from the Western dream, it is important that we realize we are awakening to a world of expanding opportunity. The anticipated needs, threats, and challenges of our global future are in reality emerging opportunities for the people of God to make a difference. You are invited to join millions of Christians all over the world in the joyous conspiracy that is bringing the news of God's future to a world that without him looks increasingly bleak.

For Discussion and Action

1. What is the Western dream? Do you agree it is no longer attainable for all the peoples of the earth? If so, why?
2. What impact will the development of the last frontiers—stellar space and sea space—have on global society in the eighties and nineties? Is their development likely to significantly change the global forecast of dwindling resources?
3. Who is largely responsible for the "shrinking global pie"? Who is likely to be most hurt by this trend, and what issues does this new reality raise for American Christians in terms of our use of resources?
4. What are some of the predictions for the future of the poor, especially in the Southern Hemisphere? What implications does this forecast have for the mission of the church in the next two decades?
5. How do you respond when you read predictions such as those made in this chapter? What are your feelings—anger, guilt, skepticism, concern, helplessness? What are some ways we as individual Christians can respond responsibly to these predicted problems?
6. What are the reasons given for the predicted urban boom in the remainder

of the century? What can the church do to respond to this potential human tragedy before it is too late?

7. List some of the transnational forces which are working to globalize or collectivize the planet. What transnational trend is likely to challenge the collectivization of culture?

8. What "basis for hope" is offered by secular futurists such as Herman Kahn, Alvin Toffler, etc.? What is the basis for our hope as Christians, and how does that hope change the way we look at the future of the world?

9. What are the spiritual origins suggested in this chapter for the problems facing our world today and tomorrow? Do you think the conversion of individuals from the tyranny of selfishness and sin to a life of service can contribute to changing the world? How?

10. How does working to alleviate suffering and deprivation relate to the church's task of worldwide evangelism?

3.

Awakening from the American Dream—
A Nation in Transition

The short stout man stretched his stubby arms as far as they would reach around the massive elm, but he was unable to circle its girth with the long yellow ribbon. As I strolled the grounds around the United States Capitol, I saw every tree and shrub festooned in bright yellow ribbons flashing in the sunlight. Just behind where the man with the ribbon was losing his battle with the elm, workers were dismantling the huge platform where, just a few days before, Ronald Reagan had been inaugurated president.

AWAKENING TO YELLOW RIBBONS AND A NEW AMERICAN FUTURE

Washington and the rest of the nation were preparing to welcome the fifty-two Americans who for over a year had been held hostage by Iranian militants. I can remember only one other time when I witnessed such good feeling, unity, and national celebration—the end of the Second World War. *The New York Times* called the hostages' return a "national catharsis," and I am sure they were right.

I am convinced that the euphoria over the hostages' relief and the fanfare surrounding the 1980 presidential election reflected a deep longing on the part of Americans to feel good about ourselves as a people, to recover a new sense of direction as a nation. And Ronald Reagan's election has given many a genuinely needed sense of hope. During his inaugural address, Reagan spoke to the needs of countless Americans when he declared, "We are not doomed to decline." Certainly he is right about our spirit as a people; there is no reason to believe our spirit is "doomed to decline." We dare not ever allow our constitutional freedoms to decline. However, it is essential that we thoughtfully reexamine our national purposes if we want to avoid serious moral decline in the decades ahead.

The reality is that the eighties and nineties will mark the end not only of the Western dream of unrestrained growth, but also of the American Dream of unrestrained affluence. As a consequence of the rapid depletion of nonrenewable resources, the United States is entering a major transitional period from a time of high growth and prosperity to a future of scarcity and limits.

We have, in this time of transition, the opportunity to choose what direction we will take as a nation. We can attempt to maintain the party at all costs—to return to the "good old days" of expanding prosperity. I believe that to choose that course is to choose the road to rapid moral decline. To attempt to return to high growth and ever-increasing levels of consumption can only cause increased deprivation for the planetary poor, and the Bible teaches from Isaiah to Amos that God judges those who prosper at the expense of the poor.

But we have another choice. In the eighties and nineties, we have the opportunity to discover a new dream for our nation—a dream that reaches beyond progress and prosperity. We have the opportunity to rise above narrow national interests and to become more fully a nation for others. It is the responsibility of those of us who are Christians to be advocates for righteousness, justice, and peace—to begin to help our fellow Americans discover a new sense of national purpose in this time of transition. Rufus Miles states, "The very idea of participating in a thoughtful search for a different destiny for Americans can be a deeply satisfying adventure." [1]

In this chapter I want to outline what I believe will be the new human challenges that are likely to flood American society in the eighties and nineties, particularly as they relate to the poor and forgotten people in our midst. And I will look at ways the church can respond to these challenges, creating compassionate new ministries in the face of new crises. Each anticipated challenge is an emerging opportunity for us to make a difference in our own neighborhoods, our communities, and in the nation as a whole.

AWAKENING TO DECLINING EXPECTATIONS AND INCREASING SCARCITY

The eighties are the first decade we have entered as a people which we didn't expect to be better at the end than at the beginning. Surveys indicate that Americans sense we are entering a time of transition; in one poll 62 percent of the respondents agreed with the statement, "Americans should get used to the fact that our wealth is limited and that most of us are not likely to be better off than we are now." [2]

In the next two decades our lives are likely to be dramatically changed by mounting shortages of energy, water, and other resources on which we have become dependent. One of the major reasons for this is the incredible wastefulness of our throw-away society. Our lifestyles are roughly equivalent to those of our neighbors in Western Europe, and yet we use twice the resources they do. It is estimated that 65 percent of the food served in U.S. restaurants and 25 percent of the food served in American homes finds its way into garbage cans,[3] and research indicates we waste half the energy we purchase.

Amory Lovins, in his article, "Energy Strategy: The Road Not Taken?" and the Harvard University energy study both maintain the United States could learn to live "within our energy income" if we mounted a serious national program of conservation (our cheapest energy source) and the creative use of energy alternatives. Such action not only would improve our economic situation and reduce our political vulnerability; it would also mean more energy at lower prices for other planetary inhabitants—particularly the poor. And it would greatly reduce the chance of young Americans' being sent to war to maintain our energy-extravagant lifestyles. Unfortunately, our national energy policy seems to be moving in the opposite direction.

The depletion of resources is not the only future problem now being created by our throw-away society. We are only beginning to discover the hazards of living in the midst of our garbage. Some estimates suggest that over 75 percent of our cancers are environmentally induced. With Love Canal and Three Mile Island fresh in our memories, we are now being told we are sitting on a "toxic time bomb." Douglas Castle, administrator of the Environmental Protection Agency, says new revelations on waste disposal "will shock our nation," that over 90 percent of the millions of tons of hazardous waste produced each year is disposed of in ways which don't conform to responsible standards.[4]

Even as environmental hazards increase, there is evidence that Americans are already backing away from environmental protection as a national priority. "Jobs first"—not environment—is already becoming the watchword of the eighties,[5] and "increasingly, environmentalists are being driven to weigh social and economic costs of pollution control against its benefits." [6] The environmental and energy policies of the Reagan administration reflect this change in national priority. In the future we can anticipate a further slackening of environmental regulations, with increasing health problems and contamination of the air, water, and food supply as part of the hidden price tag for attempting to stimulate the economy.

AWAKENING TO SLOW GROWTH AND DOUBLE-DIGIT INFLATION

The economy itself can be expected to follow the pattern of "more of the same" during the eighties and the nineties. The average growth in productivity dropped from 3.2 percent in the period from 1947 to

1966 to 1.7 percent in the years between 1966 and 1977.[7] At the same time, the plight of the United States auto industry, soaring interest rates, the escalating cost of energy, the high cost of government, and a host of other factors conspired to keep the country in an inflationary situation. This combination of slow growth and high inflation will continue in the next two decades, predict Wharton economists and other economic forecasters such as Chase Econometrics.[8]

This is hard for many Americans to accept. "The principal economic reality of the '80s," states Richard Barnet, "is that we are in a slow growth economy without the political or economic understanding to deal with it. Our present economic ideas and governmental tools are inherited from a unique moment in economic history, the two decades from 1950 to 1970, which was a period of rapid growth which is not likely to be repeated." [9]

Many of the current proposals to strengthen the economy by balancing the federal budget, reducing inflation, stimulating jobs, and cutting taxes—including the Reagan administration's proposals—have in mind a return to the high-growth national lifestyle we enjoyed in the fifties and sixties.[10] I imagine almost everyone wants to see inflation reduced, jobs increased, the federal budget balanced, and taxes cut, but there is the question of whether it is possible to achieve that kind of sustained high economic growth in the coming decades. I think not; without access to large quantities of inexpensive resources—particularly oil—chances that we will be able to sustain high economic growth are slim, though the current administration's program may well bring a brief upturn.

Besides, there are hidden costs to assuming a high growth policy in the eighties—health hazards, environmental decline, and increased suffering for the poor that are competing with us for limited planetary resources. We do need to grow as a nation, but we need to combine growth with a concern for benefitting the greatest number of people and for using resources justly. The church has the opportunity—and the responsibility—to speak out for justice in economic growth, to encourage our nation to pursue a course of responsible growth in the eighties and nineties.

AWAKENING TO THE DECADES OF THE AMERICAN POOR

Who are likely to be hurt most by continued inflation and scarcity of resources in the decades ahead? Who are likely to pay the greatest share of the costs of stabilizing the economy? Who are likely to be the first to leave the party? That's right, it will be the poor—the seniors, the Blacks, the Indians, and the Hispanics. Those who are already on the bottom rungs of the ladder will be the first to feel the crunch. But as we approach the end of the decade, the middle class is likely to lose record numbers from the party as well.

On a hot, sticky summer day on the Northside of St. Louis, an old woman climbs off a bus with a small bag of groceries. She had worked at a factory for twenty-five years, then was laid off without a pension when the factory went out of business. "Her husband died ten years ago. She lives alone on a small social security check. . . . She kicked her grocery bag: 'I pay double the prices and get half as much. . . . It's over now,' she said. 'We had some hope here ten to fifteen years ago. Back then it was only poor Blacks they said were worthless. We could fight against that. But now the dollar is worthless too. Nobody can fight that. . . .'

"The foreboding of this woman—one of twenty-five million citizens the government says is poor—is part of what most politicians and economists now accept as unavoidable: the poor are about to be devastated by the onrushing economic chaos." [11]

Senior citizens are going to be around in record numbers in the eighties, and they will make up a larger percentage of the population. A shrinking labor force will be struggling to support the pension and social security systems essential to the survival of their elders. There is a growing possibility that younger workers may rebel against this burden and that the pension and social security systems will undergo major change.

As the senior citizen population swells, the number of those living on fixed incomes will swell, too. They will be the "new poor" of the eighties, the first ones of the middle class to leave the party. It is extremely difficult for many of these people to apply for public assistance, and some will choose to go hungry rather than receive help from the government.

Increasingly, the poor are going to have to choose between heating and eating. The inflationary spiral in home heating fuels is going to grow worse now that oil has been deregulated. 16.2 million households with incomes 125 percent of the poverty level are presently spending more than 10 percent of their disposable income on heating. The problem is that next winter their expenditure for heating energy will be 25 percent of their income. In some areas like New England, it will range as high as 50 percent.[12]

"Keeping Warm" is the title of a brochure produced by the United States government for senior citizens. The booklet instructs seniors in winter survival strategies, such as wrapping their feet in old newspapers and shoving them back in their shoes. One section encourages them to find someone who has heat and hang around as long as possible—

as a conscious survival strategy. Some Lutheran Churches I have worked with in Pennsylvania are contacting utility companies in their area so they can assist seniors who have their heat cut off. This growing need provides an important opportunity for Christians throughout this nation to create innovative programs to enable the poor to provide for basic food and energy needs.

Housing for the poor is likely to be one of the major domestic crises of the eighties. Jim Wallis, Editor of *Sojourners,* told me that one hundred thousand people were projected to be displaced from inner city housing in Washington, D.C., by 1984. No one has any idea where they will move. And this story can be repeated in every urban community in the nation. The combined forces of the condominium boom, the white flight back into the city, the steady destruction of affordable housing stock, and the outrageous inflation of housing and rent prices in many areas are combining to literally push the poor into the streets. Though some low-income housing programs are available, they will be woefully inadequate for the need in the next decade. Families are already reported living under bridges and viaducts on the East Coast.

By anticipating where the housing crisis for the poor is going to be most critical and by responding innovatively, the Church can lead in meeting this challenge before we are confronted by an urban disaster. For example, members of the Sojourners Fellowship have successfully enabled the poor in their neighborhood in Washington, D.C., to purchase and gain control of seven apartment houses. If hundreds of churches joined this type of compassionate ministry, thousands of seniors and urban poor could have decent housing in the eighties and nineties.

Even though the Reagan administration is likely to significantly increase the number of jobs in the early eighties, the competition for those jobs is going to dramatically increase. Senior citizens unable to make it on their fixed incomes are already flooding back onto the labor market in record numbers. Some are proposing postponing retirement until age seventy in an attempt to correct this problem.[13]

In addition to seniors, there will be significantly more women entering the work force in the eighties. In 1970, 50 percent of the women aged twenty-five to fifty-four were working or seeking employment outside the home. That figure jumped to 60 percent in 1979, and is projected to climb to 70 percent by the end of the eighties.[14]

Even with the baby boom behind us, young people will be seeking employment in record numbers; handicapped persons and aliens will also become increasingly competitive in seeking jobs. As economic conditions become tougher, so will the job market, and unemployment statistics can be expected to climb.

In the coming decades, unemployment will continue to be highest among Blacks (closely followed by Native Americans and Hispanics). Despite Affirmative Action programs, the number of unemployed Black family heads almost tripled between 1969 and 1978, and unemployment among Black young people has been running between 20 and 40 percent.[15] Black unemployment has consistently run at least double the national average.

This percentage is likely to grow as we move into the decade, since the quality of public schooling is likely to continue its sharp decline. This will be a problem for all who attend public schools, but especially for young inner city Blacks; Barnard C. Watson, vice president of Temple University, declares, "The education too many children receive in these [inner city] schools is nothing short of a national scandal, an absolute disgrace." [16] The growth of the private school movement and the trend toward discontinuing integration efforts will probably contribute to the drop in quality of public education.

To make matters worse for Black citizens, the income of Black families is falling in comparison to that of their white counterparts, primarily because, while the number of wage earners in white households has increased, there has been a decrease in the number of multiple earners in Black families.[17] The number of Black families considered "poor" is likely to continue rising, particularly in light of federal cutbacks in job programs and increased automation of unskilled and semiskilled jobs currently available. John McDermott, a Chicago reporter, said, "There is a new kind of poverty here. . . . What we have is a group permanently unemployed and permanently dependent. There is a growing social chaos within this group, complete social isolation. Their only window to America is the television set." [18]

Endemic poverty and crushing unemployment also plague many Hispanic communities in the United States—Mexican, Puerto Rican, Cuban, Central and South American. Hispanics are going to become a much larger and more vocal minority group in the eighties, one that will demand greater economic and social justice in a society of scarcity. The Native Americans will continue to be the poorest of the poor. Thirty-four percent of the Indian people in the United States still make less than four thousands dollars a year.[19]

While the seventies were the "Decade of Me," the eighties are likely to be the "Decade of Us and Them," unless Christians embark on major ministries of reconciliation and justice. The Miami riots that shocked the country in the summer of 1980 were an important signal of the depth of rage brewing as the rich get richer while the poor get poorer. Given shrinking resources and growing competition for jobs and housing, we are likely to see growing polarization and conflict between rich and poor, and between the various ethnic groups as well.

But it's not just the folks on the bottom rung who will feel the crunch of the eighties and nineties. Have you noticed how much you are paying for food, shelter, and energy lately? The party is over for everyone!

As I have already mentioned, the seniors will be the first to leave the party, but middle-class young won't be far behind them. The birthright of the middle-class young has usually been to automatically start off a third again as good as mom and dad. If the folks live in a modest bungalow, the offspring expect to start life with a split-level ranch style. If mom and dad have an old Chevy, the young expect to drive a brand new set of wheels.

Well, no one has told them yet, but we are likely to lose many of the young from the middle class by the end of the decade. Growing numbers will be unable to afford a new or used house, postsecondary education, or the kinds of health care to which they have become accustomed.

The eighties and the nineties will present Christians in the United States with a special responsibility for the growing numbers of American poor. The Bible repeatedly warns, from Isaiah to the New Testament, that those who live well at the expense of the poor will face judgment. Listen to God's warning through Amos: "You trample on the poor and force them to give you grain. Therefore, though you have built stone mansions, you will not live in them; though you have planted lush vineyards you will not drink their wine. For I know how many are your offenses and how great your sins. . . . Seek good, not evil, that you may live" (Amos 5:11–12, 14, NIV).

In an American future marred by the specter of growing poverty, American Christians will have a special opportunity to "seek good, not evil" by sharing our resources with the poor and helping them become self-reliant. What better way to plant Mustard Seeds, to make a difference in an American future of hunger and need.

AWAKENING TO A FUTURE OF
LIMPING LIBERALISM AND GALLOPING CONSERVATISM

In the sixties, when the United States was experiencing such extravagant levels of affluence, we were inclined to invite the poor, the Black, the Hispanics, and the Indians to the party, too. We benevolently passed legislation and set up programs opening up employment and educational opportunities to those on the bottom rung of the ladder. And for a while during the War on Poverty during the sixties, the gap between rich and poor was actually narrowing.

With Richard Nixon's policy of "Benign Neglect" that all began to change. Not only is the gap between the American rich and poor widening again; many of the gains made during the civil rights movement are being seriously eroded. What happened is that many middle-class Americans discovered it wasn't possible to provide equal opportunity for all citizens without it costing them something. As it became clear that the poor could only achieve equality and justice at the expense of the middle class, the liberalism of the sixties began to die a slow, painful death [20] (although in its wake we are likely to see new coalitions of those on the left formed to challenge the new domestic and foreign policies).

One of the major reasons traditional liberalism is in eclipse, I believe, is that liberals are often unwilling to get personally involved in the struggles of the poor or to make any sacrifice for the cause of social justice (although they may "support" these causes). For example, one night on the television program, "Sixty Minutes," liberal black and white congressmen who advocate busing for racial integration were interviewed. When they were asked where their kids went to school in Washington, D.C., each of them explained with various rationales that it was necessary for their children to go to private schools. Similarly, middle-class white social workers often commute into the inner city to help "deprived" kids, then retreat to their surburban sanctuaries in the evening. It seems to me that many liberals have never come to grips with this serious problem of incongruence between what they believe and what they live.

Another reason liberalism is on the way out is the liberal tendency to see all human care as a governmental responsibility. Until the 1600s, the church was the only agent of human concern in Western culture. With the introduction of the Elizabethan poor laws in the early 1600s, the state first got involved in the delivery of human services. In our early American experience, increasing numbers of services were provided by local governments. Finally with the passage of the Social Security Act of 1935, the federal government became involved.

The Social Security Act and other federal measures granting help to the poor did correct a number of abuses in enabling the poor to have more equitable access to financial assistance. However, one of the unanticipated consequences of implementing such legislation was that it undermined vast networks of informal community, church, and family care structures in American society. These informal systems of providing for persons in need were often extremely effective, compassionate, and inexpensive.

Governmental intervention into human services significantly increased the tendency toward formal, institutional, professional, cost-intensive systems of care. And many churches have in recent decades relinquished the care of those in need almost exclusively to the state.

Belatedly, however, we are discovering the state doesn't necessarily "do it better." We are finding that often the state's interest is in keeping the lid on racism, poverty, and injustice—not in ending these abuses. We are discovering that many governmental care systems—prisons, state hospitals, and welfare departments—are brutalizing, dehumanizing, and corrupting, and that these systems often provide more assistance to the middle-class professionals who run them than to the poor they are supposed to serve. And of course, as conservatives point out, such programs are expensive; it is becoming harder and harder in a time of diminishing resources to provide the cash-flow intensive services many liberals support.

While political liberalism is suffering a lingering death, then, a new political force has galloped to our rescue—neoconservatism. Since 1976, America has been making a slow veer to the right which culminated in a sharp right turn during the 1980 presidential election.

I believe this is understandable in light of our "shrinking pie." As we become increasingly aware that there isn't enough to go around, our natural instinct seems to be to "conserve" as big a piece of the pie for ourselves and our loved ones as possible.

The dominant conservative outlook is that the future should be left not to state planners but to the free market mechanism. They genuinely believe that a system in which all people are free to get as much as they can for themselves will work for the common good.

This general economic and political outlook underlies the conservative attitude toward the poor. While political liberals were inclined to "help" the poor by setting up programs and institutions, the conservatives have tended to ignore them, concluding that certain problems—particularly the problems of the poor—are essentially insoluble. They tend to think that, "whether by nature or by nurture, by constitution or culture, the members of this group have been so seriously injured that they are to a large degree ineducable, unemployable, and alien to middle-class norms of behavior. They are, to boil it all down, 'shiftless.' " [21]

Today's conservatives, certain the state shouldn't be called upon to try to solve the intractable problem of the poor, are moving beyond Nixon's policy of "benign neglect" to active neglect of the "shiftless." The trend is toward cutbacks in government services at all levels, and the result, unless the church and other concerned parties step in to fill the gaps, will be disaster for large segments of the American poor. While it is true that government does not necessarily "do it better," it is also true that, as programs are dismantled without putting anything in their place, thousands are going to suffer.

(Actually, I am persuaded that the problem is deeper than a question of economics. There seems to be within the American psyche a deep animosity towards our poor. We find greater tolerance in our hearts for the Mafia and for those involved in white-collar crime—after all, they keep their yards up and they're obviously successful in their work—but we seem to hate the welfare mother who is struggling to simply keep life together. In my younger days I was a social worker, and I am fully aware that there are some welfare recipients who take advantage of the system—just like some corporations and labor unions do. However, my experience has shown that the majority of the poor are genuinely in need and are not trying to rip off anyone.)

Mary Clay is paralyzed from the neck down because of a spinal injury. She and her fifteen-year-old son have been able to continue living in their home, which is "bought and paid for," because the state of Washington has provided chore services. As a result of state cutbacks, however, it is likely these chore services will be discontinued. The consequence will be the breakup of Mary's family. She will be placed in a nursing home and her son in a foster home, and they will be forced to sell their house to pay expenses. Ironically, in the long run it will cost much more for Mary to live in a nursing home. After the money from the sale of her home is used up the state prefers paying nursing home payments to paying for chore services . . . because "the federal government picks up half the tab for nursing costs." [22]

In the eighties and nineties, thousands of Mary Clays are going to have essential assistance cut and sometimes have their homes broken up. They will fight back, but they have no political leverage and they will lose. Those who are intent on conserving and expanding their piece of the pie at the expense of the "shiftless" poor will win.

That may not be the end of it, however. Already, undercurrents of rage are flowing among those who have been left out of the party. As resources dwindle, as fuel, food, and jobs become scarcer, these undercurrents can be expected to intensify. In ignoring the poor, neoconservative America may be igniting a time bomb under what is left of the American dream.

Of course, at this point there has been no serious attempt to cut *all* essential services to the poor out of the federal budget. However, it would be an error to assume there is any safeguard for the future of the American poor in the face of galloping conservatism. There is no way the United States can embark on a major increase in arms expenditure, balance the budget, and provide across-the-board tax cuts without someone paying. Evidence suggests that the poor will be saddled with an unjust share of the costs of these adjustments.

Increased suffering for the poor and the social unrest that goes with it are not the only dangers to be found in the new conservatism. Riding on the coattails of the conservative movement, although repudiated by most conservative leaders, are the most reactionary elements in American society. The "new" Ku Klux Klan has set out to achieve an image of social respectability as it expands its blatantly racist activities across the United States. Small organizations are already forming to "conserve" power and wealth along essentially racist lines through training citizens in civil violence. Their extreme conservatism is based on an incredible range of conspiratorial fantasies, many of which reflect an alarming growth of antisemitism. *Time* magazine reports that there are twenty-five thousand "Christians" involved in the formation of these paramilitary groups, and that these groups are committed to doing anything they have to do to survive in the future—including blowing away hungry people.[23]

Perhaps the most serious threat of "galloping conservatism" is that in a time of crisis it could be easily transformed into full-blown fascism. When people are afraid they are susceptible to trading away their civil freedoms to protect their "things." One of the archapostles of conservative economics, Milton Friedman, has already said that, given the choice between preserving American constitutional freedoms and the economic freedom to make a dollar without interference, he would choose economic freedom hands down.[24] How tragically ironic it would be if conservative Americans bartered away their constitutional liberties to preserve their affluent lifestyles!

The political climate in the United States in the eighties and nineties is likely to include more than just the struggle between the traditional political forces of left and right. In the next two decades, we will see the emergence of new brokers of power. OPEC and other organizations are accumulating vast amounts of capital, and the ways in which that capital is used will shape all our futures. As a result of the new emphasis on supply-side economics, increasingly smaller numbers of corporations will control larger and larger shares of the total productive capability of the planet, and will influence the political direction of our nation. They have already become a potent political force, raising enormous "war chests" to defeat citizen initiatives in housing, recycling, and a host of other issues. " 'If corporate interests can dominate both legislation and referenda with their dollars,' warns the Director of the Public Citizen's Congress Watch, 'then the golden rule prevails—he who has the gold rules.' " [25]

One of the most important political and economic struggles of the eighties and nineties will be between the forces that want to centralize society—economically, politically, and culturally—and those who want to decentralize. An example of economic centralization is the oil giants' attempts to buy up all the new solar technology they can, intending to monopolize the sun so they can continue to sell us energy through their large centralized systems. Some smaller firms, on the other hand, are trying to develop independent energy systems that can be hung on individual roofs—that is economic decentralization.

The centuries-old controversy between those who want to strengthen the power of the federal government and those who want to keep power on a local level is another aspect of this struggle between centralization and decentralization. Among the strongest advocates of decentralization are the two thousand special interest groups in the United States. These groups, ranging from the Committee to Defeat Union Bosses to Common Cause, work for reducing centralization of government by increasing the political power of the average citizen.[26]

Among the potentially most powerful groups in the eighties and nineties will be those who are passionately committed to a cause—whether political or social or religious. Highly committed people have the capacity to be either a societal threat (as in the case of terrorist groups) or a source of societal renewal (as in groups such as Catholic Workers, Bread for the World, and Sojourners, all of whom represent a new breed of religious organization who are seriously working for social change).

There is a broad spectrum of new brokers of power who are seeking to shape the American future. Some control vast resources. Others control production and information systems. As a historian, however, I am betting in the long haul that the future will belong to those who have the highest level of commitment.

Where does the church fit in with regard to the political developments we are likely to see in the next two decades? Undeniably, all Christians need to be actively involved in influencing the directions of the government. We must be the voice of conscience speaking out on ethical issues like the family, abortion, and social values, and challenging the abuse of power by those who control resources. Certainly the church must take a leading role in rapidly activating and expanding informal, low-cost care networks to supplement and replace government programs that are either being dropped or who fail to provide adequate care for needy individuals. Community, church, and family care systems must be quickly catalyzed to assume a major share of the responsibility in meeting human needs in the eighties and nineties, and the church is in an optimum position to do this. Personally, I am convinced the church can "do it better" if we grasp the opportunity. (In chapter nine we will consider this possibility in more detail.)

In order to work for Christ's kingdom in the eighties and nineties, however, the church will have to disavow its mindless support of secular agendas of the left, right, or middle. As Pat Robertson of the 700 Club has stated, the church of Jesus Christ dares not become captive to either the political right or left.

In the past few decades, several mainline denominations have seemed to work more or less unquestioningly from the rhetoric of the left. This has often resulted in alienation of grassroots churches, who see all too clearly the failures of liberalism. On the other hand, many conservative Christians seem to have confused the gospel of Jesus Christ with the party line of the right. In fact, it is often impossible to get even a piece of tissue paper between the views of the political right and the new fundamentalist religious right; from ignoring the plight of the poor to promoting American supremacy and nuclear stockpiling, their agendas are the same.

A number of people on the religious right have been persuaded by books like Tim LaHaye's *Battle for the Mind* [27] to see the pervasive secularism of modern society as a "humanist conspiracy." They've actually come to believe that the small handful of individuals who signed something called the "Humanist Manifesto" are conspiring through government, public education, the media, labor unions, and liberal organizations to create a one-world society that is atheistic and amoral. Although there is no evidence that this small group of people is in any way involved in a worldwide conspiracy, this viewpoint has led some of the religious right to seek to remove from office anyone who is not politically conservative, in an effort to thwart this imagined conspiracy. In the process, they have become unwitting tools of the political right.

Can't we free ourselves from being held hostage to either the political left or the political right? Can't we develop our own political agenda directly from our unique biblical perspective, and call society to march to a new drumbeat based on God's plan for human society? Can't we become God's voice speaking out both for social righteousness and for economic justice for all people?

As the people of God, we must struggle for reconciliation and unity regardless of our backgrounds or political outlook. We can't afford to be fragmented. Christians of all traditions and political persuasions need to get to know one another, discuss our differences, and be reconciled as brothers and sisters committed to a common mission.

Recently, our Seattle chapter of Evangelicals for Social Action hosted representatives of the Moral Majority for the State of Washington in a day-long session, getting to know one another as persons and listening to one another's ideas. In the course of the session we discovered, to our surprise, several areas of common concern—such as the family and abortion on demand. Perhaps more importantly, we discovered we could be reconciled together as believers in Christ, in spite of our major differences on political issues and strategies. In such dialogue and common purpose lies a new dream for the future—for American Christians on both the left and the right.

AWAKENING TO OMNIPOTENCE, OMNISCIENCE, AND IMMORTALITY THROUGH SCIENCE AND TECHNOLOGY

As the United States faces a future of increased deprivation and need, many look to the power and wisdom of science to help us not only maintain the Great American Party, but also to make it a more spectacular event than anything ever before experienced by humankind. These technological optimists look to advances in science and medicine to solve the energy crisis, do away with hunger and disease, give us unchallenged military superiority, and create a technological wonderland. (Someone has even seriously proposed a "technofix" solution to the problem of unrest—the construction of geodesic domes over large American cities. To insure that the hungry and frustrated don't riot during long, hot summers, the airflow could be manipulated to vary the oxygen mix and induce lethargy! [28])

It is true that in the coming decades we will witness an unprecedented surge in technology. By far the largest population explosion of the century, declares Buckminister Fuller, will be the computer population boom. He predicts the exponential generation of computers will decisively outstrip the human population of this planet by the year 2000.[29] And while inflation in most goods and services is likely to trouble our future, anti-inflation will be the story in the computer market. The use of the silicon chip and the increasingly inexpensive production of microcomputers are already creating a computer revolution which will put computer technology in the hands of virtually every citizen. *Computerworld,* a trade magazine, trumpets, "If the auto industry had done what the computer industry has done in the last thirty years, a Rolls Royce would cost $2.50 and get two million miles to the gallon." [30]

In the future, microcomputers will be available to run our appliances, project our budgets, monitor our use of energy, and provide access to virtually unlimited quantities of information. As the computer is wedded to the TV set—particularly the cable TV—the possibilities will increase exponentially. In the eighties and the nineties the TV set will be transformed into a home information center, capable of doing everything from delivering mail to creating art and music.[31] Such systems may even be used for instant citizen initiatives or referenda.[32] Through cable

TV, persons in certain types of occupations will be able to commute to work electronically and thus save energy. It will be possible to hold electronic conferences and to significantly eliminate the incredible expense of fixed-site meetings. We will probably become even more dependent on our home information centers than we are on our old-fashioned TVs.

What we will be witnessing through the wedding of computers and television will be the decentralization of information, the creation of a citizens communication network, and the eclipse of the television industry as we know it. All three consequences will significantly change the character of American life. Cable TV and other video equipment will put the viewer back in the driver seat; no longer will three networks be able to exclusively decide what is good for American viewers.

We are already on the verge of this communications revolution. CATV now has fifteen million homes subscribing to its service. By 1985, the number of cable TV homes will double to thirty million— 35 percent of the viewing market. On top of this, it is predicted there will be forty million videodisc machines in the United States by 1990.[33]

But communication technology is just one aspect of the technological explosion that will change our lives in the eighties and nineties. We can expect to see increased emphasis on the development and use of biological and medical engineering—the technologies of life and death.

In 1980, in a historic five to four decision, the Supreme Court ruled that new forms of life created in the laboratory could be patented. That decision was the harbinger of a whole new age. Over one hundred applications for patents on new organisms and processes for creating life forms have been waiting in the wings for that decision. Developers of these new life forms promise that they will gobble up oil spills, clean up toxic waste sites, duplicate photosynthesis, enable plants to fix nitrogen, create inexpensive chemicals, produce synthetic protein, and manufacture antibiotics.[34] "Theoretically, any process occurring in nature can be harnessed for man's use," reports Irving Johnson, Vice President of Research for Eli Lilly.[35]

The economic incentives for moving into the business of creating new life forms are unprecedented in modern business. Because of the tremendous financial rewards of creating "biological factories," General Electric and other established corporations are being joined by new firms such as Genetech and Genex in this gold rush of the eighties. Genetic engineering is being touted as the solution to many of the human challenges we will confront in the future.

But not all scientists share this euphoric optimism. "Dr. Liebe Cavalieri of the Sloan-Kettering Institute feels that the A-bomb, nerve gas, biological warfare, and the destruction of the ozone level are all less of a threat to human existence than recombinant DNA. 'All these dangers can, in theory if not in practice, be limited or controlled,' notes Cavalieri. 'The threat of a new life form is more compelling, for once released, it cannot be controlled and its effects cannot be reversed.' " [36] Jeremy Rifkin insists that the central issue is the human intervention into the mystery of life itself. He believes it is only a question of time until scientists alter human life. [37] We will have the capability to genetically remake the human species and alter human nature.

With scientific knowledge and technological power comes not only the ability to create life, but to control life and death. Not far in the future, it is likely that families will be given the opportunity to select the sex of their unborn children, and sperm banks will consciously be used to manipulate the gene pools out of which many of tomorrow's children will spring. Genetic therapy will increasingly be used not only to treat genetic disease in individuals, but also to alter the gene pool in an effort to eliminate genetic disorders such as sickle cell anemia and hemophilia. [38] After we have corrected genetic disorders, it is probable that momentum will grow to "improve" the human organism.

At the same time, the advocacy of active euthanasia and the legalization of suicide will increasingly become issues of public debate. In a society of growing scarcity in which a person's worth is directly tied to his or her economic productivity, the criteria for sustaining life could be the ability to be a productive citizen. In an overpopulated future, the planned termination of "surplus" people could come to seem desirable to many others.

The explosion of science and technology in the eighties and the nineties will offer both opportunities and challenges for the church. Certainly the boom in computers and communications will give local churches new tools for effective social action and evangelism programs in their communities. But the features that make cable TV and computers so attractive also make them extremely vulnerable to abuse. Any time a viewer orders diet pills or expresses an opinion on the ERA through cable TV, that information can be intercepted and stored. A detailed profile can be maintained on every viewer. Churches and Christian organizations need to develop the capability to anticipate possible uses and abuses of new computer communication technologies and to play a leadership role in monitoring their future application.

It is even more urgent for Christians to be aware of the challenge presented by the new technologies of life and death. The development of ways to control birth and death and to create new life forms raises serious ethical questions for the future. Whose values will be used to determine how genetic engineering is used, or when and if a life should be terminated? What will be the long-term consequences of manipulating the gene pool or legitimizing suicide? The church has an opportunity and an obligation to anticipate and address these unprecedented ethical issues while there is still time.

The heady power of science has made some drunk with a sense of omnipotence. "We must redo the human," asserts F. M. Esfandiary, a technological extremist. To do this, he says, "we must begin by redoing the human body. The body has been our greatest hangup. Our most serious obstacle to a higher evolution." Esfandiary then outlines how humans can transcend their humanity, seeking nothing less than immortality through science. He advocates the increased fusing of man and machine to augment human potential, and urges that we use our expanding knowledge of the human brain to surgically and electronically develop superhuman mental processes.[39]

But it is no mere coincidence that C. S. Lewis, in his novel, *This Hideous Strength*,[40] used just such an idea to picture the final chapter of human history. He depicts a scientific research center, built over the site of Merlin's well, in which the brain of the leader is artificially kept alive by a network of wires, tubes, and computers. The brain continues to direct, to communicate, to "live" after its body has died. What for people like Esfandiary is the highest expression of human hope—man transcending his own mortality through science—was for Lewis the most demonic expression of human science. Lewis could find no more horrible specter to communicate his urgent concern for the human future than the fusion of man and machine with the intent of overcoming human limitations.

Modern science is committed to the absolutely unrestricted pursuit of scientific knowledge, and the pursuit of knowledge is in reality the pursuit of power. Since we took the first bite of the apple, man has longed to know as God knows, to control as God controls—indeed to be a god. This longing for omniscience, omnipotence, and—yes—even immortality is inherent within the human species. Modern man, through science and technology, has taken increasing responsibility not only for controlling his present but for shaping his future. He has really come to believe his own illusion that he is in charge, that he can, through his own rational efforts, become godlike.

As Christians we need to ask ourselves, as we look at the technological revolution around us, "From whence does our salvation come? Where does our security lie? From a Christian perspective, what place should science and technology play in society?" And we need to recognize that economic, political, and scientific systems that are not under the Lordship of Christ are part of the principalities and powers of this world. Their agenda is not the agenda of Christ. Their trust is not in the initiative of God but in the power of the human initiative to shape our future. Far from being value-free, modern science is, as Theodore Roszak has pointed out, filled with pervasive and relatively invisible values that are influencing all culture.

In a future in which science and technology play an increasingly crucial role in our lives, it will be especially important for the church to reexamine the fundamental commitment of science to the unrestricted pursuit of knowledge and the increasing intention of science to control the very substance of life and death. It is our responsibility to help steer science and technology in light of our ethical concerns for the human future.

AWAKENING TO INDIVIDUALS AND FAMILIES IN TRANSITION

All the projections discussed in this chapter—dwindling resources, continued inflation, growing conservativism, and the scientific revolution—will have a staggering impact on the American family. As our supply of resources grows smaller, an antiwaste morality will necessarily gain popular support in the eighties. However, right alongside it will be new waves of consumer products and services that we will need like we need a plastic buggy whip. The cosmetics industry already has plans to persuade men to increase their consumption of cosmetics 75 percent. Fun will be commercialized on an unprecedented scale; in the eighties and nineties we will see an explosion of electric gaming, travel in solar-propelled derigibles, space travel simulation game centers, sensory stimulation chambers, and the possible introduction of games of violence such as rollerball. We will become a people even more preoccupied with immediate gratification, and we will be willing to pay for it.[41]

In the next two decades, the middle-class family will find itself increasingly stressed by growing scarcity, high inflation, societal dislocation, moral decline, and growing awareness of the plight of the poor. The danger is that these stresses will cause families to draw into a defensive posture and simply struggle to maintain their security and lifestyles. (On the positive side, these pressures may force people to do more for themselves and in cooperation with each other. Many families may become active participants in the "decentralist" movement, joining food co-ops and working as community volunteers.)

The stresses of our rapidly changing future will also stress relationships within the family. The family is in no danger of disappearing; in fact, there is a resurgence of emphasis on the importance of family life. But fragmentation is likely to slowly increase. At present, there is one divorce for every 1.8 marriages, and that percentage is growing. One of the serious societal consequences of fragmentation in the eighties and nineties will be a dramatic increase in single-parent households.

Those of us who share a prolife concern must recognize that a significant reduction in the number of abortions will significantly increase the number of unwanted and neglected children in our society. To be prolife without immediately preparing for the care and adoption of growing numbers of rejected and abandoned kids is both irresponsible and immoral.

Unfortunately, it is likely that families—Christian and non-Christian alike—will continue to educate their children in the self-indulgent, materialistic values of American culture. Young people raised with no internal system of ethical choice other than their own self-gratification will continue to disappoint themselves and society. Sexual promiscuity of all kinds will increase as personal morality declines in the eighties. And at the same time, as we mentioned earlier in the chapter, large numbers of middle-class young people will be hard-pressed to support the lifestyles they have come to expect as their birthright.

We in the church have the opportunity and the challenge to educate our young people now for the future, to show them ways to simplify their lives voluntarily rather than have simplified lives imposed on them as a result of economic developments. Instead of maintaining youth programs that seem to concentrate on running kids around to parties and keeping them distracted until their hormones settle down, couldn't we design programs and model lifestyles that will enable them to live full, useful lives of simplicity and service in the coming two decades?

Failing to do this, we are in danger of losing a whole generation of middle-class young people from the church. A pastor at a Fuller Seminary conference on ministry in the eighties told me that the exodus had already begun in his church in Southern California. He explained that many of his young marrieds were each working a job and a half to two jobs in a heroic effort to maintain their place at the party. He stated that the young marrieds not only had no time to serve anyone else; they didn't even have time to come to church!

Unless the church helps the young to fundamentally redefine their notion of the good life, we will witness growing numbers devoting their lives to the preservation of their middle-class lifestyles and abandoning their involvement in the service of Christ—just when we need them most! What an opportunity for the church to educate young and old alike in the celebration of service and the simplification of lifestyle.

The combined impact of mounting stresses outside and inside the family in the eighties and nineties will likely result in increasing numbers of alienated young people and emotionally disturbed adults. Such loneliness and alienation will continue be reflected, as it is now, in a growing dependency on chemicals, an increasing rate of physical illness, and increasingly violent behavior.

Church of the Redeemer in Houston, Texas, is one of a number of churches that has quite literally opened its arms to the lonely, alienated, addicted, and violent members of society. They bring strangers with all kinds of problems right into their homes and love them. They don't have any sophisticated programs; they simply become family to these victims of the stress of contemporary life. And God is using the Mustard Seed of their love to transform lives. In fact, the leadership of the Church of the Redeemer today is comprised of people who just a few short years ago were on the streets. In the eighties and nineties we will need thousands of Churches of the Redeemer, communities whose primary ministry is reaching out to the hurting individuals and families in their communities.

AWAKENING TO THE FUTURE OF THE CHURCH— "BUSINESS AS USUAL" WON'T TOUCH IT!

The eighties will be a time of transition for the American church as well as for the whole of American culture. Two-dollar-per-gallon gasoline will signal the slow death of the gigantic commuter cathedrals as the church becomes increasingly decentralized. This will mean a much greater involvement of laymen and laywomen in the leadership of small house churches.

There is compelling evidence that a new movement of lay activism is forming across denominational lines. This expanding group of lay people are deadly serious about using their lives to make a difference in this world. There are those inside and outside the church who are uncomfortable with these who take their faith seriously. But they haven't been able to stop the movement from growing, and it will continue to grow.

Most mainline denominations will be faced by continued decline in the eighties and nineties, while the evangelical churches will generally experience growth. The electronic church will also continue to grow. Currently Christian programing claims 130 million listeners a week for radio and 14 million per week for television. Pat Robertson of the 700 Club believes his network will gross sixty-five million dollars in the next three years. Jerry Falwell plans to move one-fourth of his programing into prime time and to bring in two billion dollars in revenue between 1984 and 1988.[42]

The electronic church promises tremendous opportunity for evangelism in the 1980s if it can be made part of a united Christian effort to serve a world of increasing need. As we anticipate the continued growth of the electronic church, we need to ask: (1) How can its ministries be integrated into the larger global mission of the church? and (2) How will it encourage the work of local churches instead of drawing persons and resources away from them? (3) How will they steward the enormous resources they are raising from American Christians in the global mission of the church to hungry, oppressed and unreached peoples?

In the eighties and nineties there is likely to be a growing emphasis on evangelism in mainline churches, evangelical churches, and Christian radio and TV. The identification of the so-called "hidden people" in the United States and the growing sophistication of strategies of evangelism will probably result in increasing numbers of Americans who become Christians. But a rediscovery of the biblical meaning of discipleship will be necessary to ensure that individuals are converted to more than a culturally captive Christianity. The challenge will be to disciple these new Christians, to help them discover the excitement of living under the total lordship of Christ.

The church is likely to face fierce competition from cults in the next two decades. At this moment, Alvin Toffler estimates, roughly three million Americans are involved in some one thousand cults.[43] Efforts to counter cultic growth by illegal kidnappings, forced institutionalizing, and "deprograming" not only dangerously undermine constitutional freedoms; they simply won't work. Unless we can at least match the level of commitment found in cults, there is absolutely no way we will be able to counter their growth. Unless we reach out as aggressively and lovingly to the forgotten ones in our society, unless we demand at least as high a level of commitment from ourselves and our young people as they do, we had better get out of the ballgame and let others who are deadly serious about their mission take the field.

But in order to meet the challenges of the eighties and the nineties, the church will have to do more than reach out. We will also have to become a people of the inward life. Many Christians today are rediscovering the importance of the inward journey. The Cursillio movement, the charismatic movement, and the rapid sale of books by Richard Foster, Henri Nouwen, and others all illustrate the growing interest in meditation, contemplation, and prayer.

The American church in the eighties and nineties will face an opportunity unlike any it has ever faced. And given the unprecedented global and national challenges facing the church in the final two decades of the twentieth century, a business-as-usual approach won't touch it. Doing 3 percent more of what we did last year will be totally irrelevant to the avalanche of human needs that will confront us in tomorrow's society.

Stop and listen to that hungry child quietly sobbing in the doorway in São Paulo, Brazil. See that teenager, strung out on drugs in New York City, who desperately wants to change his life but doesn't know where to turn. Smell the incredible stench of the refugee camp in Somalia where thousands live on the brink of death. Hear the suckling sound of a child trying to nurse on his mother's dry breast on a back street of Calcutta. Feel the desperation of an older couple in your neighborhood who simply don't have enough money left to buy food.

Jesus is calling his church from the future . . . from the sounds, the forms, the pain that will flood tomorrow's society. We dare not ignore his call or fail to pay attention to the signals. We are being given a historic opportunity to join the Mustard Seed Conspiracy that is changing the world.

For Discussion and Action

1. What impact is the end of the Western Dream likely to have on the future of the American Dream? What are some possible alternative dreams and directions for the American future?
2. What are the likely consequences of America's pursuit of increasing levels of affluence, consumption, and waste? What are some alternative economic directions?
3. What will be the likely consequences of maintaining our present low growth economy? What will happen if we attempt to return to the high growth economy of the fifties and sixties? In either case, who will benefit and who will be hurt?
4. What is likely to be the future of the American poor in the eighties? What specific problems will they face? List some innovative ways your church can respond to these emerging opportunities in advance of crisis.
5. Give some reasons for the decline of traditional liberalism. What are likely to be the consequences of the dramatic turn to the political right, especially for the poor? How can the people of God find their own unique, biblically derived political agenda that is clearly distinct from the agendas of the right and the left?
6. What are likely to be some of the new scientific and technological developments in the eighties and nineties? What kinds of ethical issues do they raise for the church?
7. What pressures will the changes in the next two decades put on families and individuals? Where do you see these pressures already at work? What are some creative ways your church can begin to enable families and individ-

uals to respond to these changes without withdrawing into protective isolation?

8. List some examples of the impact the dramatic changes of the eighties and nineties are likely to have on the church in the U.S. How can we respond imaginatively to these changes in order to more fully carry out the mission of Christ to a world of exploding need?

9. What will happen if the church adopts a "business as usual" posture in the face of the escalating global and national challenges of tomorrow's world?

10. Consider the following list of potential crises in the eighties and nineties: housing shortages, food and energy shortages for seniors, increasing numbers of single-parent households, growing numbers of alienated young people and an increasing polarization between the haves and the have-nots. List creative ways the church could turn each anticipated challenge into an opportunity for ministry and for working with God to change his world.

4.

Awakening to the Great Escape, the Secular Agenda, and the American Dream

"Do you realize if we start feeding hungry people things won't get worse, and if things don't get worse, Jesus won't come?" interrupted a coed during a Futures Inter-term I recently conducted at a northwest Christian college. Her tone of voice and her serious expression revealed she was utterly sincere. And unfortunately I have discovered the coed's question doesn't reflect an isolated viewpoint. Rather, it betrays a widespread misunderstanding of biblical eschatology (having to do with the last days) that seems to permeate much of contemporary Christian consciousness. I believe this misunderstanding of God's intentions for the human future is seriously undermining the effectiveness of the people of God in carrying out his mission in a world of need.

In this and the next chapter we will, against the backdrop of a future of increasing deprivation, ask, "What are God's intentions for the human future?" In chapter five we will examine how we as his people can understand his intentions and act out his plan in the light of what the Bible tells us. But first, in this chapter, we will look at some commonly held attitudes toward the future—attitudes I believe do not reflect the biblical perspective. We will look at three specific responses: 1) The Great Escape, 2) The Secular Agenda, and 3) The American Dream. And we will examine how the values of these responses compare to the values of the religion of Jesus.

THE GREAT ESCAPE AND THE INCREDIBLE COPOUT

The response of the coed at the Futures Inter-term reflects what I call the Great Escape view of the future. So much of the popular prophetic literature has focused our attention morbidly on the dire, the dreadful, and the destruction of all that is. When we get caught up in this literature of despair we tend to dwell on what is going wrong instead of looking at the positive ways God is acting in his world. As a consequence, when we look into the future all we see is the world going "to hell in a handbasket." This singularly dismal spectre leads many to conclude nothing can be done to alter the growing plight of the world's poor, to change unjust economic structures, or to end human oppression. There is the feeling that, while such suffering is undeniably tragic, God intended it to happen and there is no point in our working to try to alleviate it.

This attitude limits hope to the expectation of one's own personal escape—and perhaps in getting a few more people in the lifeboat while there is still time. In virtually every generation since the resurrection of Christ there have been a few believers who have decided their only hope for the future was their own personal escape. For example, in the early 1800s there was a small handful of Christians who sold all they had and waited on a mountain for the return of Christ. Their eschatology had convinced them they couldn't make a difference in their world . . . and they didn't.

About the same time, another group of Christians converted through the Finney awakening believed they were supposed to make a difference in their world . . . and they did. Born-again Christians were in the forefront of every major social reform in America during the 1830s. They spearheaded the abolitionist movement, the temperance movement, the peace movement, and the early feminist movement. Christian colleges such as Wheaton advocated working in the world for God's kingdom; board members, administrators, faculty, and students at Oberlin College were even involved in regular acts of civil disobedience freeing slaves through the underground railway.[1] During those years, the structure of American institutions and the fabric of American life were dramatically changed as a direct consequence of Christians taking initiative to make a difference in their society, and the fruits of their labors can still be seen today.

The irony of the Great Escape approach to the future is that, while it claims to take God seriously, it unwittingly moves God outside history, insisting that even he is powerless "in these last days" to feed the hungry, bring a global awakening, or change unjust economic structures. It portrays God as able to redeem sinners and to communicate with his children, but at the same time unintentionally fashions him into an impotent absentee landlord who has lost control of his world and of human history. For those who believe the forces of darkness are fully in control, the only role an absentee God can play is to bring down the final curtain at the end of history.

This viewpoint reflects a degenerative view of history and a fatalistic view of the future. Those who subscribe to this position tend to see human history as running relentlessly and inevitably downhill to total destruction, and they conclude that there is nothing anyone—certainly not Christians—can do about it. Of course, if we have a totally deterministic view of history and are convinced God can't work through his church to change the world, we can't help being fatalistic.

However, the eschatology of escape reflects more than a degenerative view of history and a fatalistic view of the future. It betrays a frightening lack of a sense of responsibility for the world in which God has placed us. This latter-day fatalism can become an excuse from obligation, from personal involvement of our total lives in advancing the cause of God in a world of escalating human deprivation. It has caused millions of Christians to psychologically and literally take their lives and resources out of the "ballgame," since they have persuaded themselves they can't possibly make any difference anyway. The Great Escape becomes an incredible copout from all Christ called us to be and to do.[2]

Apparently a growing number of conservative Christians no longer even believe that God is going to pull them out of this mess before times get really tough. You will find Christians in the forefront of the new survivalist movement. Survival condos in the mountains are being bought by the wealthy, and huge quantities of freeze-dried food are being stockpiled by middle-income Christians.

This survivalist movement seems to be motivated by both fear and anger. Out of fear thousands have totally given up on the future. Out of anger, thousands are arming themselves. Kurt Saxon, who has written about survivalism, expresses serious concern that we are moving into a new feudalism in which many survival schools rely on paramilitary tactics: "They are learning to kill and nothing else. . . . They . . . will become predators after catastrophe, preying on the local population," he warns.[3]

The increasing involvement of conservative Christians in the survivalist movement is indicated by a growing number of books such as, *Eat, Drink and Be Ready,* by Monte L. Kline and W. P. Strube, Jr., which instructs Christians on how to sock it away for number one so they can survive during the coming tough times: "We . . . have been forewarned by the Scriptures of signs preceding Christ's second coming which will result in food shortages. Our choice also is to respond to God's revelation by preparing a food reserve and continue to live for the Lord, or to 'Eat, Drink, and be Merry, for. . . .' You must make that choice either to prepare for something sure to come or to ignore the warning of Jesus Christ, hoping that what he predicted will not come true in your lifetime. If you can do that you are braver than we are. That gamble may cost you your life. Remember it's better to be five years too early than five minutes too late." [4]

"Five years" early or "five minutes" late is really beside the point. Christ never called his followers to be survivors. If he had been a survivor, he would have found a way to avoid the cross. As his followers, we must be prepared as he was to lay down our lives for others. If we have enough extra resources to sock away food reserves for ourselves, we are mandated by God's Word to use that money to help the world's poor avert the apocalypse which is for them only moments away, and to trust our personal future to our Father's care. The whole Christian survivalist movement is just one more form of selfishness—putting ourselves, our needs, and our survival first rather than concentrating on God's agenda for serving a world in need.

PROMOTING THE SECULAR AGENDA AND THE HUMAN INITIATIVE

While some Christians tend to see history on the skids to inevitable decline and destruction, others tend to be more optimistic. Products of the Enlightenment of the seventeenth and eighteenth centuries, they look forward to the gradual improvement of society through social progress, education, and liberal political initiatives. They see society gradually moving up a treadmill of progress towards a more humane social order.

In the past, Christians who subscribed to this particular approach believed the kingdom of God on earth would be awaiting us at the end of the treadmill if we just kept improving society. Few look forward any longer to the attainment of a full-blown utopia, but many still believe we can see gradual societal improvement. The better future seems to be pictured as a strictly temporal realm in which society experiences continual economic and social improvement.

Christians who subscribe to this view naturally tend to believe in the possibility of change. But many of these Christians set out to promote change by simply climbing aboard whatever movement for progressive social change happens to be passing through town at the moment. And they seem to derive much of their agenda for change directly from the causes they join—whether abortion on demand, homosexuality, or victimless crime.

The problem with this secularly derived approach to change is that it often doesn't seem to take theology—or even God—very seriously. Walter Brueggemann states, "It has been hard for liberals [involved in social action] to imagine that theology mattered, for all that seemed irrelevant. And it was thought that questions of God could safely be left to others who are still worried about such matters. As a result, social radicalism has been like a cut flower without nourishment, without any sanctions deeper than human courage and good intentions." [5]

To what extent have various social agendas subscribed to by Christians been checked against a biblical theology? Are the images of the better future that Christian activists are struggling to attain derived from Scripture or from secular society? If we are to be effective in working for Christian social change, don't our agendas for action and our visions for change have to be derived from a strongly biblical theology?

So totally merged are the agendas of some churches with those of secular causes, that it is not only difficult to separate them; sometimes it is hard to figure out where God fits into them at all! Rather than depending on God as an active initiator and collaborator in the agenda for human change, those who subscribe to the gradualist view of the future seem dependent on the treadmill of social progress and on human initiative to bring us to that better future.

It seems to me that many gradualist Christians haven't taken God any more seriously than have their fatalistic brothers and sisters. In this context, God becomes merely a passive deity whose function is to sanction the activities of our institutions, governments, and churches working for social change. If we buy into this viewpoint, then the future is totally up to us. Our God becomes an impotent cultural deity; our hope is really in man and his initiative to bring change.

BUYING INTO THE AMERICAN DREAM AND LIVING FOR NUMBER ONE

Both those Christians who are waiting for the Great Escape and those expecting human initiative to gradually improve society often get caught up in another image of the future. We buy into what is often called the American Dream, and into all the values that are a part of it. Even now, as the American Dream seems to be slipping from our grasp, many are working to renew it at all costs. It might help us, therefore, to understand how the Dream developed, in order to understand its power and to see how it relates to the religion of Jesus.

Images of the Future in the American Past

Since its inception, America more than any other nation has been invested with dreams of a new future. A few English Christians caught up in the Reformation dreamed of a future in which the intentions of God could be fully realized. John Winthrop stood preaching on the foredeck of the Arbella in 1648 as it sailed into Massachusetts Bay: "God has called us to be a city set on a hill for all the eyes of the world to see." The Puritans who had risked the sea were resolute in their commitment to act out the future intentions of God in this new land. But their vision was destined to fall on hard times, and the Puritan vision had little influence on the American Dream.

Other Europeans journeyed to the new continent and colonized Georgia, Virginia, and New York. Their visions for the new land were visions of power, prosperity, and progress. Many who had lost hope in the old risked all they had on the new. And in their baggage they brought their dreams for a better temporal future.

Two of the nation's founders were particularly influential in shaping the dreams and visions for this new land. Both Benjamin Franklin and Thomas Jefferson labored to midwife a new political experiment in which power derived from the consent of the governed and the constitutional freedoms of the individual were guaranteed. This experiment was to become a model of constitutional freedom and human rights. But perhaps what is less well recognized is that Franklin and Jefferson, in addition to being involved in the birthing of a new political order, were consciously involved in the fabrication of a new secular religion— what I call the Religion of America. They created this new religion to help achieve their dream for this new land.

Franklin and Jefferson both viewed the new religion as subordinate to and supportive of the new American political order and their dreams for a new society. As Deists, they even made the passive God of their new religion of America subordinate to the state and to their dream; they cast him as a figurehead diety silently sanctioning those who were energetically erecting a new order.

The shapers of the American dream drew many of their ideas from the Enlightenment. Somehow the personal pursuit of perfection and the kingdom of God that had characterized the vertical quest of the church was, in the Enlightenment, transformed into the horizontal pursuit of social progress and a new temporal order. Many of the founding fathers including Franklin and Jefferson fully believed that free men pursuing their own aims in a free society would inevitably progress . . . towards a new temporal, political, economic and social kingdom . . . right here on earth. Their new civil faith taught that economic and political progress would inevitably result in moral progress for the whole society. They genuinely believed that societal perfection could be achieved through human initiative.

Franklin gratuitously offered himself as the first Adam of this new order and this new religion. He intoned that if anyone would look to his remarkable example of rising from rags to riches, from obscurity to prominence, they too could rise and the nation would rise with them.[6]

Franklin insisted that if the American people were going to rise, possess the western frontier, and become an economic and political power, they must have a new system of ethics. One of his major contributions to the Religion of America was his revision of traditional Christian values to meet the needs of the new order.

For example, he said the Puritans were absolutely right in claiming virtue is important. But they were mistaken when they taught that virtue is an end in itself. Virtue is not the goal of life, he said; virtue is the *means*. If we live virtuously, we will become successful. Success, not virtue, is the goal of life. Sound familiar?

Through his innovative adult education program called *Poor Richard's Almanac,* Franklin indoctrinated a whole people in the secular values of the new religion of America. Those values included industry, power, acquisitiveness, thrift, respect for authority, conformity, prosperity, prestige, and most of all personal success. The acquisitive, aspiring self was at the very center of Franklin's gospel.

So effective were Franklin's efforts that these acquisitive, materialistic values are at the core of the Religion of America and the American Dream to this day. In fact, the gospel of success and prosperity preached in many of our churches has a great deal more to do with the gospel of Benjamin Franklin than with the gospel of Jesus Christ.

Thomas Jefferson borrowed from the millennial language of the Christian faith to describe his dream for a new temporal paradise spanning a continent comprised of the "chosen people of God." But in Jefferson's civil faith the "chosen people" were simply any individuals who had the good fortune to be born on American soil.

Influenced by John Locke, Jefferson put the autonomous individual, not God, in the center of the new order and the new faith. Believing the individual to be inherently good, Jefferson insisted that he or she should have the power to decide how he wanted to be governed and to violently tear down any government not in his own best interest— to decide whether God existed and to be the sole arbiter of conscience. Essentially, he saw the autonomous self as the final authority in politics and religion. And he insisted that the supreme power of the individual had to be maintained not only by keeping government at an absolute minimum, but also by keeping economic systems as small as possible. Jefferson genuinely believed that if each person in the new order was given total freedom to pursue his or her self-interest, the common good would be the result.[7]

The economic theory of Adam Smith, who was also influenced by Locke, became an essential component of the American dream, although Smith, a Scot, was not directly involved in the founding of the new nation. Smith argued that if everyone was given total freedom to pursue his own economic advantage, the entire society would automatically progress. In a theory which kept God passively stuck in the woodwork of history sanctioning the works of man, Adam Smith assured his readers they could trust the "blind hand" of the free market mechanism to bring them to a better future. And Adam Smith, by influencing many American founders, became the guiding light of our economic system.

The image of the better American future as articulated by Franklin and Jefferson profoundly confused nationalism and religion, economics and piety, the pursuit of religious perfection with the pursuit of social and economic progress. The depth of this confusion can be seen in a speech made in 1826 by John Quincy Adams, then President of the United States.

In this address Adams was trying to interpret an amazing event to a questioning American people. Two former Presidents, Thomas Jefferson and John Adams, had died within five hours of each other on July 4 of that year, fifty years to the day of the signing of the Declaration of Independence. Citizens believing strongly in divine providence were asking themselves what God was trying to tell them, and John Quincy Adams, obviously influenced by the new secular faith of Franklin and Jefferson, declared, in effect, I will tell you what means. It means that the Declaration of Independence is indeed the Word of God and America is called to become the political savior of the world! [8]

Of Parking Places, Pencils, and the Pursuit of Pleasure

The confusion of our constitutional republic with the secular religion of America is with us to this day. We tend to assume our national and personal agendas are automatically the agendas of God. Our acceptance of the American Dream can be so complete that we fail to even question just how compatible it is with Christian values.

Specifically, what is the life goal advocated by the Religion of America and how compatible is that with the religion of Jesus? Let's answer this question by witnessing another confrontation at another Christian college. . . .

"God doesn't care if I get a parking place?" responded an irate student to the off-the-cuff remark I had just made in chapel. "Last week I broke my pencil and discovered God had put another pencil in my pocket," interrupted another young man. "If God doesn't care enough about us to find us parking places or replace broken pencils, why should we be Christians?" "Why indeed," I countered. "Doesn't God care about every detail of our lives?" yet another student challenged. "Including the deoderant you use?" I queried. "Sure—including the deoderant I use."

It went on like that all afternoon. There was scarcely any response to my call for a more radical brand of discipleship in the eighties.

No way. They wanted to talk about parking places, and they were angry. I was stopped in hallways, buttonholed on stairways, and confronted in classrooms. I was developing a very uneasy feeling for my personal safety and sincerely wished I had never mentioned parking places.

But the damage was done. I had obviously touched a very sensitive nerve in my audience, but the intensity of their emotional response baffled me. I lingered on campus longer than I had planned, trying to figure out why my passing comment had provoked such a hostile response.

I had never intended to suggest for a moment that God doesn't care about us personally. I was only attempting to challenge the popular myth that one of God's primary functions is insuring that American Christians have a life free from inconvenience—that they never have to drive around the block twice or sharpen a pencil. I find such a singularly self-referent faith repugnant while kids are starving in Somalia and Christians in Haiti are dying from the lack of three dollars' worth of antibiotics.

Later, while I was sitting alone in the Student Union with puzzled thoughts and a cold lemonade, it came to me. Suddenly I began to understand why the students had reacted so explosively to my comment. I believe they, like so many contemporary Christians, have unwittingly borrowed the life goal of a non-Christian religion and made it central to their Christian faith. The life goal, of course, comes from the Religion of America. Thomas Jefferson told us that the goal of life is the individualistic "pursuit of happiness"; this goal was at the heart of his new political experiment and the cardinal doctrine of his new secular faith.

I believe an authentic study of the Gospels shows us that the individualistic pursuit of happiness should not be the life goal of a Christian. In fact, it would be difficult to find a goal for human life that is more antithetical to everything Jesus represented. Jesus called his followers not to seek life, but to lose life. In fact, he warned those who would follow him that if they sought life they would by that very act lose it (Matt. 10:39). He insisted paradoxically that only those who gave their lives away in service to the needs of others would find life.

Look at Jesus' life. He had no concerns for his own needs, no place to lay his head. Jesus said he came not to be ministered to, but to minister. He lived as a servant who never turned away from any person's need, and he died as a sacrifice for every person's sin. He was that kernel of wheat that fell into the ground and died that it could bear much fruit.

If we would follow Jesus, we must take up our towels and our crosses, deny ourselves, and lose our lives in service to the needs of others as he did. For the Christian, happiness is never a goal to be pursued. It is always the unexpected surprise of a life lived in service. In fact, in Matthew 6:33 we are taught that followers of the Way shouldn't even be concerned about the satisfaction of their basic needs, let alone their personal happiness. If we seek his kingdom first, God will provide our needs.

One of the most unfortunate consequences of placing the life goal of the religion of America in the center of Christian faith is that it radically alters our relationship to God. Instead of serving God, we do a flip in our minds and expect him to serve us. We tend to picture him as a gigantic cosmic bellhop whose sole duty is to indulge our desires, spare us inconvenience, and insure our success in every venture.

This unfortunate reversal is most apparent in prayer meetings where petitions are focused almost exclusively on the needs, desires, and ambitions of those present. "Pray that God will help me find my lost tea towels . . . pass my exams . . . locate a new apartment . . . find a used Mercedes . . . heal my heartburn." [9] Seldom a prayer for the often urgent needs outside of the prayer group. Many of us have been influenced by a egocentric culture to unwittingly participate in egocentric faith.

The reaction of the college students to my casual comment about parking spaces shouldn't be a surprise to any of us. The "me first" preoccupation of our secular society has fully permeated every generation of Christian life, including the present generation of young adults. (By the way, as I returned to my car after that long day of struggle, I saw something fluttering on my windshield. I personally discovered God doesn't seem to be bothered by my getting parking tickets, either!)

The Good Life—The American Dream in Miniature

At the very core of the American Dream is a notion of what "the good life" is. That notion is based on Jefferson's insistence that the individual should have total autonomy to pursue happiness and Franklin's insistence that the individual will find happiness and success through being acquisitive. "The good life" has come to be inextricably tied up with consumerism, materialism, and the pursuit of power and self-actualization—with the expectation that such a quest will bring happiness and well-being. We have actually come to believe that happiness has something to do with how much we accumulate in our garages, how much we ring up on our charge accounts, and how much we throw into our garbarge cans. TV's Archie Bunker speaks for many of us when he says, "There's three great things that happens to a man during his lifetime: buying a house, a car, and a new color TV. That's what America is all about." [10]

There are a surprising number of people who believe that's what being a Christian is all about, too. Zig Ziglar, one of the leading proponents of the "success gospel," a man who used to "sell cookware lucratively, now makes a silk-lined living telling the upward seeking that the here and now inheritance of God's promises assures great material blessings." He told three hundred pastors at a meeting at the First Baptist Church in Dallas "that anyone who thinks otherwise is guilty of 'stinkin' thinkin'." [11] "Will Herberg, a contemporary Jewish philosopher, claims that Americans have 'faith in faith,' that they think believing in God assures them of economic prosperity and personal achievement." [12] Horatio Alger's rags to riches yarns still pervade our spirit. And we really seem to believe our destiny is to strike it rich, even in tough times. Benjamin Franklin's acquisitive self is still alive and well.

You see, what's happened is that our whole notion of the pursuit of happiness has gotten caught up in the pursuit of money. We have convinced ourselves that we cannot really be happy unless we steadily increase our income year after year and decade after decade. We have gotten ourselves hooked on a "materialistic rat race where everyone has to make increasingly greater amounts of money and consume ever greater amounts of resources to be happy." [13]

Those who succeed in this "Let's Make a Deal" lifestyle are not only pursuing happiness but prestige and power as well. We have become a people obsessed by power. Our gargantuan war technology, our domineering foreign policy, our predatory competitiveness, our macho male folk heroes reveal our absolute mania for control.

The American male particularly is programed from the moment he enters this world to pursue power and achievement. His very soul depends on it. He must learn to carve out his Ponderosa, manage his household, and maintain his power in the workplace. Hierarchical male-dominated structures within organizations (including the church) have become power centers. In fact, numbers of conservative churches are caught up in what I call "evangelical pyramid power" in which power radiates from the top exclusively through male "chain of command" systems. I suspect this preoccupation with power has much more to do with cultural influences than with any biblical teaching on headship.

But the search for power and prestige in contemporary America is not a purely male phenomenon. Women by the droves are buying books and attending seminars that teach how to climb the ladder of success. Magazines that once specialized in the home and family now urge their feminine readers to learn the "politics of power." The more women enter the marketplace, the clearer it becomes that, although women have yet to rival men in actual power, in our society the drive for power is a characteristic of men and women alike, an integral part of what we think of as "the good life."

Perhaps the American notion of "the good life" can be seen most clearly in our homes. We live in single-family, detached dwellings, and it seems to me that more often than not the adhesive that bonds our families together is consumption. We no longer work together. We have precious little time for one another because of the demands of the rat race. We seldom serve others as a family, and even in our religious activities we are segregated by age and gender. The one thing most American families do together is consume; we are absolutely gifted in consuming Big Macs, sitcoms, and tennis lessons.

Not only is the American home the foremost symbol of the good life; it is also the basic training ground for the young in the self-seeking lifestyles of American culture. Robert Cole, a psychologist, charges, "Very little is asked of a lot of American children with regard to compassion and thinking of others. The emphasis is on psychology to cultivate the individuality and self-importance of a child. One sees that in home after home, children are encouraged to look out for themselves and get what they can. Very little emphasis is put on pointing the child's eyes and ears away from himself or herself and towards others.[14] Doesn't this dawning awareness raise the question of whether the role of the church is to simply preserve the family as it is or to help transform it into what it should be: a family for God and for others?

Erma Bombeck, reflecting on the plastic lifestyles of many American families, contemplates how future anthropologists would characterize our contemporary consumer culture:

Our garage bulged at the seams with lawn spreaders, leaf sweepers, automatic mowers, snowplows, golf carts, bobsleds, skis, ice skates, boats, and camping gear. Our electric kitchen crackled with efficiency of micro-ovens, dishwashers, ice cube crushers, slow-cooking pots, electric knife sharpeners, brooms, sanders, waxers, blenders, mixers, irons and electric ice cream freezers and yogurt makers.

The once-silent streets had been replaced by motor and trail bikes, transistors, and piped-in music in the shopping center parking lot and the air was thick with charcoal. . . .

I couldn't help but speculate how future historians would assess the suburbs. . . . Would they be able to break the code of neon signs that flapped in the wind: 'go-go,' 'carry-out,' 'drive-in,' or a sign that instructed 'speak clearly and direct your order into the clown's mouth?'. . . . Would they probe the sand boxes and come up with a Barbie and Ken form, and figure we got sick?

Or would they piece together scraps of PTA notices, home parties, church bazaars and little green stamps (thirty to a page) and ponder, 'how did they survive?' At that moment the ghosts of one hundred million settlers are bound to echo, 'we drank!' [15]

Indeed, millions of suburbanites seem to find that "the good life" is only endurable under sedation. As a matter of fact, there is growing evidence that we Americans are an amazingly unhappy people. Granted, some of the advances of our modern society have resulted in longer lifespans, better health, and more creature comforts. Anyone who has traveled overseas returns with a profound respect for our nation, our constitutional freedoms and the opportunities we have in our free society. But when I return from abroad I usually find myself also aware of the contrast between the contented, simple lifestyles of my friends overseas and the high-stress lifestyle of the consumer society in the United States.

I come back to people whose lives are victimized by the trivia of broken power mowers and the pressure of overbooked schedules. If our national intake of alcohol, valium, and assorted other chemicals or our statistics on mental health problems, suicide, and stress-related illness are any indication, we aren't enjoying "the good life" as much as we think.

I suspect one of the major reasons we are belatedly discovering high consumption isn't all that satisfying is that, contrary to popular opinion, humans are primarily spiritual and social—not economic—beings. We have been conditioned to believe that ever-increasing consumption of goods and services will not only make us happier but will increase our self-worth and power. In fact, we have come to derive our very identity from what we produce and consume: "The earth and your family name can be ignored; it's your personal patterns of consumption that tell people all about you. And so if you are what you own, the more you own, the more you are." [16]

What we have done is reduce persons, made in the image of the living God, into economic objects. This is a tendency that characterizes all of Western culture; as a matter of fact, the economic, materialistic view of life many Americans hold has more similarities to the Communist outlook than we like to acknowledge. "Communist materialism is doctrinaire and oppressive. Capitalist materialism is pragmatic and cancerous," asserts John White. "Communist materialism claims that matter is all there is. Western materialism assumes that matter is all that matters. Many people who would not consider themselves to be materialists in the strict sense of the term live as though material things were of supreme importance." [17]

Lewis Mumford, in tracing the history of the Western value shift to an industrial consumer-oriented culture, accurately notes, "Within the span of a few centuries the focus of interest has shifted from the inner world to the outward world. . . . All but one of the [seven deadly] sins, sloth, was transformed into a positive virtue. Greed, avarice, envy, gluttony, luxury, and pride were the driving forces of the new economy. . . . Unbounded power was harnessed to equally unbounded appetites." [18]

The Good Life of Self-Actualization

During the seventies an important shift took place in American values and in our definition of "the good life." Polls conducted by Yankelovich and others revealed that new self-fulfillment motives had begun to join accumulating motives: "People still want material rewards, but they no longer feel that it is necessary to give so much of themselves to achieve them. Also, they often see their self-fulfillment in addition to financial security. . . . What they want is more of everything." [19]

What we are witnessing is a values split along generational lines. Many older Americans committed to the pursuit of profits, prestige, and power have been willing to make major sacrifices and defer gratification until the waning years of life. Many of the young aren't willing to wait. They want both their material gratification and their sense of personal fulfillment now.

It is my opinion that the growing immorality of modern society can be directly traced to what Christopher Lasch calls "the narcissistic preoccupation with self." And I fear that in many instances churches, youth ministries, and Christian colleges are unwittingly contributing to this growing immorality through encouraging an overemphasis on seeking personal fulfillment.

The "narcissistic preoccupation with self" has found a great deal of encouragement from the self-actualization and relational movements in psychology. "When therapists speak of the need for 'meaning' and 'love,' they define love and meaning simply as the fulfillment of the patient's emotional requirements. It hardly occurs to them . . . to encourage the subject to subordinate his needs and interests to those of others, to someone or some cause outside himself," observes Lasch. "Love as self-sacrifice or self-abasement, meaning a submission to a higher loyalty—these sublimations strike the therapeutic sensibility as intolerably oppressive, offensive to common sense and injurious to personal health and well-being." [20]

In the philosophy of self-fulfillment, the autonomous self is seen as fully endowed with all the resources necessary to achieve its own healing and integration. Self becomes the ultimate source of meaning and the ultimate arbiter in all life's decisions. I suspect Jefferson might be very pleased. A book called *The Aquarian Conspiracy* [21] is the bible of this latter-day religion of self that is likely to seriously challenge biblical faith in the eighties.

I am not trying to suggest that God is not interested in us as individuals. God wants us to develop our potential, to be our best selves. But the biblical purpose of personal growth is not the individualistic pursuit of happiness, achievement, success, self-gratification, or even self-actualization. God's intention is that we become whole, loving people so that we can worship him and serve others. Instead of being autonomous selves "doing our own thing," we are called to be surrendered selves living totally under his lordship in communities of shared life. And instead of being acquisitive selves striving and competing for our own selfish gain, God calls us to be servant selves who put the needs of others before our own (see Rom. 12:10).

Taking Back the American Dream

What is the American Dream? The American image of the better future? Listen to the crusading words of Robert Ringer, author of *Looking Out for #1:* "The time has come. The citizens of this country . . . must take America back. . . . By 'taking back America' I mean nothing short of restoring the American Dream. This means each individual regaining his right to his life, his liberty, and his pursuit of happiness." [22]

Ringer and others seem to genuinely believe that if a nation of individuals and individual nuclear families all look out for themselves, the nation will somehow be renewed. "Progress" will prevail, and for the advocates of the American Dream progress almost invariably means economic progress. They still believe we will climb to ever-increasing levels of affluence if we maintain an environment of complete economic freedom and trust the blind hand of the market mechanism to determine the winners and losers.

The problem is that the American economy reached the point of satisfying the basic needs of its citizens early in this century. In order to keep the party going and the economy growing we are having to create enormous numbers of new consumer "needs" and promote increasing consumption as a way of life—all this at the expense of the world's poor and of future generations.

Sometimes I wonder how some Christian businessmen I know are able to simultaneously hold a fatalistic view of the future—they are convinced everything is headed for immediate and total calamity—and an optimistic view of the American future—they expect everything to be 4 percent better every year. I heard that one of the leading writers on biblical prophecy, a man who has predicted the imminent end of everything, has invested the profits from his books in twenty-year long-term growth bonds.

Early in this chapter, it was pointed out that Christians who hold a fatalistic view of the future seem to view God as an absentee landlord whose primary act is to bring down the final curtain, and that Christians who hold a gradualistic view of the future tend to view God as an impotent bystander who is depending on us to supply the initiative to get the job done.

Advocates of the American Dream have a slightly different idea of where God fits into the realization of their future, but they still see him as essentially powerless. In his discussion of morality, Ringer questions who should make the rules and who should rule in American society. He asks, "Shall it be God? This might be a satisfactory solution to many people, but unfortunately God seems to have more important things to do than to make frequent appearances on earth. And in His absence, there seem to be several million differing interpretations of His laws." [23]

Ringer's comments reflect a view of God not unlike the one reflected in the Religion of America. He really isn't the active Lord of history; he is a passive national deity who has some ceremonial value to national interest but is essentially disinterested. History is controlled not by God but by the free market. Is it possible for Christians at one and the same time to believe that God is the Lord of history and that history is controlled by the so-called blind hand of the free-market mechanism?

The American Dream and the Cultural Captivity of the American Church

How has the church in the United States responded to the often self-seeking and materialistic values of American culture? Brueggemann charges that "the contemporary American Church" is totally unable to challenge the values of American culture. He argues that the church has been so enculturated by the ethics of consumerism that it has little power to believe or act. "This enculturation is . . . true across the spectrum of church life, both liberal and conservative." [24]

It is absolutely essential that we in the church realize the fundamental problem isn't "out there" somewhere. The problem isn't something called "secular humanism" that terrifies many conservative Christians. "The enemy" isn't the emergence of the religious right that strikes fear in the hearts of many mainline Christians. There is no reason to worry about being gobbled up by outside forces . . . the church is already being eaten alive by the Religion of America. The life goal and values of this secular faith have penetrated and adulterated our beliefs and values more than any of us are willing to admit.

Ivan' Illich, in his book *Deschooling Society,* talks about a "hidden curriculum" in our schools, a hidden set of values that are reflected in the design of our schools, the lifestyles of the staff, and the ways in which the teachers relate to students. He contends that this "hidden curriculum" has more influence in shaping the learner than the visible curriculum has.[25]

What hidden values are reflected in the design and affluence of our churches, our comfortable institutional lifestyles, and the lifestyles of our congregations? What values are reflected in the ways your churches use the time and resources of their members? Are our values and the values of the members of our churches really much different from our secular counterparts who are devoted to the individualism, consumerism, and materialism of American culture?

Don't we often preach Franklin's gospel of personal achievement, acquisitiveness, and success from many pulpits? Don't we teach the gospel of self-actualization, fulfillment, and personal happiness from many others? Haven't we often by word and deed put self in the center of the gospel of Jesus, even as it is in the Religion of America?

The cultural seduction of the church is based on a completely irreconcilable dualism that traces back to the Enlightenment. Francis Bacon drew a line between what he called "the Works of God" (the natural world) and "the Words of God" (the realm of the Spirit).

This unfortunate dualism has distorted our understanding of the role of God and his people in history. We have come to see the spiritual dimension as narrowly including evangelism, church planting, worship, devotional life, tithing, etc.; in this dimension God is seen as alive and well, actively involved in the ministries of the church and the personal lives of Christians. The physical dimension, on the other hand, involves personal lifestyle decisions, recreation, business, economics, politics, social action, and science and technology. In this physical dimension we still tend to think of God as a passive spectator locked outside history. This dualistic thinking about God and his world has caused us to present a mixed message to the world; we preach about a totally nonmaterial future life with God while at the same time encouraging Christians to pursue a materialistic future for themselves.

Today, in the early 1980s, American Christians tend to confuse the symbols, values, and agendas of the American state with the symbols, values, and agendas of the church, just as they have done since the time of Jefferson. This is evident in books such as *The Light and the Glory* [26] and in much of the rhetoric of the religious right.

But "Civil religion is an inherently false religion," charges Jim Wallis, "because it is the religious expression and incarnation of the dominant values of the present order that is passing away—values and assumptions that live in sharp contrast to the priorities of the kingdom of God. When conformity to such false religion infects the churches, the very meaning of the gospel may be lost or blurred as those in congregations become unable to make a choice or even perceive the need to make a choice between God and Caesar." [27]

We need to ask ourselves whether we are educating our young in the values of Jesus or in the values of the dominant national culture. Does the "hidden curriculum" of American culture, which emphasizes the values of materialism, individualism, and nationalism, have the upper hand, or do the "others serving" values of Jesus have the greatest influence in our Christian educational systems? In all honesty, are our church schools, day schools, Christian colleges and seminaries educating the young to fit into society or change it?

There is even a growing tendency in the church to turn Jesus into a consumer item; from bumper stickers to Christian entertainment, we are finding ways to market our Lord. Our entire culture is oriented to hype, and unfortunately the church is becoming increasingly involved in image advertising. "If it works do it" has become the pragmatic watchword of the Christian image makers. Malcolm Muggeridge once angered an audience when he "dared to suggest that Jesus, coming in our time, would turn down free time on television and would indeed consider such an offer a fourth temptation of the devil. . . . The idea was unthinkable." [28]

How should we as Christians respond to the pervasive influence of the values of culture on the values of our faith? Jim Wallis responds, "The greatest temptation of the people of God has always been to worship other gods and therefore to disobey the first commandment by putting their trust in finite realities rather than in God alone. Unmasking idolatry and turning back to God is a continual task. In our day we must resist the church's servitude to the contemporary idolatries of American life and society, to name a few: the consumptive mentality; the will to power and domination; the oppressions of race, sex, and class; the arrogance of national destiny; and the efficacy of violence. In so doing we can liberate our selves from the tyranny of false gods and be free to serve others in God's name." [29] It is time we faced up to the reality that the American Dream and the Christian image of the future are not synonymous, and that we as American Christians need to discover a new vision for the future . . . a vision of hope for all peoples . . . a biblical vision that challenges the principalities and rulers of our darkened world.

IN SEARCH OF A BIBLICAL VIEW OF THE FUTURE

This chapter began by asking, "What are God's intentions for the human future?" Frankly I don't find much biblical basis for subscribing to the Great Escape, the Secular Agenda, or the American Dream as the answer to this question. How can we approach the Bible in a way to genuinely discover God's intentions for the human future? To be honest, I question whether some Christians take the Bible seriously enough in attempting to derive direction for life and mission. On the other hand, I believe conservative Christians have another problem—a problem of perspective.

What would happen if we asked prophecy buffs to write birth pamphlets for expectant mothers? Imagine how those pamphlets would read. They would focus on the pain, the agony, the trauma, and certainly the chronology of the birth process—but never on the beauty of the newborn. If widely distributed, these pamphlets would undoubtedly bring us to zero population growth overnight.

We desperately need to wrench our attention away from our morbid fascination with the birth process and to rivet our gaze on the beauty of the consummate newborn future of God. We need to abandon our fixation on figuring out the chronology of the last days and earnestly strive to discern God's intentions for the human future.

Of course there is going to be a traumatic birth process, but the only reason the Scripture tells us about it is so we will be ready and active in his service. Jesus insisted, "No one knows, however, when the day and hour will come—neither the angels in heaven nor the Son, the Father alone knows" (Matt. 24:36, TEV).

In spite of this patently clear statement, Christians spend outrageous amounts of time and resources in the Great Christian Guessing Game attempting to outguess one another regarding the timetable of the last days. I suspect the five foolish virgins may well be prophecy hobbyists sequestered away in ivory towers fiddling with wall charts while the forgotten ones slip into their imminent apocalypse.

Jesus instructs his followers, "Watch out, then, because you do not know what day your Lord will come. If the owner of a house knew the time when the thief would come, you can be sure that he would stay awake and not let the thief break into his house. So then, you also must always be ready, because the Son of Man will come at an hour when you are not expecting him" (Matt. 24:42–44, TEV). Therefore, the only thing we can know for sure is that he will come when we aren't expecting him.

Jesus follows these instructions with three parables to explain what it means to "be ready." These parables make it abundantly obvious that being "ready" means being totally committed in our inward lives and outward service to the advance of his kingdom.

In fact, immediately after Jesus shares his parables on being "ready," he concludes the section by describing what will happen to those who are ready and those who aren't ready for his "final exam": "Then the King will say to the people on his right, 'Come, you that are blessed by my Father! Come and possess the kingdom which has been prepared for you ever since the creation of the world. I was hungry and you fed me, thirsty and gave me a drink; I was a stranger and you received me in your homes, naked and you clothed me; I was sick and you took care of me, in prison and you visited me' " (Matt. 25:34–46, TEV). I am sure you remember what he said to the others! Even though Jesus assures us that we will never be able to figure out when he is going to return, he makes it clear what he expects of us until he does return. We can understand God's intentions for our own lives and indeed for the human future.

So let us join hands in a journey through the Scriptures to discern God's intentions for our lives and his world. It is clear from the passage just quoted that Jesus not only has a very special concern for the poor and forgotten ones, but that in a real way he is incarnated in their very lives. As a consequence of this reality we will pay particular attention to what God's intentions are for the poor.

By discerning God's intention for the human future, we will be able to discern his intentions both for our own lives and the mission of the church now. This insight will give us a wholly new basis for understanding what God expects of his people. And it will provide the church with a whole new premise for more sharply defining our role and mission in a world of increasing human need.

For Discussion and Action

1. Describe the "Great Escape" view of the future. How does such a view of the future seriously compromise our ability to mission to the increasing needs of tomorrow's world?

2. What is the "Secular Agenda" view of the future, and what are some of the likely consequences of adopting this view?

3. What are the secular values of the "Religion of America" and the "American Dream" advanced by Franklin and Jefferson and other shapers of American thought? What are some examples of ways these values are still with us today?

4. Specifically, what is the life goal of the Religion of America, and in what ways is it in tension with the life goal of the religion of Jesus?

5. How does the American notion of the "good life" reflect the values of the American Dream?

6. What are some of the indications that the "good life" we Americans are taught to pursue really doesn't make us as happy as we were told it would?

7. What is the gospel of self-actualization? How does it compare with biblical views of personal maturity and growth?

8. Can you think of specific ways the values of the American Dream have permeated your life, your church, your Christian school, etc.?

9. How can the church effectively challenge the secular values of the dominant culture in its midst and in the larger society?

10. How do you think we can go about finding a biblical alternative to the three views discussed in this chapter—a view that will enable us to compassionately serve a world of exploding need?

5.

Awakening to the Present and Coming Future of God

Let's take a journey together into another time and place. . . .

As far as the eye can see there is no sign of life. No water. Not a single green blade. Stretched out before us in all directions is an arid wasteland . . . a silent desert. The scorching sun reflects off crumbling rocks, burning sands and a few scattered bones. There is not even the whisper of a breeze.

Suddenly rising up in front of us out of this vast wilderness is an enormous mountain, as lifeless and forbidding as the desert that surrounds it. Large rugged boulders stand guard at its base. Without warning, dark clouds roll across the sky like so many artillery cannons readying for battle. Shadows cover the land. The rough jagged shoulders of the huge peak almost seem to become one with the menacing sky. The desert is abruptly plunged into a dense, suffocating darkness, and the still air is almost electric.

The skies are suddenly rent by blinding light and deafening sound. The entire earth begins to convulse beneath our feet as though in labor. In a flash of light we can see the mountain shaking violently, throwing huge rocks down its heaving sides at the trembling earth. Sheets of slashing rain join the assault.

No sooner has the storm started than it is over. The desert is silent again, and the mountain is still. Steam begins rising from the entire valley as a spectacular rainbow arches from the valley floor right over the top of the mountain. Somehow in that brief moment everything seems to have changed. A sense of newness fills the air.

In the distance a shining ribbon reflects in the sun. It rushes towards us. At the last moment the river sharply turns and races past the mountain. A single bird follows the river on its serendipitous journey. The rain has cooled the desert and the air smells surprisingly like springtime.

Thousands of small dark dots begin appearing on the horizon. Like the river, they seem to be slowly coming towards us. At first it is impossible to make out what they are, but as they begin to come closer we can see they are people, thousands of people, coming toward us from all directions. Some stop at the river to drink. Others just keep struggling forward. Those who are able help the feeble and the small children over the rocks. They walk right past us and begin scaling the boulders at the foot of the mountain.

One young man with cerebral palsy struggles with the greatest difficulty to get past the boulders and begin climbing the mountain. As he violently wrenches his body up the trail he suddenly stands erect. By the time he disappears from sight his stride seems to become more confident.

The desert is flooded with people coming from every direction—all kinds of people. There's a family of Haitian refugees. That man with the machete looks like a sugar cane worker from the Philippines. The older couple over there with the threadbare clothes look like they might be from Central Europe. And those kids chasing each other must be from one of our inner cities in the United States. The only thing they seem to have in common is that they all look very poor.

A group of three men and two women who look like they are from Central America are having particular difficulty getting started up the mountain. They are chained together at the ankles, scarcely alive. Others help, and they finally get started up the trail. They only take a few steps when they stop abruptly in the middle of the trail. They stand staring at one another absolutely dumbfounded. Their ankle chains are lying open on the ground.

A scream rings out behind them. "I can see! I can see!" shouts a middle-aged black man who literally throws down his cane and runs straight up the mountain. He doesn't even bother to use the switchbacks. The shout brings the small group of Latin Americans back to life. They begin spontaneously singing and dancing right in the middle of the switch-back, their faces transformed with jubilation.

A thin Indochinese woman slips up behind them, holding her dead, emaciated baby close to her breast. She looks up in startled surprise at the celebration; she seems totally incapable of comprehending this explosion of emotion. Then, above the singing and shouting an infant's cry can be heard. The dancers immediately sense what is happening and sweep both mother and child into their celebration. Singing and dancing, they climb the mountain together.

Looking back, we can see that not only is the valley filled with people from every tongue and tribe and nation pressing toward the mountain; the valley itself is remarkably changed. Majestic cedars have appeared from nowhere. We can see small springs surrounded by acacias and myrtles. The desert is now covered with luxurious grasslands sprinkled with wildflowers. Groves of olive trees rich with fruit cluster at the base of the mountain. Birds play in the trees.

The mountain has come to life too. A single blade of grass has sprouted in the middle of the trail. The face is carpeted with rich vegetation and flowering shrubs. Terraced gardens of citrus and pomegranate trees line the crowded trails. Climbers help themselves to the oranges and pomegranates. And the rough mountain switchbacks suddenly open before us on to a wide, smooth roadway.

As the first climbers reach the rim of the mountain, they find themselves on a vast plateau, and in the distance they see the skyline of an enormous city that looks like it is descending directly out of the brilliant sky. The city glistens in the sunlight with jeweled loveliness like a bride waiting for her intended. It looks like it is made of transparent gold. The jubilant crowds, arms around one another, wind their way through Edenic gardens chanting "further up and further in."

The gates of the city glow like great blazing pearls. They seem to lift their heads in respect as the immigrants enter. As the throng moves through the gates there appears to be a tremendous sense of homecoming. People coming up different trails run to embrace loved ones as if they haven't seen them in a long time. Sons and daughters, brothers and sisters, moms and dads, grandparents act as if they are home at last. The best of all that's been seems to have come alive again. The past, the present, and the future have become one.

A thousand voices in a hundred different tongues sing an incredibly lovely song. In one street some spontaneous folk dancing begins. Jews and Arabs, Afrikanders and Angolians, Protestants and Catholics from Northern Ireland, and people from every political, ethnic and cultural background are dancing up one street and down another, embracing, caught up in the spirit of the mountain and the city.

Even wild and domesticated animals join in the celebration. I don't know where they come from, but no one seems afraid. A small, curly-headed child rides by the dancers on a lion. It is like a circus, a family reunion, and a meeting of the United Nations all at the same time. The dancing column, singing at the top of their voices, follows the lion and child toward the center of the city.

A small group stops dancing and starts dismantling some military weaponry someone has found outside the city. It looks like they are trying to fashion some missile casings into pipes to construct an irrigation system for raising water from the valley below.

The boy on the lion leads the celebrants into a huge square in the center of the city. Every tree in the vast square is decorated with lavish garlands of flowers welcoming the guests. Beds of spring blossoms raise their heads and join the chorus of welcome. The atmosphere in the square hangs heavy with the fragrance of springtime and a growing sense of anticipation.

Underneath the trees are hundreds of long oak tables beautifully deco-
rated with fruit and flowers. They are covered with large jugs of wine
and plates stacked high with bread. The entire square looks like a gigantic
wedding reception. A solitary figure puts down his shepherd's staff, picks
up a towel, and prepares to serve the guests. People begin filling the
square. As they enter, their jaws invariably drop in wonder at the stunning
beauty and the gracious hospitality. But the singing only stops for a
moment.

Part of the procession is still following the boy on the lion toward
the head of the square. There at the very center of the city a serene
crystal river flows from a brilliant light which illuminates the entire
city. Somehow the mountain, the city, and the river are all one.

As the procession approaches we see a small group of people having
enthusiastic foot races alongside the river; . . . a line of crutches and
canes marks their track. An elderly American couple sit down on a
bench in the sun in front of the temple and watch a group of kids
from England and Ireland playing together. Everywhere you can hear
those who had been imprisoned rejoicing. They keep shouting, over and
over, "All oppression is ended, all sins forgiven!"

Following the child, they crowd along the riverbank to give grateful
thanks. Some are still singing; others are quietly praying. Still others
with faces almost on fire with joy extend their hands toward the heavens
with praise. The singing, the praising, the laughing, the crying all blend
in beautiful harmony. Over a period of what seems to be hours, thousands
come to the river, kneel down to pray, and go away renewed.

In the square a child's voice suddenly rings out above the happy sounds:
"Proclaim the feast of the Lord!" People begin moving toward the tables.
The poor, oppressed, and forgotten ones are made the special guests of
honor. Quietness settles on the entire assembly. The child speaks again
with great reverence. "Here on Mount Zion the Lord Almighty will pre-
pare a banquet for all nations of the world—a banquet of the richest
foods and finest wine. Here he will suddenly remove the cloud of sorrow
that has been hanging over all nations. The Sovereign Lord will destroy
death forever!" (Isa. 25:6–8).

" 'Now at last God has his dwelling among men! He will dwell among
them and they shall be his people, and God himself will be with them.
He will wipe every tear from their eyes; there shall be an end to death,
and to mourning and crying and pain; for the old order has passed
away!' Then he who sat on the throne said, 'Behold! I am making all
things new!' " (Rev. 21:3–5, NEB).

We took this journey as a way to focus our attention on the incredible
imagery of hope and redemption to be found in the Old and New

Testaments of the new age of God. This narrative only scratched the surface of what God is planning for his people and his world. Let's walk through the Scriptures together and see if we can discover God's intentions for the human future and our lives today. *The reality is that the party is over, but the good news is that the celebration of God has just begun!*

IMAGES OF THE FUTURE IN THE JEWISH PAST

The Beginning of Promise, the Birth of Hope

What are God's intentions for the human future as revealed in the panorama of his relationships to the children of Israel? In the images of creation and the Garden, the intentions of the Creator are clearly good. We are shown a world of rhythmic night and day, darkness and light—a world of spectacular variety, color, and sound, with birds piercing the heavens and fish filling the sea.

God created beings fashioned in his own image, and we are told his intentions for those new beings were good. They were to be caretakers of his Garden, and they had the opportunity for the most intimate relationship with their Creator. They are shown communing with their God in the cool of the day. Tragically, the Fall ruptured that relationship and somehow twisted the world and all those who would inhabit it.

However, the intention of the Creator for his world and his people remained inviolate. "The Lord had said to Abram . . . I will make you into a great nation and I will bless you . . . and all peoples on earth will be blessed through you" (Gen. 12:1–3, NIV).

When God made a covenant with the children of Israel, he promised a future in which they will be a great nation and a future in which all the inhabitants of the earth will be blessed. The history of God's relationship to Israel is a history of the redemption of a people as prologue for his redemption of a world. God chose to identify himself with a poor band of displaced Semitic tribes. It is unprecedented in the history of religions that deity would be pictured on the side of the poor instead of the powerful.[1]

Experiencing the Liberating Future of God

God's covenant relationship with Abraham, Isaac, and Jacob found a new expression in the deserts of Egypt. Let's visit this band of enslaved Semites with whom God had chosen to identify himself, in order to learn his intention for their future. There were over half a million men working in this tropical oven for the Egyptian state. Moses brought God's word to the Pharaoh, whose response was immediate: "Make these men work harder and keep them busy, so that they won't have time to listen to a pack of lies" (Exod. 5:9, TEV). The slaves were forced to get their own straw while keeping up their quota of production of bricks. Beatings increased. Life was becoming intolerable.

Then God dramatically took the initiative to free his people by sending a series of natural disasters on Egypt. Not until that memorable night of Passover, when the firstborn of Egypt were struck down, did Pharaoh relent. After four hundred thirty years of slavery, the tribes of Israel marched out of Egypt, delivered by the hand of God. They scarcely believed what had happened to them, and when they saw the armies of Egypt coming after them they momentarily regretted they had ever paid any attention to Moses. But Moses told them, " 'Don't be afraid! Stand your ground, and you will see what the Lord will do to save you today; you will never see these Egyptians again' " (Exod. 14:12–13, TEV).

No sooner had Moses spoken than the entire mass of refugees ran into a natural barrier—the Red Sea. Moses raised his hand and the sea dramatically parted and the children of Israel scurried to the other side. We see a hilarious celebration on the far shore as the Red Sea thunders back together, swallowing the Egyptian hordes. The thunder of the sea must have been completely drowned out by the euphoric shouting and singing of these liberated slaves. Over a million people could be heard singing at the top of their lungs, "I will sing to the Lord, because he has won a glorious victory; he has thrown the horses and their riders into the sea" (Exod. 15:1, TEV). In this amazing act God revealed that his intentions for his people were political as well as religious. He determined to achieve nothing less than their liberation from slavery and oppression. Many of those who are oppressed, exploited, and enslaved today see in this amazing act a foreshadowing of the liberating future of God.

Creating a Countercultural People of God

A new nation was born through the initiative of Yahweh. This new people lived with a tremendous sense of destiny. Yahweh repeatedly gave them a vision of a future filled with promise: "Now if you obey me fully and keep my covenant, then out of all nations you will be my treasured possession. Although the whole earth is mine, you will be for me a kingdom of priests and a holy nation" (Exod. 19:3–6, NIV).

Unquestionably, one of God's primary intentions for the human future

was to create a people for himself . . . a new community . . . a holy
nation. As a priestly people this new community found their solidarity
in the worship of their Creator, Liberator, and King.[2] God intended
that they, as a holy nation, would incarnate a way of life and a system
of values radically counter to those of the prevailing culture. They
were to be a showcase of his righteousness and his future. They were
called to be a servant people.

In the Ten Commandments, we see God's intention to establish a
new standard of righteousness for his people. In his instructions on
worship we see that God's intention is to be reconciled to his people.
In his instructions on diet and sanitation we see that God is concerned
about the physical well-being of his people. And in the institutions of
religious festivals there is a foreshadowing of his new age of celebration.

Celebrating the Jubilee Future of God

Suddenly on the Day of Atonement, a trumpet could be heard
throughout the entire land proclaiming a year of Jubilee and celebration.
The Lord explained to Moses, "In this way you shall set the fiftieth
year apart and proclaim freedom to all the inhabitants of the land.
During this year all property that has been sold shall be restored to
the original owner or his descendants, and anyone who has been sold
as a slave shall return to his family. You shall not plant your fields
or harvest the grain that grows by itself or gather the grapes in your
unpruned vineyards. The whole year shall be sacred for you; you shall
eat only what the fields produce of themselves" (Lev. 25:10–12, TEV).

The entire Jubilee celebration was premised on the biblical principle
that the earth is the Lord's, that we are only stewards of the earth
and its resources. In this celebration we see that God's intentions for
his people were not only religious and political, but economic and social
as well. He purposed to create a new social and economic order by
making it difficult for a few to achieve a vast accumulation of wealth
at the expense of the many. Every fifty years there was to be a "fruit
basket upset," and the poor were to receive back land and resources
they had lost. Just as they were to be given a new opportunity to
help themselves economically—a new beginning—God intends to create
a new order in which economic and social justice is built into the
very fabric of his new society.

Longing for the Promised Land of God

Perhaps no image of God's future for his people more fully reflected
their longings than the image of the Promised Land. Here was a tribal
people that had been enslaved for hundreds of years and then had

spent forty more wandering in the wastelands of the Middle East. They had absolutely no idea what the future held for them until Yahweh painted a splendid picture. He sketched out a fertile land of hills and valleys gushing with rivers and springs, and artesian streams. He added fields laden with wheat and barley . . . trees heavy with figs, pomegranates, and olives . . . lush vineyards . . . hives filled with honey. As he presented his people with this picture of their future he assured them, "There you will never go hungry or ever be in need. . . . and you will give thanks to the Lord your God for the fertile land that he has given you" (Deut. 8:9–10, TEV).

God intends for his people to have a homeland in which they can experience the loving care of their Creator. And the Creator longs for his people to enter his promised future, to come home to his loving care. "If God . . . has in the covenant bond demanded of Israel full obedience, he also promised if they obeyed, He would defend them and establish them in the promised land. And He is powerful to do so, and His word is faithful. What outcome then could history have but the fulfillment of promise, the establishment of God's chosen people under His rule in peace?" [3]

The Creation of the Kingdom and the Destruction of the Dream

After Israel had crossed the river Jordan and entered the promised land, they started demanding a king like other nations. Initially God resisted their demands, but eventually he gave in to his people and granted them a king. John Bright suggests that Israel's very nationhood was an essential precursor to the coming Messiah and his kingdom. "Before there could have been the hope for a prince of David's line, there had to be David. Before the hope of a messianic kingdom, there had to be a kingdom of Israel." [4]

It would be the prophets who would subsequently develop the linkage between the Davidic kingdom and God's future intentions not only for the children of Israel, but for all peoples. One of these was Amos, who lived in the eighth century B.C.

Israel at the time was enjoying a period of economic and political success unparalleled since the time of Solomon. However, it was a time of incredible disparity between rich and poor. God sent Amos to prophesy against the children of Israel for their oppression of the poor, but his message went unheeded (see Amos 2:7). And so, "only a few years after Amos spoke, it happened just as God had said. The Assyrians captured the Northern Kingdom and took thousands into captivity. Because of the mistreatment of the poor, God destroyed the Northern Kingdom—forever." [5]

The apparent reason Israel failed to respond to the message of Amos was that they had become confident they would automatically inherit the future God had promised them, regardless of their behavior. They forgot that God's future intentions for his people were not automatic, but conditional on their maintaining a covenant relationship with God and a just relationship with one another. Because they repeatedly violated their relationship to God and man, Israel was no longer the true people of God. For them to yearn for the day of the Lord, Amos said, was to yearn for their own imminent judgment.

"This meant that the hope of the establishment of the kingdom of God, the hope embodied in the dream of the day of Yahweh, began to be divorced from the Israelite state and driven beyond it." [6]

Journeying Into the Mountain Future of God

Even though the dream of the coming kingdom of God gradually became more inclusive, it remained the passionate hope of the children of Israel. In spite of their rebellious behavior, they lived in constant expectation of God's promised messianic future. The same prophets who warned them of the judgment of God for their idolatry, disobedience, and oppression of the poor also showed them the image of the future God had planned for those who faithfully served him. Isaiah, Jeremiah, Micah, Zechariah, and the Psalmists gave this new age an unusual setting within God's recreated heaven and earth. They all described the future of God in terms of a mountain and a city. Let me share three out of the dozens of passages on the mountain future of God with you:

The Lord says,

> I am making a new earth and new heavens. The events of the past will be completely forgotten. Be glad and rejoice forever in what I create. The new Jerusalem I make will be full of joy, and her people will be happy. I myself will be filled with joy because of Jerusalem and her people. There will be no weeping there, no calling for help. Babies will no longer die in infancy. . . . Even before they finish praying to me, I will answer their prayers. Wolves and lambs will eat together; lions will eat straw, as cattle do, and snakes will no longer be dangerous. On Zion my sacred hill, there will be nothing harmful or evil (Isa. 65:17–20, 24–25, TEV).

> . . . the mountain where the Temple stands will be the highest one of all, towering above all the hills. Many nations will come streaming to it. . . . He will settle disputes among the nations, among the great powers near and far. They will hammer their swords into plows and their spears into pruning knifes. Nations will never again go to war, never prepare for battle again (Mic. 4:1, 3, TEV).

> I will return to Jerusalem, my holy city . . . and the hill of the Lord Almighty will be called the sacred hill . . . I will rescue my people from the lands where they have been taken, and will bring them back . . . to live in Jerusalem. They will be my people, and I will be their God (Zech. 8:3, 7–8, TEV).

What Are the Intentions of God for the Human Future?

What are God's intentions for the human future as revealed in the panorama of his relationship to the children of Israel? At the Creation his intentions for the human future were clearly good. He promised through Abraham and his covenant to bless all the people who would inhabit planet Earth. In his remarkable liberation of a population of Hebrew slaves he demonstrated his intention to deliver the poor and oppressed. In the Jubilee God revealed his intention that his future be a future of justice for all peoples. In the picture of the Promised Land God revealed his desire for his people to live righteously, peacefully, and abundantly. In the incomparable imagery of the mountain city of our God he showed a future in which all sin, darkness, and death are to be swallowed in a new age of righteousness. All oppression, suffering and pain are to be replaced by a new age of justice. All hate, violence and destruction are to be transformed into a new age of reconciliation, love and peace.

Above everything else God was intent on creating a people for himself, a new community with whom he could share life forever. He intended that they stand apart from the self-seeking values of pagan culture and incarnate in community the righteousness, justice, reconciliation, peace, wholeness and love of his consummate future.

It seems clear that God the Creator, Liberator, and King intends nothing less than the supernatural redemption of his people and his world, and for them to live under his loving reign forever. This future begins, the prophets tell us, with a single tender new sprout in a barren land, a single light in a land of shadows. The people who have walked in darkness have seen a great light. Those who have lived in a land of shadows find the light is shining on them. They are filled with the joy of the harvest or of the discovery of a treasure. The yokes that cut into their bodies and the whips that tore their flesh are broken. The oppressors are defeated. The garments rolled in blood from the war are thrown into the fire for burning: "For to us a child is born, a son is given, and the government will be on his shoulders. And he will be called Wonderful Counselor, Mighty God, Everlasting Father, Prince of Peace. Of the increase of his government and peace there will be no end. He will reign on David's throne and over his kingdom,

establishing and upholding it with justice and righteousness from that
time on and forever. The zeal of the Lord Almighty will accomplish
this" (Isa. 9:6–7, NIV).

DISCERNING GOD'S INTENTION
FOR THE HUMAN FUTURE IN JESUS CHRIST

In the Fullness of Time the Future Came

"In the fullness of time" Jesus came. The One who was prophesied
to bring the future of God had come among men. As always, God's
kingdom conspiracy comes upon us in a surprising way—a defenseless
infant. God's grace had taken on human form. Somehow his mother
immediately sensed something of the historic implications of his birth:
"[God] has stretched out his mighty arm and scattered the proud with
all their plans. He has brought down mighty kings from their thrones,
and lifted up the lowly. He has filled the hungry with good things,
and sent the rich away with empty hands. He has kept the promise
he made to our ancestors, and has come to the help of his servant
Israel. He has remembered to show mercy to Abraham and to all his
descendants forever!" (Luke 1:51–55, TEV). God took the initiative
through her small baby to bring down the proud, the prosperous and
the powerful from their high places and exalt the poor, the hungry,
and the powerless. Historically the poor and powerless have been at
the bottom of the social pyramid. Jesus came to set society right side
up by turning the traditional structures of affluence and power upside
down.[7]

Luke shows us Jesus at the inception of his ministry entering the
synagogue in his hometown on the Sabbath Day. Undoubtedly the congregation knew him very well. He walked to the front of the synagogue,
opened the scroll to Isaiah 61, and read: "The Spirit of the Lord is
upon me, because he has chosen me to bring good news to the poor.
He has sent me to proclaim liberty to the captives and recovery of
sight to the blind, to set free the oppressed and announce that the
time has come when the Lord will save his people" (Luke 4:18–19,
TEV). Jesus quietly rolled up the scroll, gave it back to the attendant
and sat down. While every eye in the room was riveted on him, he
said, "Today this Scripture is fulfilled in your hearing" (4:21, NIV).
When he inferred this good news wasn't the sole possession of the
Jewish people, they became very angry and took him out and tried to
kill him (Luke 4:20–21, ASV).

In this remarkable event Jesus announced that God's long-awaited kingdom had finally come in his own person. He had been chosen to bring the good news to the poor, the prisoners, the oppressed, and the blind that God had not forgotten them but was inviting them into his kingdom. John Howard Yoder convincingly argues in his book *The Politics of Jesus* that Christ was not only the inaugurator of the kingdom but the realization of all that Jubilee represented: he would bring justice for the poor.[8]

When Jesus came proclaiming, "The kingdom of God is at hand, repent and believe the good news," he didn't have to explain what the "kingdom of God" meant to his listeners. They lived in constant hope of the promised liberation of God, the establishment of the mountain city of God, the creation of a new age of righteousness, justice, peace, reconciliation and love . . . the absolute loving reign of God in the lives of his people and his world.

In Jesus Christ there was a paradoxical "already" and a "not yetness" to the future of God. He was both the future made present and a herald of the future to come. However, in both the immediacy of the kingdom and its promised coming, we can discern God's intention for our lives and churches today.

Jesus Christ—a Living Preview of the Loving Future of God

In proclaiming that the kingdom of God is at hand, Jesus Christ quite literally announced himself as the future of God. Jesus is more than just the full disclosure of the Father; he is an opening preview of the Father's future.

If you want to see what the future of God is like, look at Jesus. Every time we see him make a twisted body whole with his touch and see the paralytic go running and leaping down the street, we are shown the future of God. Every time Jesus opens the eyes of the blind— that's the future of God. Every time he lovingly lifts children into his lap and plays with them and hugs them—that's what God's future is like. Every time He feeds the hungry, sets free the possessed, forgives the sinner, and raises the dead, we are shown a glimpse of what God's intentions are for the human future. "Jesus Christ is the future made present. He is the first fruits, a foretaste of the great banquet yet to be enjoyed by us in the consummate kingdom of God." [9]

The good news is that in God's future there will be no more kids with palsied bodies or damaged brains, no more people suffering through the overwhelming pain of terminal cancer. No more babies will slowly die of starvation, and no more people will struggle to survive while others live in conspicuous affluence. There won't be any more people victimized by oppressive economic and political systems, or individuals destroying themselves and others through malignant selfishness and sin. There will be an end to fragmented relationships and broken homes, loneliness, and depression. No more addicted young people. No more discrimination. No more mindless slaughter of the innocent on the battlefields of the world, no more holocaust, no more rebellion against the rule of God in his world. He will redeem his people and his creation. He will wipe away all tears from our eyes. Thank God his future has already begun and we can be a part of it!

Jesus is the very incarnation of God's intentions for the human future. In his life of contemplation we see the intimacy with the Father which we lost in Eden restored. In his servant life the Creator becomes the servant, foreshadowing God's new inverted hierarchy of last being first.[10] In his lifestyle of simplicity and self-giving we see what the lives of those who join him in his kingdom will be like.

Jesus consciously identified with the poor, the outcasts, and disenfranchised; in these we see the kind of people he will welcome to his kingdom. In his life with the twelve he incarnated what it meant to be the countercultural community of God in anticipation of God's creation of a new people with whom he will celebrate the future. In his human relationships, we see a spirit of forgiveness and trust and a significant broadening of familial relations to include literally everyone who does the will of the Father; this anticipates the creation of the new family of God.

In his confrontation with political, economic, and religious leaders during his cleansing of the temple, Jesus demonstrated that the new age of God will overthrow and redeem unjust and evil structures. In his joyous celebration of life, his uncompromising righteousness, his love of friends, his constant compassion for those in need, we are shown a kingdom of love, goodness, celebration, and joy. "This eschatological future reveals itself in Jesus as the highest good for which men can strive, as the fulfilling destiny of human life and the goal of the whole creation." [11]

"The kingdom of God, then, is a power already released in the world. True, its beginnings are tiny, and it might seem incredible that the humble ministry of an obscure Galilean could be the dawning of the new age of God. Yet it is! And the conclusion is victory." [12] By his grace he can even use our insignificance to manifest his victory.

The Kingdom of God in the Words of Jesus

The victory of the future of God was the central theme of the ministry of Jesus. He talked about the kingdom more than any other subject. Michael Green asked during the Lausanne International Conference on World Evangelization in 1974, "How much have you heard here about the Kingdom of God? Not much. It's not our language. But it was Jesus' prime concern. He came to show that God's kingly rule had broken into the world: it no longer lay entirely in the future, but was partly realized in Him and those who followed Him. The good news of the kingdom was both preached by Jesus and embodied by Him . . . so it must be with us." [13]

What can we do to join Jesus in making the kingdom the primary theme of our lives and churches? Let's look again at what he had to say regarding the future of God. In his Sermon on the Mount he described the characteristics of the kingdom and the qualities of those who would enter it:

"Happy are you poor; the Kingdom of God is yours! Happy are you who are hungry now; you will be filled! Happy are you who weep now; you will laugh! Happy are you when people hate you, reject you, insult you, and say that you are evil, all because of the Son of Man. . . . But how terrible for you who are rich now; you have had your easy life! How terrible for you who are full now; you will go hungry! How terrible for you who laugh now; you will mourn and weep! How terrible when all people speak well of you; their ancestors said the very same things about the false prophets" (Luke 6:20–26, TEV).

Jesus was proclaiming a future that would literally stand the world on its head. These passages weren't intended to be spiritualized; they mean just what they say. The economic, social, and political inequities of every culture have been turned right side up and God promises his kingdom to the poor, the hungry, the suffering, the oppressed, the humble, and the pure in heart, to those whose greatest desire is to serve God and his kingdom, to the merciful and to those who work conscientiously for the cause of peace. They will enter singing and dancing into the wedding feast of the new age. And the other side of that coin is also intended to be taken literally. Those folks who have already had their party in a world of suffering, deprivation and death are in serious trouble.

God wants all people to laugh, to dance, to live fully now and to join him at that future feast. But our invitation to the kingdom isn't any more automatic than the Children of Israel's. He calls us to seek *first* his kingdom in every area of our lives.

Following the beatitudes, Jesus outlines what are to be the ethical expectations of a kingdom people (Luke 6:27–42). These right-side-up principles are problematical to many; a few theologians even try to catapult them to the other side of the apocalypse. But while this convenient act may seem to render Jesus' principles less troubling, I am unable to find any biblical basis for it.

Jesus taught that we are not to get angry with others; we are not to come to God until we are reconciled with our brothers and sisters; we are not to commit adultery or even indulge in exploitative sexual fantasy. Under Jesus' teaching, divorce for any cause other than unfaithfulness falls short of his ideal. As his followers we are instructed to abandon the temptation to "get even"; we are to take insults and abuse without striking back or getting defensive. We are to go the second mile. Not only are we to care about people we are close to; we are taught to reach out with affection to people we don't know and even to people we see as enemies. When we do respond to our Father's love or the needs of someone else, we are to do it secretly so we don't derive any fringe benefits from our religious behavior.

Christ didn't offer these principles as new commandments, regulations, or conditions for the kingdom. But I believe he made it pretty clear that he does expect his followers to take them seriously in order to reflect the right-side-up values of the new age.

Jesus liked to use parables to describe the kingdom to his followers and to show them what the future of God will be like. Receptivity and sensitivity were required to detect God's word hidden in these simple stories; often Christ had to explain his parables even to his closest followers. But these stories portrayed the coming of the Lord's kingdom more vividly than any mere exposition could.

For example, in his parable of the four soils (Matt. 13:18–23), Jesus showed that the kingdom works secretly and quietly among persons willing to receive it, and that where it is received it will bring forth an amazing amount of fruit. The presence of the kingdom in a world that appears to be abandoned by God is the theme of the parable of the tares (Matt. 13:24–30); only when God's future fully comes will those who comprise the hidden kingdom come into their own.

The parable of the mustard seed (Matt. 13:31–32) depicts the exciting reality that the insignificant and the unexpected can silently change the world. Small acts of kindness, small projects of hope, small struggles for peace and justice in the name of Jesus are Mustard Seeds of the kingdom, and these seeds will grow into vast trees under which all the peoples of the world will discover the sheltering love of God.

There are still more parables that expand our understanding of the kingdom. It is like yeast, permeating and penetrating every people and culture, changing all of human society (Matt. 13:33). It is like a treasure or a precious pearl, of inestimable value but costing us absolutely everything we have—our time, our resources, our ambitions, our very lives (Matt. 13:44–46). The parable of the net (Matt. 13:47–49), as in the parable of the tares, make it clear that there is going to be a sorting process. Those unwilling to pay the price of the treasured kingdom are unlikely to possess it; they will be left with only themselves.[14]

Jesus used paradox as well as parables to dramatically illustrate how the values of the kingdom are diametrically opposed to the basic direction of human society then and now. He insisted that the only way to find life was to lose it. He taught that the first would be last and the least the greatest of all. He explained that those who would be leaders had to be servants, and that we had to become as powerless, receptive, and trusting as little children if we wanted to have anything to do with his kingdom.

Jesus described God's future most often as a feast, a banquet, a wedding party. Jesus told about a wedding party that a ruler prepared for his son. A number of guests were invited who decided they really didn't want to come, and chose to be about their own business. The host was furious and instructed his servant, "Hurry out to the streets and alleys of the town, and bring back the poor, the crippled, the blind, and the lame" (Luke 14:21, TEV).

The story of the prodigal is also an analogy of the kingdom. Almost before the rebel is out of the hog trough, his father is falling on his neck, loving him and forgiving him. A marvelous celebration and homecoming await all who are able to turn away from their sin and failure long enough to see the Father running to embrace them. The wedding banquet and the homecoming party are always waiting for those who want to come home again.

As a matter of fact, Jesus' final description and incarnation of the kingdom of God was a feast. The Last Supper, the wedding party, and the homecoming celebration are all prototypes of the great banquet of the kingdom. Every time we celebrate the Eucharist, we participate in the very life of our Lord as we will partake eternally at that final feast. Listen to Jesus' words: "This is my blood, which seals God's covenant, my blood poured out for many for the forgiveness of sins. I tell you, I will never again drink this wine until the day I drink the new wine with you in my Father's Kingdom" (Matt. 26:28–29, TEV).

The Future Comes on a Donkey's Back, on an Executioner's Scaffold and on a Spring Morning

The surprising kingdom of God came riding on a donkey's back. "Tell the city of Zion, Look, your king is coming to you! He is humble and rides on a donkey . . ." (Matt. 21:5, TEV). And the praises to David's Son had scarcely died down when the scaffold started to go up. The future had become a threat to the present. The religious, political, and economic powers were intimidated by this King that rode on a donkey's back; somehow they sensed his kingdom would upset their world and would unmask them. They thought if they killed the King they would stop the encroachment of his kingdom.

They couldn't have been more mistaken. God is able to use absolutely every apparent defeat and failure—even a cross—as the stuff out of which he will erect his new age. Nothing can stop the coming of his future.

John Bright declares, "that future coming power nothing can defeat. To be sure it might seem that the cross had been its defeat, for there Christ was delivered into the grips of the powers of this earth and was 'crucified, dead, and buried.' But don't be deceived! The cross was not the defeat of the power of God, but precisely its victory. In the cross and the resurrection . . . the decisive blow has been dealt to the power of Evil. Satan there suffered a defeat without tomorrow; his back is broken, he is beaten, done for! The struggle may drag on for many a weary year yet, but the outcome is not in doubt. The Servant's work has been done; Victory has already been won!" [15]

In the eighties we Christians need to drag our attention away from the clamor of evil as it struggles in its final death throes. We need to focus our attention on the reality that in the cross the powers of darkness have been totally defeated and victory of the kingdom has already been won. "For the darkness is passing away, and the real light is already shining" (1 John 2:8, TEV).

Early one spring morning surprised screams broke the silence of the Jerusalem countryside. He had risen from the dead! The resurrection of Jesus Christ is the most significant sign of the coming of the kingdom of God on earth. The apocalyptic hope of a resurrection from the dead was assured in Christ's rising.

In the death and resurrection of Jesus the problem of the suffering of the innocent was also solved. Jürgen Moltmann states, "In Jesus' sacrifice is found the sacrifice of God Himself. In Jesus' sufferings, God suffers; in His death God Himself tastes of damnation and death . . . Jesus' resurrection is the answer to the cry of the forsaken . . . Jesus' crucifixion stands as a symbol of God's continual sharing in the suffering and injustices of our present world; Jesus' Easter resurrection stands as a promise to those who are dissatisfied with the present eon that God himself is preparing a new future in his kingdom." [16]

The Beginning of the End—The Opportunity to Collaborate with God in the Coming of His Kingdom

Predictably, Jesus taught his disciples about the kingdom of God in the forty days after his resurrection. He had already instructed them to pray a radical prayer: "Thy kingdom come, Thy will be done, On Earth as it is in heaven" (Matt. 5:8, RSV). Now he taught them to pray that the transcendent future of God would continue to invade and radically change the human present, even as it had during his life and ministry. His parting instructions were to wait in Jerusalem for the gift of the Father.

At Pentecost the Spirit of God rushed upon the gathered disciples and the church was born; in supernatural power, unity, and love it broke the limitations of old wineskins and boldly invaded the world. Thousands answered the call of the kingdom, and churches were established throughout the Mediterranean region. This small beginning, this Mustard Seed, soon was credited with turning the world upside down. God's future had come among men, and the world would never be the same again. In every age and culture the surprising future of God would change the lives of men and nations, in anticipation of the day Christ returns and his kingdom fully comes.

During the days of the early church, the Holy Spirit continued to instruct believers, through the letters of Paul, in the values of the kingdom of God. Paul described the future of God as a time of a new humanity. He eloquently described a kingdom in which there is no distinction between Jews and Greeks, men and women, slaves and free—a future without racial, cultural, and sexual discrimination.

In his letter to the Roman believers, Paul compellingly described what it will be like when this new humanity comes into its own:

> In my opinion whatever we may have to go through now is less than nothing compared with the magnificent future God has in store for us. The whole creation is on tiptoe to see the wonderful sight of the sons of God coming into their own. The world of creation cannot as yet see reality, not because it chooses to be blind, but because in God's purpose it has been so limited—yet it has been given hope. And the hope is that in the end the whole of created life will be rescued from the tyranny of change and decay, and have its share in that magnificent liberty which can only belong to the children of God! (Rom. 8:18–21, Phillips).

And in that great day the principalities and powers of this world will be totally defeated (Col. 2:15), and every knee shall bow and every tongue confess that he is Lord to the glory of God.

The author of Revelation, like the prophets, pictured the consummation of the future of God in a holy city, a new Jerusalem. Listen to the vision:

> Then I saw a new heaven and a new earth; for the first heaven and the first earth had passed away, and the sea was no more. And I saw the holy city, new Jerusalem, coming down out of heaven from God, prepared as a bride adorned for her husband; and I heard a great voice from the throne saying, 'Behold, the dwelling of God is with men. He will dwell with them, and they shall be his people, and God himself will be with them; he will

wipe away every tear from their eyes, and death shall be no more, neither shall there be mourning nor crying nor pain any more, for the former things have passed away.' (Rev. 21:1–5, RSV).

THE FUTURE OF GOD AND THE MISSION OF THE CHURCH

What are God's intentions for the human future? As we have seen, the Scripture makes it clear it is not God's intention that we fatalistically sit around and wait around for our own personal escape. Nor are we likely to discover God's intentions in the various contemporary secular agendas for social change. And the self-seeking values of the American Dream are diametrically opposed to the other-serving intentions of the religion of Jesus.

God's intentions for the human future as shown in his Word are, quite simply, the redemption of his people and the re-creation of his world. The Scriptures convincingly teach that his intention from the beginning was to create a servant people who would worship him and incarnate the values of his new age—a people who would unreservedly devote their lives and resources to seeking his intentions in their own lives, in their communities, and in the larger society.

The Scriptures also convince me that God's intentions for human society include more than the saving of souls; what he intends is the redemption of whole persons. All too often we have focused narrowly on the spiritual dimension of God's redemption, not recognizing the biblical truth that God intends to redeem us totally—mind, body, and spirit. The future of God is not the creation of some vaporous spiritual realm out there somewhere. He intends to create a new heaven and a new earth—even the earth will be redeemed!—and in his re-created earth a redeemed people will live eternally with their God in a celebrative society of righteousness, justice, peace, reconciliation, wholeness, and love.

If those are God's ultimate intentions, can he have a different set of intentions for today? If he intends to create a new world of righteousness in which people no longer destroy others through selfishness and sin, a new age of justice in which all oppression and exploitation is ended, a new order of peace in which violence is totally vanquished, and a new society of love and reconciliation that is free from racial, sexual, and cultural discrimation, can he have a different agenda for us now?

No! His intentions for our ultimate future are his intentions for today. God is changeless. In his very nature he always and in all times opposes sin, selfishness, injustice, oppression, discrimination, and violence, and it is his intention to destroy these works of Satan wherever and whenever they exist.

In other words, the church today can derive its sense of intention, direction, and mission directly from what Scripture tells us about the future intentions of God. Remarkably, God invites us, his children, to join with him in working for his intentions now. He calls us to work for righteousness, justice, peace, reconciliation, wholeness, and love. That is the mission of the church today . . . to seek first his kingdom.

"We live between something that happened and something that will happen," observes John Shea. "We live between the already and the not yet. The kingdom of God is at one and the same time present and coming. Jesus came proclaiming the marvelous news that the future of God has arrived" [17]—and it has, but not in its fullness. He challenged his followers to set aside every other agenda and to seek first the future of God. In every age God longs to move through his broken, failing church and to manifest even in a partial way his incredible new age.

How specifically can an understanding of God's intentions for the future lend direction to us in the church as we face the challenges of the next two decades? For one thing, it can enable us to see ourselves and our mission more wholistically, to abandon the fruitless discussions as to whether evangelism is more important than social action or vice versa. In the life and ministry of Jesus it was absolutely impossible to draw a line between his life of love, his words of love, and his works of love. His life and ministry were a seamless garment, and so must be our lives and mission as we work for his kingdom; there simply isn't a biblical basis for elevating one dimension above another.

Above all, it means rediscovering the meaning of being a countercultural people of God, incarnating in our individual lives and our communities of shared life the radical values of the new age of God. "The existence of a future kingdom is a catalyst that changes the present," writes Chris Sugden. "The present order must be changed into ever-increasing conformity with that order which is God's will for it and that will one day supersede it . . . Our work now is not building the kingdom of God on earth, but the invasion of this earth by the kingdom. . . ." [18]

The invasion of the kingdom of God is coming through his initiative and his initiative alone. He has taken the initiative to manifest his future through the body of Christ—through your life and mine—to change his world. He has chosen to use the insignificant to confound the mighty. Regardless of whether we choose to cooperate with his loving conspiracy or not, his kingdom will come.

And it is obvious from our brief journey through the Scriptures that God is not an impotent deity stuck in the backwash of history. The God who breathed worlds into being, who walked in the Garden in the cool of the day, who made a covenant with Abraham, Isaac and Jacob, who liberated the children of Israel, who established a Holy Nation, a Kingdom of Priests, and who sent his own Son to live, suffer, and die in our midst in order to rise again to take us into his new future—that God is alive and well and is actively directing the course of human events, in spite of the forces of darkness. His kingdom will come and his will be done on earth as it is in heaven.

Yes, the party is over. But the good news is that the future of God has just begun, and that he invites us to the incredible celebration and adventure of being a part of the inbreaking of that new age. Only he knows the difference he can make in our lives and our churches and in our world if we seek his kingdom intentions first.

For Discussion and Action

1. What are some of the biblical images of hope you discovered in the narrative on the mountain city of God? What are some other biblical images that could have been used?
2. What do the Creation, the Covenant, the Exodus, and the Jubilee reveal about God's intentions for the human future?
3. What did the image of the Promised Land mean to the children of Israel? How did their behavior in the Promised Land cause them to lose exclusive claim to the kingdom of God?
4. What are the primary characteristics of the new age of God as revealed in the Old Testament? How were Old Testament prophecies about the Messiah linked with God's intentions for the human future?
5. What impact did Mary prophesy the birth of her Son would have on human society? What implications does this prophecy have for the way we look at the future of our world?
6. In what ways was Jesus a living preview of the future of God?
7. What did Jesus teach about the kingdom of God and about God's intentions for the human future?
8. How was the suffering, death, and resurrection of Jesus God's answer to suffering and death in the world? What is the relationship of the resurrection to the future of God?
9. What are some images of God's future described in the Letters of Paul?
10. Summarize God's intentions for the human future as shown in his Word. How can understanding God's intentions for the future lend direction to the mission of the church as we seek to respond to the increasing needs of tomorrow's world?

6.

Seeking First the Future of God through Creative Lifestyles

The entire living room shook as we enthusiastically danced the Jewish hora and sang the Hebrew songs we had just learned. People burst into applause as the dance ended. We were celebrating the Feast of Tabernacles. As people began to sit down, I shouted, "It's not over yet! Get the stuff on the front porch." People started dragging in two-by-fours, evergreen boughs and tools. "What are we going to do with all this?" a friend asked. "Build a booth," I responded. "Build a what?" a guy under a long beam hollered. "A booth . . . we are going to build a booth."

BOUGHS, BERRIES, BOOTHS, AND THE GOOD LIFE

I explained that building a booth was an integral part of celebrating the Feast of Tabernacles. Every year Jews all over the world celebrate the sojourning experience of the children of Israel in the desert by building booths and living in them for eight days.

"Don't worry," I said. "We don't plan to keep you in the booth for the full eight days." It started a bit slowly and then people really began to get into it. You could feel the energy level rise as the frame went up. Three guys were securing the frame with crosspieces while at least a dozen people tied boughs, branches, and berries all over the frame.

We jammed all forty of us into the booth in the middle of the living room. We sang Jewish songs and praised God, had an outrageously good time; I think a lot of people would have stayed in the booth all night if we had let them.

"I don't know when I have had so much fun . . . dancing, singing, building the booth, and just learning about our Jewish heritage," was the feeling expressed over and over again that evening. What we had done was to make a decision to consciously change our lifestyle through adding a new dimension of celebration. To enrich our Christian lives, we had decided to celebrate all the Jewish holidays that year.

So much of the literature on the simplification of lifestyles seems to be only about "cutting back and giving up" a chunk of the "good life." And I want to holler, "Wait a minute—who ever said that the rat race we are caught up in has anything to do with 'good life'?" Instead of talking about "cutting back and giving up," the first thing we need to do is fundamentally redefine our notion of just what "the good life" is from a biblical perspective. I think we have a priceless opportunity to bring much more celebration back into our lives as Christians, even as we work to live more simply and responsibly. As harbingers of the new age of God we should be the ones that are teaching the world to sing, dance and rejoice in our certain hope.

In this chapter we will explore ways we can translate the compelling imagery of the future of God into our lives and lifestyles. We will discuss practical ways to celebrate life more while consuming less. And we will ask, "What does it mean to seek first the future of God in commitment, discipleship, stewardship, and lifestyle?"

TAKING JESUS SERIOUSLY

"Two different worlds we live in" is the opening line to a romantic ballad that accurately characterizes the dualism many contemporary Christians live by. It seems to me that most of us tend to live compartmentally. We have one compartment for our churchgoing, our committee meetings, our church potlucks, Bible studies, and Sunday school classes. And then, unfortunately, we lump the rest of our lives in a separate compartment. The two compartments often seem to have little relationship to one another. And we rarely stop to seriously consider what a commitment to Jesus means in terms of our whole lives.

Some churches seem to be satisfied with "commitment by association"; they assume that anyone who hangs around a church must be a Christian. Other churches demand commitment by conformity to certain cultural expectations. How can we get a handle on what Jesus means by commitment? It seems to me that if we as Christians intend to take Jesus seriously, we must logically begin by making him Lord of all the compartments of our lives and seeking his kingdom first in all that we do.

But taking Jesus seriously isn't as easy as it sounds. His life and values are so completely alien to our life and culture. "Christians spend a lot of time and energy explaining why Jesus couldn't possibly have meant what He said. This is understandable: Jesus is an extremist, and we are all moderates. What is worse, He was an extremist in His whole life—not just some narrowly 'spiritual' areas . . . but in every-thing," observes John Alexander. "So we have to find ways to dilute his teaching." [1]

And we have been remarkably effective at diluting his extremist teach-ing and truncating his radical gospel. That explains why we can have a nation of two hundred million people, sixty million of whom profess to be Christian, and yet make such an embarrassingly little difference in the morality of our society.

Jesus Christ stands in the midst of history calling every one of us to repent of sin and the tyranny of self and to surrender our total lives to be re-created by the power of God. Through our faith in Jesus Christ we will be changed. He desires nothing less than to enable broken, selfish persons like us to begin maturing into completed kingdom persons who live for God and others. Paul has assured us that "God, who began this good work in you, will carry it on until it is finished on the Day of Christ Jesus" (Phil. 1:6, TEV).

E. Stanley Jones affirms that "self surrender is the greatest emancipa-tion that ever comes to a human being. Seek first the kingdom of God and all things will be added to you including yourself." [2] Every cell of our being is made for the kingdom. As we surrender our lives to loving our Father and others he begins changing us into the integrated, delightful kingdom people he intended us to be. However, the surrender of ourselves to the life-transforming lordship of Christ cannot be limited to the private, personal, pietistic compartment of our lives. Jesus in his extremism insists that we surrender all our relationships, our re-sources, our careers, our futures—our total lives—to his lordship.

Not surprisingly, a number of people during his life and ministry and since that time have felt the price is too high. But those few who gladly relinquish all they have to possess the pearl of great price not only experience the personal redemption of God; they become collabora-tors with him in the redemption of a world. "To be Christian is to be possessed and dominated by the kingdom of God," Jim Wallis ex-plained. "Salvation must not be seen as merely an individual event but, rather, as a world event in which the individual has a part. The kingdom of God has come to transform the world and us with it by the power of God in Jesus Christ. The cross of Christ is not only the symbol of our atonement but the very pattern and definition of our lives, the very means of the new order that has invaded the world in Christ." [3]

Richard Foster has written, "If we don't seek the kingdom of God first . . . we don't seek it at all." [4] As disciples we are called to set aside every lesser priority and devote our entire lives to seeking his kingdom. I believe that means we must embrace God's intentions for the human future and make them fully our own. Whether layperson or clergy, we must totally commit our lives to the inbreaking of his new age and struggle to make a world of difference in response to a world of need. Specifically, that means that every Christian seeks God's guidance in how to use his or her gifts, time, and resources working for righteousness, justice, peace, reconciliation, wholeness, and love in this broken world. God's intentions become our intentions as his people.

REDEFINING THE GOOD LIFE . . . A CELEBRATIVE ALTERNATIVE

We are the people of the dream, the people of God's consummate wedding feast, and we are called to incarnate the good life of God in a world that understands so little of life or genuine happiness. But to do this we must redefine the meaning of the good life.

How do we begin? I believe we do it by categorically rejecting the popular notion that the good life has anything to do with the individualistic pursuit of happiness, with consumerism, or with materialism. We begin with a paradox. We affirm that in losing life we will find life—that, like the mustard seed, by falling in the ground and dying we will branch, blossom, and bear fruit beyond anything we could imagine. We affirm that, by taking up our towels and serving instead of seeking to be served, we will discover the true meaning of life and celebration.

The Christian notion of the good life is inextricably bound up in the king we serve and the kingdom we seek. Look at Jesus. Where do we find him in the New Testament? We always find him either with his Father or with people. He really didn't have much time for anything else. We could learn from him how to be more fully present to our Father, to his creation, and to others.

Celebrating the Life of the Inward Journey

As we begin to redefine our notions of the good life, we must begin where Jesus began, in our relationship to God. In the New Testament we see Jesus frequently retreating into the desert or mountains to spend long periods of time with his Father. This was the very source of his life and being, and is meant to be the life-source for us, too. As we learn to dwell beside his streams, drink from his waters, and live in his presence, we get a foretaste of that celebrative relationship we will enjoy with him in the mountain city of our God.

But many of us have a hard time getting alone with God. We Americans are an outward people. We flood our consciousnesses with TV, radio, stereo; we stay busy because we are so afraid of facing ourselves or our Father alone. We know little of the inward dimensions of life. Even those of us who are Christians have little time to spend with our Father and little contact with the inward realm of the Spirit.

A few years ago I made a discovery about my own prayer life. Prayer for me had been a matter of dragging my problems into the presence of God, chasing them around a few moments, and then saying amen. But belatedly I discovered that worrying in God's presence is not prayer. Deeply frustrated by the barrenness of my inner life and upset over a major personal crisis I was facing, I sought help. It came in the person of one Richard Foster, who gave me the first three chapters of a book he was writing, *The Celebration of Discipline.*[5] That providential encounter helped turn my prayer life around, and Foster's writings are still helping me discover the incredible joy of the inward journey.

For the first time in years I am focusing on the Person, not on my problems. I have learned to release my frustrations, anxieties, and failures to the Father, and I have learned the exhilarating delight of just being with him, of meditating on who he is and on the new future he is bringing in to being. I have also learned to intercede for those in need.

I am just a beginner in this kind of prayer, but I am a believer in the richness it brings to a Christian's life. The people I know who take significant time to celebrate the God "in whom we live and move and have our being" are among the most vitally alive people I have ever met. You can sense they are intimately connected with God; they have a deep inner joy and peace that have absolutely no relationship to their circumstances, their patterns of consumption, or the realization of their personal ambitions.

As the people of God we have the opportunity, in prayer, to allow our Father to express his love for us and fully share in every aspect of our every day. We can let his life course through ours, changing us and empowering us to be members of his new servant humanity, to collaborate with him by his power in the re-creation of his world. Henri Nouwen affirms, "In a world that victimizes us by its compulsions, we are called to solitude where we can struggle against our anger and greed and let our new self be born in the loving encounter with Jesus Christ. It is in this solitude that we become compassionate people, deeply aware of the solidarity of our brokenness with all humanity and ready to reach out to anyone in need." [6]

Reading the Bible, studying it, and meditating upon it can add to the celebration of our inward lives. I have found particular value in actually picturing myself in episodes in the Bible, for example, the aftermath of the Resurrection. I invite the Holy Spirit to flood my imagination and to enable me to experience what it must have been like to be a disciple, to taste the bitter despair and have it transformed into the exulting victory of being in Christ's risen presence.

Many believers, through prayer and meditation and God's Word, have found their way back to the Father, but many of us have yet to be reconciled to God's creation—his world. As Western Christians we have been programed to see the world as nothing but a set of random molecules and a grab bag of resources.

As we draw closer to the Creator on our inward journey, we need to develop new eyes for looking at his world. We need to learn to see the way Ransom, the hero of C. S. Lewis's science fiction trilogy,[7] learns to look at the universe. Rapidly traveling through space towards a distant planet without benefit of a space ship, Ransom suddenly looks around, and he doesn't see what most Western Christians would likely see—cold, dead, sterile, empty space. In a flash of awareness he sees space literally exploding with spiritual life—so filled with the presence of the living God that it can't begin to contain it all.

To live the good life, we need the eyes of a Ransom; we need to rediscover and celebrate the sacredness of God's creation. We need the heart of a St. Francis of Assisi, to become spiritually reunited with God's good world. "The simplest and oldest way . . . in which God manifests Himself is . . . through and in the earth itself. And he still speaks to us through the earth and the sea, the birds of the air and the little living creatures upon the earth, if we can but quiet ourselves and listen." [8] To experience the celebrative life of God we have the opportunity to take significant time not only to encounter our Creator but to become reunited with his creation in anticipation of that day when we will be harmoniously one with his new heaven and new earth.

Celebrating the Life of the Shared Journey

When Jesus wasn't off in the mountains with his Father, he could be found down in the villages with his friends. He thoroughly enjoyed people—all kinds of people. In fact, he was repeatedly criticized because he had such a good time at dinner parties and wedding banquets with the wrong kind of people. Today, instead of showing up as a guest of honor at a religious leadership luncheon at a posh hotel, he would more likely be found on skid row having a spontaneous party in a doorway with a group of friends from the streets. His celebration of relationships broke across all the traditional economic, racial, sexual, and cultural barriers, foreshadowing his future.

Recently I took a trip to observe a World Concern project in Haiti. Chavannes Jeune, a young Haitian who had been studying in the United

States, accompanied me. Chavannes had been away from his homeland for only six months, and yet when the people from the valley where he had worked saw him they went crazy. They threw him up in the air. They carried him on their shoulders. They sang. They laughed. They kept Chavannes up all night partying, visiting—just enjoying him. I was envious. Usually when I return to my community, people don't even know I was gone, let alone celebrate my return.

We American Christians tend to be so caught up in our schedules, our activities, our projects, and our efforts to preserve our place at the party that we have no time left over for what was one of the central obsessions of Jesus' life—celebrating his relationships with other people. Our brothers and sisters in the Third World have much to teach us about how to put aside our quest for acquiring and possessing, and simply to relish the people around us.

We don't even have to go to the Third World to learn this lesson. I have friends in Hawaii for whom it isn't unusual to take three days off work and three hundred dollars out of the bank to prepare food for a niece's christening. For many Hawaiians the celebration of relationships has a much higher value than personal accumulation of resources or getting ahead on the job. To celebrate life more we might try discovering, as the Hawaiians have, the extravagant pleasure of giving away our time, our money, and ourselves to our families, our friends, even to people we don't know. "Give to others, and God will give to you. Indeed, you will receive a full measure, a generous helping, poured into your hands—all that you can hold. The measure you use for others is the one that God will use for you" (Luke 6:38, TEV).

I know so many Christians whose lives have been made immeasurably richer by opening their homes to Indochinese refugees. They have learned it really is in giving that we receive. It is by breaking out of our middle-class white ghettos that we have the opportunity to receive the gifts so many of God's other children are waiting to share with us. It is in loving and enjoying others that we begin to experience what life will be like in God's new transcultural community.

Of course we need to learn to particularly enjoy our brothers and sisters who follow Jesus—his new community. In the community of God's people we find healing, forgiveness, reconciliation, affirmation, love; we find the kingdom, if we take the time to know and care and be with one another. (In chapter 8 we will discuss more fully our celebration in community.)

We are a people who share a dream and live in anticipation of a hope. Our dream can be summed up in the word *shalom*, which means that at every point our awareness of God transforms us into a harmoni-

ous community of loving care—his family.⁹ Our hope is that one day
we will exuberantly rejoice over our lives, our relationships, our community being made fully whole through his kingdom initiative.

Celebrating the Joys of Servanthood
and the Relinquishment of Power

Once we learn to know and enjoy the marvelous people God has
placed on this earth, we can learn as Jesus did to become servants of
the kingdom. Instead of pursuing social preeminence and power, we
will in our personal lives and Christian organizations give up our pursuit
of prestige and power. This is absolutely central to the religion of Jesus.
Believe it or not, there is genuine joy to be experienced in giving away
your power in order to empower the poor and the powerless. There
is no greater satisfaction in life than the realization that God is giving
you an opportunity to participate with him in the inbreaking of his
future.

Join me on a trip to Southwest Haiti. I want you to meet three
friends. Larry, Lucy, and Joanne understand the meaning of servanthood
in rural Haiti. They are members of the World Concern team who
moved into the Haitian valley and adopted the lifestyle of the people
who lived there. These three Christians voluntarily gave up their place
at the party, along with electricity, running water, supermarkets, sanitation systems, stereo headphones, and personal comfort. They willingly
relinquished the power and prestige of their middle-class lifestyles to
empower the people with whom they live and to help them more effectively meet their basic needs. However, they learned servanthood is never
a one-way street. They will tell you they received at least as much
from their Haitian brothers and sisters as they gave. Life is much more
full for them today because they have discovered Jesus' secret of giving
it away.

"The most miserable people in the world are the people who are
self-centered, who don't do anything for anybody, except themselves.
They are centers of misery with no exception," insists E. Stanley Jones.
"On the contrary, the happiest people are the people who deliberately
take on themselves the sorrows and troubles of others. Their hearts
sing with a strange wild joy, automatically and with no exceptions.
We are structured for the outgoingness of the love of the kingdom. It
is our native land." ¹⁰

I know of very few Christians who seem to understand the possibilities
of servanthood or the sheer satisfaction of service. Of those involved
in ministry, far too many seem to be serving Jesus out of duty and

obligation. We need to rediscover the celebration of servanthood and turn people on to an amazing opportunity in anticipation of entering the kingdom of the servant.

Celebrating the Right-Side-Up Values of the Kingdom

To follow Christ into the celebration of servanthood, we must also join him in celebrating the right-side-up values of the kingdom. Not only will we find a whole new level of life satisfaction from giving ourselves away, we will discover a heightened joy from incarnating the countercultural values of the kingdom.

I know a couple who committed their lives to Christ last year and who determined to break out of a compartmental Christianity. They made a commitment to apply the extremist teaching of Jesus to their entire life, not just the spiritual dimension. Now, Jan had undergone oral surgery three years before and the surgeon, in the course of his work, had broken her jaw. When he refused to compensate her for his obvious blunder, she and her husband Jeff had filed suit to reclaim damages and lawyer fees. The case had dragged on for three years!

Then, two weeks before the insurance company was to send them a check, Jan and Jeff changed their minds. They asked themselves, "How can we follow Jesus' teachings to love this doctor and forgive him for breaking Jan's jaw, and still take him to court?" Jan said, "The revolutionary love of Jesus makes it totally impossible for me to do anything but love him and forgive him." So they dropped the case. As a consequence of their decision, Jan and Jeff will not only lose a fifteen-thousand to twenty-thousand dollar settlement; they will wind up owing their attorney four thousand dollars.

Is this a Christian notion of the good life? Absolutely! I saw my friends right after they made their decision, and I have never seen two happier people. They were jubilant because they had obeyed the teachings of Jesus and were learning to trust God for every aspect of their lives—including raising four thousand dollars to pay off the attorney.

We Christians know too little of the joy of forgiving those who take advantage of us, turning the other cheek, going the second mile or any of the other countercultural values of the coming kingdom of God. We don't think God really expects us to take such values seriously in our everyday life. We think it is possible to seek our own rights and the kingdom at the same time. But I'm convinced God is preparing us for his future by challenging us to live out the right-side-up values of his future now.

Celebrating the Past and the Future and the Present

One of the reasons that we know so little of the joys of the right-side-up kingdom is that we have become a people who, influenced by a culture of narcissism, live very superficially in the present moment, getting what we can to satisfy our immediate desires. We have abandoned the past and give little thought to the future.

The children of Israel were not a people preoccupied with the present. Their very identity and mission was inextricably bound up with their sacred past and their promised future. As the New Israel we have much to learn in order to more fully celebrate our past and our future so that we can live more meaningfully in the present.

As the people of God we need to learn how to get in touch with our past and genuinely savor it. We need to learn how God has acted through his people in other days and to celebrate his acts. We are discovering in our home that there is a vital richness to be found in celebrating the feasts and holy days of Judaism and Christianity. Congregations could offer church history courses that not only focus on our Judeo-Christian past but that help laymen and laywomen identify where their own forebears participated in that Christian past. As we become more conscious of the acts of God in the history, our present faith and our hope for the future will be enriched.

Perhaps nothing is more essential to a Christian definition of the good life than the celebration of the consummate future of our God. We have the opportunity to celebrate the future of God by immersing ourselves in the breath-taking biblical imagery of his new age (see chapter 5). And let's celebrate God's incredible future by creating a new generation of Christian music, drama, and art. Along with the bless me songs, let's sing songs that raise our consciousness of a world of desperate need and a future of overcoming hope—songs like Ken Medema's "Kingdom in the Streets." Let's balance Christian drama that is preoccupied with private piety with powerful dramatic treatment of issues of hunger, justice, peace, and reconciliation. Let's capture in Christian art images of the consummate future of God to fill this generation with hope.

By learning to passionately celebrate our past and our future, we can learn to more fully celebrate the present. As we are liberated from self-seeking to seeking first the future of God, the present is transformed. Unlike our contemporaries, we are completely liberated from the rat race and from the anxiety that goes with it.

We are also freed from our need to acquire and collect things as we discover the joys of living in the present moment. E. F. Schumacher, author of *Small is Beautiful,* describes the journey of people learning a different concept of the good life: "Many of them had a better time than they had ever had in their lives because they were discovering the new freedom—the less you need the freer you become. They discovered and kept discovering that they were carrying far too much baggage and so they dropped pieces right and left, all the way, and the more they dropped the happier they became." [11]

As we join the celebration of the present and learn how to really live, we will be surprised to discover that we don't need things nearly as badly as we thought we did. It will no longer be a question of giving up a chunk of the "good life" to follow Jesus. As we begin to derive our identity, security, and life satisfaction from our relationship to the Father and to our brothers and sisters, we will find we need things less and less.

I discovered after praying the Lord's Prayer for over twenty years that when I prayed "Give us this day our daily bread," I wasn't really counting on God to provide my daily bread, or much else for that matter. In all honesty I was counting on the American economic system and my employer to provide my daily bread. I was counting on scientific health care systems to keep me healthy. I found I rarely prayed for God's healing unless the health systems failed to do the job. I was counting on the American military establishment and our nuclear stockpile for my personal security. I am embarrassed to discover how little I really trusted in God.

As I am seeking to authentically find the good life of God, I'm still struggling, but he is beginning to free me from counting on anything but him for my life—my present and my future. And I'm finding that even small things are beginning to take on a stunning new beauty. I feel like Emily, in Thornton Wilder's play *Our Town,* who discovered too late the singular joy of just being alive. Looking back on her community, her family and her life one last time before she goes to her grave, she cries out, "Goodby, goodby world. Goodby Grover's Corners . . . Mama and Papa. Goodby to clocks ticking . . . and Mama's sunflowers. And food and coffee. And even ironed dresses and hot baths . . . and sleeping and waking up. Oh, earth, you're too wonderful for anybody to realize you." She stoops, hesitates and then asks with tears in her eyes, "Do any human beings ever realize life while they live it?—every minute? " [12]

God has made us for life and he has made us for his kingdom. It is when we put ourselves aside and put his kingdom first that we really begin to live every minute . . . becoming more fully present to God, his good creation, and others than we have ever been before.

Celebrating the Good Life of God

As we embark on God's good life together, it is important to remember that it doesn't exclude suffering, pain, and even failure. We must be ready to change, take risks, to abandon what is comfortable. We must be ready to be obedient, even if our efforts aren't successful. Above everything else, we must be ready to passionately labor with our Father to manifest his new age of justice, righteousness, peace, and reconciliation, wholeness, and love. We may even be required to lay down our lives for his sake.

But the good news is that we no longer have to go through it alone. God goes with us, giving us strength and comfort. And our lives are no longer at the mercy of our circumstances. We can, like Paul, discover the wellsprings of joy even in the prison experiences of life.

We have the opportunity to fundamentally redefine the good life—to be Christmas, Easter, Pentecost, Jubilee, and the wedding celebration of the kingdom all at the same time to the folks around us. What's holding us back? We're supposed to be the living celebration of God. God is not looking for armies of outstanding Christian leaders. He is just looking for a few ordinary Christians, a few Mustard Seeds. If we're willing to abandon our compartmentalized Christianity and follow him, life won't get any easier, but it will never be boring. And we will learn that there is no life more satisfying than the life that is lived for the kingdom.

CREATIVE LIFESTYLE AND BIBLICAL STEWARDSHIP

When people followed Jesus their decision always altered their lifestyles and radically changed the way they used their time and resources. They were never the same again. Look at Peter and Andrew. They were hard-working fishermen trying to get ahead. Then suddenly they encountered Jesus, and he told them the good life is catching men, not fish, and losing life, not seeking it. You didn't hear them say, "Well, I have a couple of free hours Tuesday night and some free time Saturday mornings." No. They immediately abandoned their old lives, their vocations, their boats, their relationships—everything.

As Peter and Andrew glimpsed the future of God it wasn't hard for them to give up the obsessions of men. They apparently didn't even take time to sell their business or their boats. Their lives took on an entirely different focus. Instead of spending the better part of their waking hours trying to provide for their own needs, and getting their business to grow, they worked with Jesus, using their energy and their time to proclaim the good news that God's future had arrived.

As Jesus healed the sick, set free the possessed, and demonstrated the loving future of God to the poor, the disciples discovered what it meant to live the good life of God. And that discovery dramatically changed the ways in which they used their time, talents, and physical resources.

Jesus repeatedly emphasized that following him meant radically changing the ways we set priorities for our lives and resources. To the rich young ruler who asked how to have eternal life, Jesus responded: "Sell all you have and give the money to the poor, and you will have riches in heaven; then come and follow me" (Matt. 19:21, TEV).

Every sermon on this passage I have ever heard plays fast and loose with what I believe Jesus was teaching here. Preachers I have heard explain that this was a "salvation test," that once Jesus was sure the young man was willing to give up his wealth he would let him keep it. But I don't find any scriptural justification for such a culturally convenient interpretation of this passage.

It has never occurred to us that Jesus was telling us God really wants us to change the way we use resources to bring justice to the poor! I have heard the passage on the prodigal son preached in terms of God's love for both the prodigal and the older brother, but I have never heard the passage on the rich young ruler preached in terms of God's love for both the rich young ruler and the poor.

Listen to what Jesus told his disciples as the young man walked away dejected: "It is much harder for a rich person to enter the Kingdom of God than for a camel to go through the eye of a needle" (Matt. 19:23, TEV).

I believe Jesus meant exactly what he said. He literally intended that he and his followers would incarnate the future of God by working for justice for the poor. And for Jesus, that struggle for justice began not in programs but in the radical lifestyle changes of those who followed him.

Is it possible we American Christians are the rich of whom Jesus speaks? Or is he talking only about Arab shieks or J. Paul Getty as the rich of the world? It may be hard to realize, but Americans, including many of our low-income citizens, are among the richest 1 percent of the people who have ever lived on this planet. Coming to grips with our lifestyles or affluence in relationship to God's concern for equity and justice for the poor is not easy—not for me, you, or any of us. But there are ways we can begin adopting the just lifestyles Jesus calls us to.

One popular way many Christians rationalize the radical expectations of Jesus in relationship to their lives of evident affluence is by adopting what I call the doctrine of "passive availability." To put it simply, those who subscribe to this viewpoint insist all they have is really God's.

Should he ever want it all he has to do is hit them with white lightning and show them a blinding vision from on high and they will release it for his work. Until such a time, however, they will continue to enjoy what they have as the sign of the personal blessing of God on their lives.

But there is a problem with the popular doctrine of "passive availability." No one can find any Scripture to support it. Those who choose to follow Christ are called by Scripture to unequivocally follow the doctrine of "active redistribution"; that is, we are called to actively redistribute all of our time, talents, and resources to seek first his kingdom in our world. There's no waiting for visions. We have already had our marching orders. Jesus stated simply, "None of you can be my disciple unless he gives up everything he has" (Luke 14:33, TEV). He leaves to question that we have to let go of our lives and resources—right now. The question is not *whether,* it's how: how can we most fully invest all of our lives and resources to manifest God's new age of justice in a world of growing need and tragic inequity?

What we need is to reassess our understanding of Christian stewardship. I believe the prevailing teaching on the tithe is wholly inadequate in terms of both biblical validity and practical application. Of course one can understand the Old Testament origins of the tithe, but the New Testament introduces us to a much higher level of expectation. Jesus never asked for a part of a person's life or for a percentage of his or her resources. (Imagine Christians singing, "10 percent to Jesus I surrender, 10 percent to him I freely give.") Jesus demands nothing less than that we actively invest *all* our lives and resources in the advance of his kingdom.

I was startled to hear Tom Skinner, a well-known evangelist, say to a group of Christians, "Let's be honest, we tithe to ourselves." I had to stop and think a moment. But Tom is absolutely right. Most of the tithe we bring into the "storehouse" we turn right around and take out in services, facilities, and programs for ourselves and our families. Precious little of it ever gets out of the local church for programs of evangelism or social action in our own communities, let alone the rest of the world.

Where can we find a new doctrine of stewardship that is solidly biblical in its foundation and clearly equitable in its transglobal application? "A cartoon in the *New Yorker* showed a portly man and his wife looking through the picture window of their living room at a lovely vista of fields and trees. The man was saying: "God's country? Well, I suppose it is. But I own it." [13] Our lifestyles often reflect the same level of smug possessiveness as this cartoon.

One of the fundamental teachings of the Bible is that "the earth is the Lord's." If we accept that as a premise in hammering out a new concept of stewardship, it moves us in a wholly new direction. If the earth is the Lord's it is no longer a question of, "How much of mine do I have to give up?" Rather, it is a question of, "How much of God's should I keep? How would God have us use the time and resources he has placed in our care in order to have the greatest possible kingdom impact?" If we start with the premise that the earth belongs to God, we can no longer make personal lifestyle decisions or institutional spending decisions without regard to the welfare of the rest of the people with whom we share this planet, the environmental consequences, or God's agenda for the global future.

In practical terms, that could mean a Christian family in San Diego might seriously reconsider buying a motor boat when they learned a Christian family in the Philippines might not be able to survive a serious drought. It could mean a church in Wheaton, Illinois might reconsider constructing a multimillion dollar palace for worship when they learn that churches in Latin America can't afford a corrugated metal roof to keep out the tropical rain. We need to recognize that God has entrusted a finite resource to the international body of Jesus Christ and we have a responsibility to use that resource in concert with all our brothers and sisters for the advance of his kingdom.

This approach to stewardship would enable us to start using the global resources of God more intentionally and more equitably, with a growing sense of interrelatedness within the international body of Christ and with everyone else on this finite earth. This approach to stewardship, whether applied in individual lifestyle decisions or institutional planning, would be based on single biblical criterion. Before attending to any personal desires or institutional goals, we will ask, how can we use the resources God has entrusted to us to intentionally seek first a future of justice, righteousness, wholeness, reconciliation, and peace in those most compelling areas of human need in our community, nation, and world?

At the International Consultation of Simple Lifestyle sponsored by World Evangelical Fellowship and held in London during March of 1980, participants wrote a definition of Christian stewardship that fully supports this viewpoint. "By unfaithful stewardship in which we fail to conserve the earth's finite resources, to develop them fully, or to distribute them justly, we both disobey God and alienate people from his purposes for them. We are determined therefore to honor God as the owner of all things, to remember that we are stewards and not proprietors of any land or property we may have, to use them in service to others, and to seek justice with the poor who are too exploited and powerless to defend themselves. We look forward to the restora-

tion of all things at Christ's return (Acts 3:21). At that time our full hu-
manness will be restored; so we must promote human dignity today.[14]

CREATING LIFESTYLES OF CELEBRATION AND JUSTICE

How can we begin to fashion lifestyles that are at the same time
more celebrative and more just? How can we celebrate life more while
consuming less? The first question we all have to answer is: are we
going to join the conspiracy of the insignificant that is changing the
world? Are we going to give highest priority to God's agenda for human
society? Are we going to become families and individuals for others?
Are we going to live more fully under the lordship of Christ?

Once we have committed our lives to putting God's agenda first, it
is time to honestly assess our present situation. If we want to see what
we value most, all we have to do is look at how we spend our time
and resources; as Jesus said, "Where your treasure is, there will your
heart be also" (Matt. 6:21, KJV). I would encourage you to get a pencil
and a piece of paper and to write out your answers to the following
questions:

1. How celebrative is your life now, and to what extent is your celebration
   an expression of your Christian faith?
2. How are you presently using the time and resources God has entrusted
   to you? Be specific in listing the percentage of your weekly schedule and
   monthly budget that is presently invested in God's service among those
   in need?

The purpose in answering these questions is not to make us feel
guilty, but to help us become aware that God has placed in our hands
our talents, our resources, our very lives, to steward in ways we choose.
We can either spend them on ourselves or find imaginative ways to
lose them in service to others as a part of Christ's loving conspiracy.
In the rest of this chapter we will be exploring some specific ways
individuals can invest their time and talents in the service of Christ's
kingdom.

As you embark on this adventure, set some modest, easily attainable
goals for yourself. Begin small, but do begin. And begin with celebration!
Find some new ways to give expression to your faith this week by
taking time to celebrate your relationship to God, to the people you
care about, and to God's good creation.

So far so good—now set your cap for bigger game. Examine your
lifestyle for wasted resources that could be invested in the kingdom.
Are you wasting valuable energy by leaving your heat at room tempera-

ture while you are away? Are you wasting food by buying more than you can use before it spoils?

Estimate how much you can save through adopting a less wasteful lifestyle and find imaginative ways you can translate that savings into a benefit for someone in need. For example, some Christians are setting up food co-ops to reduce the waste involved in individual shopping practices. They take the money they save through this more responsible approach to shopping and invest it in urban hunger projects. It isn't costing them a penny out of their budgets to help in this way. Other churches are sponsoring garage sales for the hungry—investing the proceeds in self-help projects among the poor.

A Southern Baptist Church in Waco, Texas, has found a way to transform old newspapers into food for the hungry. The congregation collected all their old newspapers and sold them for over one hundred dollars. They used the money to buy vegetable seeds, and they are canvassing a ten-block-square area in their neighborhood, offering to plant vegetable gardens for senior citizens on fixed incomes. After they plant the gardens they plan to continue visiting the seniors and maintain their new friendships.

It is amazing what can be done with resources that would otherwise be thrown away. We need to become wizards in transforming waste into the tools of the kingdom. But even beyond controlling waste is the question of how we can steward our time, budgets, homes, and physical resources more justly. Once we begin celebrating life more fully and begin to get a sense of how satisfying it can be to give ourselves away to others, we are ready to ask the tough question: "How much do we really need?"

Many Christians I know are discovering they can live a very full life on about half their present income. Take out your budget and look seriously at how much you spend on eating out, on entertainment, on clothes, shelter, transportation. Prayerfully ask God to show you what you really need and what you could more justly invest in the work of his kingdom. Also, explore reducing your time schedule so you have more time to simply enjoy God, those you love, and those who use your care.

A number of Christians are discovering that cooperative living can significantly reduce the amount they need on which to live. By sharing housing, transportation, meals, and other costs, they find they need less income. They can either cut back on the hours they work at conventional jobs, thus freeing up time to invest in the work of the kingdom, or they can invest their extra income in ministry for Christ.

As you consider freeing up time and resources for his agenda, submit yourself to other Christians who share your concern. Ask them to hold you accountable for new ways in which God is guiding you to increase your celebration and service while reducing your consumption.

At the same time, it is important to recognize *why* you are simplifying your lifestyle. As Richard Foster writes, "simplicity is an inward reality that results in an outward lifestyle." [15] Simplifying the way you live and reducing your consumption is not an end in itself, but a means to an end.

The basic issue is: for what purpose are we conserving resources? I heard of a Christian family with two teenage sons who reduced their monthly grocery bill to one hundred fifty dollars by eating an almost completely vegetarian diet. However, Mom and Dad used the money they saved to go out for a steak dinner while the boys stayed home and ate soybean burgers. I am sure those teenage sons have some question as to the justice involved in the family's reduced consumption!

For us as Christians, the point of conserving time and resources is to put them to work for the kingdom among the poor, the forgotten, and the unreached. We don't need a new legalism—a set of rules such as "No Christian should eat meat or have two cars"—but we do need a heightened sense of responsibility for those with whom we share the earth. Ron Sider's books, *Rich Christians in an Age of Hunger* and *Living Simply*,[16] can provide biblical focus and practical examples for this quest.

A "WHOLE EARTH CATALOGUE" FOR LIFESTYLES OF CELEBRATION AND JUSTICE

We have the opportunity to move away from a compartmentalized Christianity to a faith in which Christ is Lord of every compartment of our lives, including our use of time and resources. This means that every aspect of our lives, from the way we vacation to the way we decorate our homes, provides an opportunity to celebrate his future and serve him. I hope the rest of this chapter will serve as a kind of Christian "Whole Earth Catalogue" of ideas for celebrating his future and serving him in the present.

For example, five couples I know who used to blow a wad eating out together once a month in exotic restaurants found an alternative. They still eat together once a month, but they host one another in their homes. They eat some delicious international dishes, with complete decor, at a fraction of the cost of eating out. In addition, they have decided to learn about the country in which their meal originated and the work of the church in that country. They invest the difference between the cost of a restaurant meal and one fixed at home in one of the Christian projects in that country.

Other families are learning to reduce food costs and increase nutrition through using the principle of complementary proteins. I have eaten some delicious dishes taken from publications such as *The More with Less Cookbook, Diet for a Small Planet,* and *Recipes for a Small Planet.* [17]

To discover whole new ways to celebrate life, Christians I know are beginning to dig into their ethnic, Christian, and Jewish heritages. For example, Christians of Swedish ancestry in Seattle include the Festival of Lights and other traditional festivities in their enjoyment of the Christmas holidays. There is much in our histories we can reclaim to enrich our celebration, including many rich customs from our American past.

The Alternative Celebrations Catalogue and *Living More with Less* [18] have all kinds of practical ideas for ways Christians can celebrate more by consuming less. For example, on Christmas or birthdays we can give *ourselves,* instead of expensive gifts, to others. We can give fishing trips, tennis lessons, home-cooked meals, poems, pictures, prayers.

How about a celebration of appreciation for no special reason except— gratitude? My mom and dad were a little surprised when they found an eight-foot scroll on their wall proclaiming "Parents Appreciation Day." But they recovered quickly, and we had a wonderful time.

By simplifying their use of time, many Christians I know have made themselves more free to savor life and enjoy others, as well as having more freedom to serve those in need. An exciting possibility is for individuals or families to arrange their schedules so one evening a week is free, not for church meetings, but for direct involvement in the lives of needy people. In a futures workshop with twenty-four Lutheran pastors in Gettysburg, Pennsylvania, I asked, "What would happen if every active lay person in your church freed up one evening a week for service in the community?" One pastor responded with obvious amazement, "There are three hundred active lay people in my congregation, and if they each volunteered one evening a week we could change the entire community!"

I have discovered most Christians can make time in their weekly schedules to be involved in such lay ministries. Even Christian students in colleges and seminaries can find time on a weekly basis to care about others if they make it a priority. Local pastors are good sources for ideas on ways Christians can use their gifts and interests to make a difference in their communities.

Many Christian families are serving others by opening up their homes. They are inviting handicapped children, international students, senior citizens, and refugees to live with them, and their lives are being made immeasurably richer in the process. In addition, I know a number of families who are having the best vacations of their lives remodeling houses together in a poorer section of Jackson, Mississippi. Others are helping build a Christian hospital in the Caribbean. Vacations for others are an option for many of us.

I know Christians who are learning to simplify their transportation needs by cutting back to a single vehicle, using public transportation, walking, and biking. Frank Herbert, a science fiction author, told me of an alternative transportation system he is putting together: he is building a windmill at Port Townsend, Washington, and ordering an electric car to plug into the windmill. He will never have to go back to Standard Oil again.

One area many Christians give very little thought to in terms of their Christian commitment is interior design. Most Christians invest thousands of dollars over a period of years decorating their homes in prevailing styles. A few Christians have opted for severe simplicity and orange crates but have lost any sense of beauty in the process. An alternative is to be pacesetters instead of mindlessly following the prevailing culture or opting for "Goodwill Basic."

How about letting people in on our joyous faith? Everything in our homes provides an opportunity to make a statement about our Christian faith.

What theme in your Christian life is most significant to you? Is it Advent, the Resurrection, Eucharist, or the Kingdom? If you were going to decorate your whole main floor around the theme of Easter, what colors, symbols, fabrics might you use? How would you creatively and tastefully express the joy of your faith so that every visitor immediately senses something of the celebration that is central to your life? Part of the creative challenge is to do it with a very modest budget.

I read of one family that built a beautiful simple version of the Lord's Table and put it in the center of their living room. They placed handsomely carved symbols of the Eucharist on the table and left the rest of the room very simple and understated to keep the focus on the table.

In our home we have developed a picture montage on the main wall in the living room. Underneath the pictures is the lettering "Thy Kingdom Come." The pictures include a long vertical picture of the rainbow of promise, a large horizontal picture of a butterfly, Hick's classic of the Peaceable Kingdom in the center, a picture of a little child with a beaming face from India, a baptismal scene from Latin America, and a few other pictures. In the dining room the raised lettering reads "Thy will be done on earth." Above is a collection of some thirty pictures of moms and dads and kids from all over the world, laughing, struggling, working, and in a few instances just barely surviving. We want guests in our home to sense the celebration of God's future that is the center of our faith.

How about being pacesetters not only in the decoration of our homes, but in our wardrobes, too? How about designing a wardrobe that reflects our celebration in traditional and ethnic styles that won't be out of vogue tomorrow? We could use much more durable fabrics and reduce our wardrobes to items we need instead of accumulating closets full of garments we never wear.

For most families housing takes a major chunk of time and income. In Seattle, the least expensive house on the market is about sixty thousand dollars, and a sixty-thousand-dollar house really costs more than a third of a million dollars over the course of thirty years. That same amount of money will buy one thousand permanent homes in India, where millions are forced to sleep in the street because of the critical housing shortage.

I can almost hear someone responding, "But we have a responsibility to shelter our families." Absolutely. But there is more than one way to do it, and a little imagination can save a lot of resources. An architect in Tillamook, Oregon, built a lovely home almost entirely out of recycled materials he had scrounged. It is a solar-oriented home with a natural wood interior, hardwood floors, and large double glazed window areas. It isn't large enough to hold a rollerskating party like some of our suburban homes, but there is plenty of space for a small family. The August '79 issue of *Sunset Magazine* reports the total out-of-pocket cost of that home was only four thousand dollars.

My friends Todd and Irma found an alternative way to shelter their family in a rural area outside of Tacoma, Washington. Their approach to housing really flowed out of their sense of Christian calling; God has called them to work with emotionally burned-out people from the cities. Instead of getting a master's degree in social work and setting up a fifty-dollar-an-hour counseling program, they bought some rural acreage and constructed a charming three-story house as the first building in a Christian community. It has a rough cedar exterior, is heavily insulated, and is beautifully finished inside in natural wood tones. The total cost for this three-story structure utilizing some timber from their own land? About ten thousand dollars.

By paying cash for this house, this family of five lives very comfortably for under five hundred dollars a month. This means they can get by on half of one income, so they have more time for their family and for the troubled people from the city who come to live with them at no cost. All this was made possible through a creative approach to shelter.

This is the kind of creative lifestyle planning we will need in the eighties and nineties if we hope to respond to the mounting challenges that will face us. What would happen in your church if five young married couples cooperatively built five modest dwellings on a piece of land for under twenty thousand dollars each, and paid for them with cash, then invested the money they saved or the time they saved to serve those in need? Those five couples could together free up twenty-five hundred to five thousand dollars a month, or up to sixty thousand dollars a year—or the equivalent amount of time—by this stewardship decision. Translated into direct ministry, that money would be enough to finance a team of five people to head a self-help project in nutrition, literacy, evangelism, and community health among ten thousand people in the rapidly growing slums of São Paulo, Brazil. Or they could free at least four people out of the ten in their own community to be involved in full-time service to urgent needs in the area or neighborhood at no cost to the church. The stewardship differential between cooperative living and individual living is enormous. We have the opportunity to free up millions of dollars and thousands of "man years" for the kingdom.

Still other Christians are relocating in poorer inner city sectors and sharing housing as a way of freeing more resources for urban ministry. There are even a few suburban Christians experimenting with sharing housing. Several people I know are looking into redesigning an urban storefront or warehouse for multiple use by an urban Christian community, advocacy ministries, a day-care center, and several small businesses. Thousands of Christians are finding innovative ways to shelter themselves for less, in order to free up more time and resources for God's initiative in history.

Not surprisingly, many of these believers are also looking into becoming more self-reliant in terms of food, energy, and technology. The people in Todd and Irma's fledgling community, described earlier, raise a major portion of their own food, are building their own solar nursery, and are surrounding their home with "edible landscape."

There is a nonreligious community in San Francisco that has achieved a very high level of self-sufficiency in an urban environment. In an old Victorian house on a small lot, a group of people have built a system of self-reliance that only takes four hours per person per week to sustain. The house is heated primarily through passive solar panels. The backyard is intensively farmed, and "Gray water" from the showers and dishwashing helps irrigate it. Above one corner of the garden is a fish tank, and above the fish tank is a beehive. The water from the fish tank is also used to water and fertilize the garden, and dead bees from the hive help feed the fish.

There are a number of interrelated systems like this all over the country in which participants achieve a high level of self-sufficiency for a minimum investment of time. However, few are being tested by Christians for the purpose of service and not survival. To the extent that we can learn to live more lightly on the earth, we will have more to share with those whose survival is in serious jeopardy. In the eighties we need "enclaves of the future" in which Christians intentionally live out every dimension of the good life of God.

Frankly, I am convinced that often the world doesn't take us seriously because we are so much like the world; we are caught up in the same miserable rat race of self-seeking consumerism and materialism. But as Christians we have the opportunity to teach the world to sing and dance and to discover that the true good life is the life that is given away. We have the opportunity to incarnate in our lifestyles the joyous conspiracy that is changing the world.

For Discussion and Action

1. What specifically are the problems of "compartmentalized" Christian living?
2. Just what does it mean for Christians to take Jesus seriously? To live under his leadership in every dimension of life?
3. What are five different ways listed in this chapter that we can redefine the concept of "the good life" to make life more celebrative?
4. When people wanted to follow Jesus, what did he tell them would be required in terms of their use of resources and the cause of justice for the poor? How did following Jesus affect the ways his disciples used their time and resources?
5. What is the difference between the doctrine of "passive availability" and one of "active redistribution"? Search the Bible for support for each doctrine. Which do you think is more biblical?
6. What is a biblical alternative to the tithe? How might such an alternative enable us to be more just stewards of a finite planet? What is a global view of stewardship?
7. What are some specific steps you could take toward becoming a family— or a single—for others?
8. What are some creative ways you could celebrate life more fully while freeing up much more of your time and resources for the work of the kingdom? Ask someone to hold you accountable as you begin this journey.
9. Can you think of some imaginative ways you and yours could house yourselves much less expensively, relocate, or share your home? How could the resources or space you freed up be used to reach people for Christ, empower the poor, and advance the kingdom?
10. Give a rough estimate (in hours and dollars) of the time and resources that could be freed up in your church if 25 percent of the congregation seriously began simplifying their lifestyles by trying some of the ideas listed in this chapter.

7.

Seeking First the Future of God through Creative Vocation

I had no sooner gotten up off my knees than I sensed everything had changed . . . everything was new. I went outside, and to my amazement even nature had changed. I had always "known" that the natural world was beautiful, but this was the first time I had really experienced it. The brilliant sun burst through the translucent green leaves overhead against the backdrop of a deep blue summer sky. Banks of irises danced in the warm breezes. I felt reconciled not only to my Father, but also to his good world.

I was sixteen years old that summer when I first discovered God's forgiveness and his love. Becoming a Christian dramatically changed my life in so many ways. My high school friends and I had been aspiring delinquents, but frankly we had not been very good at it. It wasn't particularly difficult for me to give up my half-hearted apprenticeship in delinquency.

One of the most radical changes that occurred that day was a change in my life direction. I had decided as a six-year-old to pursue a career in art. For ten years I had never waivered from that decision, and had taken every art class I could find. Yet somehow I immediately sensed when I finished praying that God had given me a whole new direction.

NEW BEGINNINGS AND NEW DIRECTIONS

From that first day of new beginnings I have had the strongest sense of Christian calling. I didn't know exactly what God wanted me to do but I knew it would involve the major part of my waking hours. I haven't always been a very obedient Christian, but I never have been able to escape his call on my life.

Two years later I went to Cascade College and discovered my experience wasn't unique. At the time we graduated I am sure that over 90 percent of the class had a strong sense of ministry calling. I would conservatively estimate that over 60 percent of us were going into "full-time Christian service" on the mission field, in a pastorate, or in Christian education. The rest of our class felt God calling them into specific vocations outside the church in health care, education, and social work. I really don't think we were any different from any other Christian college students in the late fifties. Almost everyone seemed possessed by a strong sense of calling that focused outwardly in some form of service to others.

It is my impression that Christian colleges emphasized calling and ministry much more then than we do now. I am deeply saddened at the number of beautiful, lavishly gifted young people I meet who have absolutely no sense of life direction, no sense of calling from God. They seem to be floating like so much flotsam on the sea with no idea where they are going. There are a few who are motivated to pursue some personal career goals, but there are so many whose lives seem to be directed by pure happenstance. And both groups, whether by choice or by chance, assume that whatever they are doing is God's will, simply because that's what turned up.

Actually, I find this tragic problem among Christians of all ages. At a time in the history of the church when we need literally every man, woman, and child to follow God's calling into lives of active service towards others, so many of us are squandering our lives away in jobs, professions, and leisure-time activities that often have nothing to do with God's kingdom call on our lives.

In this chapter, we will explore together the concept of Christian voca-tion—defined here as God's ministry calling on our lives. We will look at ways to put God's future first by finding his calling for our lives, and we will see how God's calling relates to our jobs and use of leisure time. And we will wrestle with the whole issue of how we can discover the will of God for our lives in our vocational calling. I will introduce you to a few people I know who have found their ministry calling and are having a positively marvelous time marching to a different drumbeat.

HIRED HELP AND PART-TIME SERVANTS

Let's begin by examining our contemporary understanding of Christian vocation. The primary expression of Christian vocation in many churches is what I call "surrogate servanthood." The attitude in these churches is that the clergy is hired to live out Christian vocation for everyone else. The laity may be involved in occasional volunteer activities and sporadic philanthropy, but the business of being Christian servants and really getting involved in the ministry of Jesus in the world—well, that's what professional clergy is hired for!

In this dualistic approach, careers for the laity are seen almost exclusively as secular activities that have little to do with the Christian vocation practiced by the clergy. The focus of life and vocation for many laypersons seems to have much more to do with the secular agenda of getting ahead and building security than with the biblical agenda of living their faith.

In some Christian churches this dualism is expressed in a different way. While the laity's primary involvement is usually in their secular careers, they often invest large amounts of their discretionary time in committees, programs, and activities of their churches. Unfortunately, little of this time and energy is focused on the urgent spiritual, emotional, and physical needs of those outside the church.

One aspect of the dualistic attitude toward Christian vocation is a remarkably noncritical view of secular employment. Any job is viewed as being as good as any other job for Christians, as long as they work hard, are honest, and say a little word for Jesus when the opportunity arises.

How did we get into such a fix? Where did we get such a naive view of work as it relates to Christian vocation? This attitude stems from the sixteenth-century reformers, who taught that all jobs should be done to the glory of God.[1] And unquestionably this is true; *all* human activity should be done to the glory of God. But the problem with this doctrine of Christian calling is that not all human activity is synonymous with the biblical concept of vocation, nor does it promote God's agenda. There are life decisions, jobs, and personal goals that are at best irrelevant and at worst diametrically opposed to God's intentions in history.

John Alexander shares one response to this question: "My main concern about jobs is not that people are doing bad things. It is that most of us are doing pointless things. Most of us might as well be packing sand down ratholes." [2] And some jobs are not simply pointless; a number are destructive! Christians are involved in the production of nuclear bombs and chemical weapons systems, and some labor union, corporate, and governmental practices exploit the poor and seriously damage the environment. Can a job that has destructive consequences, compromises basic ethical values, or at best makes no positive human contribution to God's agenda really be done to the glory of God?

Don't misunderstand me. There is nothing inherently un-Christian about being a carpenter, a businessman, or a factory worker. But as Christians we must ask why we are doing our jobs, what consequences our work will have in our society and our world, and how our work will contribute to the advance of God's kingdom.

It seems to me that the dualism of unquestioningly accepting "any job" as fine for Christians as long as they support the institutional church and say a word for Jesus is not a biblical model of vocation. Had this view been in vogue in the days of Jesus, Matthew never would have left his work with the "IRS," nor Luke his medical practice. In the New Testament, secular jobs were never automatically synonymous with Christian vocation. Quite to the contrary, those who followed Jesus often left their jobs abruptly to become as fully involved as Jesus was in the vocation of spreading the good news that God's future had invaded the present.

Again, I am not suggesting that all Christians should quit their jobs. But I am urging that we adopt a much more critical and a much more biblical attitude toward secular occupations as they relate to Christian vocation and to God's agenda for the future. If we commit our total lives as disciples to seeking his kingdom first, shouldn't that commitment be reflected in the jobs we choose and the ways we invest our working hours and our leisure time as well?

In Jesus Christ every believer—lay and clergy alike—has a vocation that should be reflected in every dimension of his or her existence—as it was in the lives of the first disciples. Every Christian has a ministry calling. And yes, that may mean some will feel challenged to change jobs, cut back working hours, or begin to challenge unethical practices where they work. But above everything else, it should mean that every area of the life of a believer centers around God's kingdom call.

Thomas Merton encourages us to realize that "each one of us has some kind of vocation. We are called by God to share in his life and his kingdom. Each one of us is called to a special place in the kingdom. If we find that place," he counsels, "we will be happy. For each one of us there is only one thing necessary: to fulfill our own destiny, according to God's will, to be what God wants us to be." [3]

But how do we find God's will? How do we become what he wants us to be? How do we discover his vocation for our lives? M. Blaine Smith in his book, *Knowing God's Will*, insists that the dominant concern of today's Christian young people and adults is how to know the will of God. And yet there is probably more confusion on this issue than any other issue in the contemporary church. [4] While there are no easy answers to these questions, I think there are some biblical principles that can provide us a sense of direction. But first, let's examine some of the common ways Christians in different traditions seek God's will for their lives.

THE PURSUIT OF THE PERSONAL, PRIVATE, PARTICULARISTIC, PLEASURABLE WILL OF GOD

Among some Christians, the dualism between the secular world and the spiritual world appears to be so complete that life decisions are seldom made on a basis of faith (except sometimes in the case of the clergy). Decisions regarding careers, for instance, seem to be handled little differently than non-Christians would handle them; job decisions are made on the basis of opportunities for increasing the levels of personal satisfaction, professional advancement, and financial compensation.

In contrast, of course, a large number of Christians *are* interested in seeking God's guidances for their major life decisions. A few receive a sense of calling from God and enter into some type of "full time" Christian ministry. However, most of the laity seem to have little awareness that God has a vocational call for their lives; as a consequence, seeking the will of God for their lives seems to be a matter of asking for guidance in the "particulars" of life—what job to take, whom to marry, where to live, and so on.

My experience in working with young people in three different Christian colleges has shown me that the pathway to finding God's will on such matters usually begins—consciously or unconsciously—with "What do I want?" "What do I want in a job, spouse, house, lifestyle?" Then, once they happen on a job, person, or living arrangement that meets their expectations, the next question typically is, "Is it God's will?" Translated, this means, "Will God let me have what I want?"

Prayer then too often becomes a means of coaxing, cajoling, and if necessary badgering God into sanctioning or granting our desires and letting us "have it our way." Some believers search the Bible for verses they can interpret as giving them the green light. Or they set out "fleeces" (see Judg. 6:36–40), prepared only to accept answers that accord with what they wanted all along. One engaged young man prayed, "Father, if it isn't your will for me to marry the young woman I have selected, close the door or blow up the church, and I will reconsider. Otherwise, I am going full steam ahead."

Some Christians believe that it isn't even necessary to pray about such decisions, that a Christian can simply trust his or her desires because God's will and a Christian's desires are synonymous. Many Christians rely on taking the pulse of their inner feelings to learn whether or not they have God's okay. Still others watch for signals in the circumstances of their daily lives.

Through whatever combination of the above, many Christians arrive at a decision and assure themselves that their decision must be the will of God or "I wouldn't be where I am." And then, once they have finally gotten the job, spouse, house, and lifestyle they wanted, they are often willing to make some spare time available to usher or even to teach a Sunday school class. The ministry decision is typically the last decision they make. The problem is that there is absolutely no way the church can hope to make any difference in the face of the human challenges of the eighties and nineties with this kind of casual, self-centered approach to finding God's will.

When we try to find God's will for the private, particular desires of our lives, it is all too easy for our own agendas and desires to get in the way of hearing God's voice. Frankly, I am suspicious of persons who confidently claim to know the mind of the sovereign God in every situation; I have seen too many situations in which such serenely assured souls made decisions that wound up embarrassing them and sometimes their churches. Is it possible that much of what we do under the guise of seeking to know the will of God reflects our need to be able to understand the mind of God and to manipulate his activity instead of surrendering our lives to his control?

I made a startling discovery as I was researching this chapter: I could find no examples or teachings anywhere in the New Testament on how to determine the private, "particularistic" will of God regarding careers, marriage partners, or choice of lifestyle. We never hear Christ praying for guidance as to where to stay in the next town, or praying about career decisions for one of his followers. For him, knowing the will of God seemed to have a totally different meaning. He taught his disciples to pray, "Thy kingdom come, they will be done on earth as it is in heaven," and to allow God's kingdom to be expressed through their lives and service.

Even though a number of Paul's prayers are recorded in the Epistles, we never hear him praying for guidance on the kind of matters that fill our prayers. We don't hear Paul praying, "Father, show me whether I should get a job tentmaking for awhile," or "Show Timothy whether or not he should get married." Even in his extensive teaching on singleness and marriage, Paul offers absolutely no instruction for finding the will of God on whom and when to marry. He too seems to have a different notion of God's will in human life than many contemporary Christians have.

Does this mean God has no particular will for us, that he doesn't have a "plan for our lives," that there is no special job, spouse, or location foreordained for us? There are some Christians who think so. They suggest God expects us to use our sanctified intelligence to make the best decisions we can in these areas. People who subscribe to this position urge that Christians learn to take greater responsibility for their decisions and to make more mature decisions that are congruent with their faith.

I certainly can't argue against the need for greater responsibility, maturity, and congruence in Christian decision making. And yet we are still left with the question of whether we are strictly on our own in making these important decisions in our lives. I really don't think so. Frankly, I am attracted by charismatic Christians who constantly refer every issue of life to God for direction. I have to believe it is possible to be more mature and responsible and at the same time more dependent on God. There must be a way to avoid the folly of singlehandedly trying to guide our own lives on the one hand and the silliness of expecting God to tell us which shirt to buy on the other.

THE PURSUIT OF THE REDEMPTIVE, COLLECTIVE, WORLD-CHANGING WILL OF GOD

What would happen if we stood this whole business of seeking the will of God on its head? Instead of beginning with the question, "What do I want?", I think we would have a better chance of discovering God's will by asking "What does God want, and how does he want me to be a part of what he is doing?" When we look at the will of God this way, the first question for a Christian to ask becomes, "What are the intentions of God for his world, and how does he want to use my life and gifts to advance his kingdom?" The answer to that question for each of us is our ministry calling—our Christian vocation—and it comes before any specific decisions as to job, spouse, or lifestyle.

Once we discover how God wants to use our lives to promote righteousness, justice, peace, reconciliation and wholeness in our needy world, we have a reference point for all our other life decisions. Then we will seek that job, career, or tentmaking position that will enable us to most fully work for his kingdom calling in our life. We will seek his guidance regarding whether we should remain single or get married in light of our ministry vocation. And of course, one of our primary criteria for marriage will be finding someone who shares a highly compatible sense of ministry calling. We will even intentionally decide where to live and what kind of lifestyle to adopt in light of God's kingdom call on our lives.

Once we decide to start with the question "What does God want?" instead of "What do I want?" we still need some specific pathways to God's vocation for our lives. We need to discover *how* he wants to use our lives in the service of his kingdom.

Kingdom Vocation: Love Incarnation

"God's will is plain. We are to love Him and to love people," advises John Perkins. "The Biblical evidence overwhelmingly states that the will of God is to love Him in a way that leaves no room for idols and to love our neighbor in a way that liberates Him from poverty and oppression either spiritual or physical." [5]

God's vocation for all his children is love. Wherever we find ourselves, in whatever work or relationships, we can be sure that it is his will to incarnate the loving life of his Son through us. Our lives should be a foretaste of the loving celebration of God's future.

My grandmother was such a person. She exuded the love and joy of God everywhere she went. In her declining years she was placed in a nursing home where she really didn't want to be. Yet instead of trying to puzzle why God had allowed her to wind up in such a place, she did what she had always done in every situation; she focused on the needs of others around her. She spent the better part of every day reading Scripture and stories to others in the nursing home. She understood God's will for her life, even though she was no longer free to make all of her own life decisions.

There are many devout Christians in the United States, in Europe, in Japan, and certainly in the Third World who don't have a lot of options regarding their life situation. It is pointless for them to pray about relocating occupationally, geographically, or relationally. They must find the vocation of God in the often-desperate struggle of their immediate circumstances.

Whatever our circumstances, it is God's will that we be salt and light and leaven to a world that has given up hope. We are called to be the loving, hope-filled presence of the kingdom in the midst of struggle, pain, and even death.

KINGDOM CALLING: A PATHWAY TO VOCATION

How can those of us who have the luxury of greater choice discern God's vocation for our lives? How can we know the specific ways he wants to use our lives to change his world? How can we use our greater freedom for the greater good of others?

The most important step is to acknowledge that he does indeed have as much intention of using our lives to make a difference in the world as he had for Andrew, Peter, or Luke. God loves each of us and longs for us to experience the profound satisfaction of using our lives and gifts "to proclaim liberty to the captives and recovery of sight to the blind, to set free the oppressed and announce that the time has come when the Lord will save his people" (Luke 4:18–20, TEV).

Paul reminds us that God's Spirit "energizes to each individual exactly as he pleases" (1 Cor. 12:11, MLB). It isn't possible either to predict or structure the way God in his sovereign wisdom calls men and women to his service. Some hear God speak to them at an Urbana Conference on World Mission. Others hear his voice through the needs of neglected senior citizens in their own communities. Still others hear God's voice through a personal crisis. For some, the vocational calling may only involve freeing up one evening a week. Others may feel led to change their lifestyles more radically.

Even though the way God may choose to call an individual is totally unpredictable, be very sure he has a vocation for every life—he has a vocation for you! He wants to use your life to make a kingdom difference in his world. Let me outline one way of listening for God's call. If you are not sure of God's vocation for your life, I encourage you to give it a try.

This pathway to vocational calling has seven steps. Before you begin, I would encourage you to purchase a journal—a dream book—as a place to record what God is saying to you as you go through the process. And be warned! If you sincerely follow this process and listen for the kingdom call of God on your life, your entire life could be changed. You just might be plunged into an adventure from which you can't turn back.

(1) *Listening for his call in his present and coming future.* We begin our right-side-up search for the will of God with the question, "What does God want for his world and for his people?" To answer this question, I would encourage you to join with a group of other Christians who are determined to put his kingdom first in an intensive study of his Word. It might be helpful to use chapter 5 of this book as a guide for your vocational study group.

As you study together ask yourself, "What are God's intentions for the future, and how does he want to use my life to be a part of his intentions?" "How does he specifically want me to be an agent of righteousness, justice, reconciliation, peace, and love, working with him to change his world?" The Bible is filled with examples of individuals who heard God's call and either responded or went their own way. Particularly note those examples and the ways in which he dramatically changed the priorities and life goals of those who responded. Listen for God's call as you study his Word. Keep a running list in your vocational dream book of all impressions you receive in your biblical study—and especially of specific areas of service God may be calling you into. Be ready for immediate induction into the army of the Lamb and the battle for his kingdom.

(2) *Listening for his call in the lives of needy persons.* The Scriptures teach that Jesus is uniquely incarnated in the lives of the poor and forgotten ones. Therefore, if we listen, I am convinced we can hear God calling us through the pain and suffering of the hungry in Brazil,

the alienation and loneliness of seniors in a retirement home in Atlanta, the hopelessness and despair of drug addicts in San Francisco, and the fear and hopelessness of neglected children right in your own community.

In your study group, review chapters two and three of this book for an overview of future areas of human need. Read newspapers, news magazines, and mission newsletters together. Watch films and TV specials on human conditions. What areas of human suffering and need particularly grip your heart? List them in your journal. Discuss them. Pray over them. It may well be that Jesus is calling you through a specific area of spiritual, emotional, or physical need into an area of compassionate service you have not yet dreamed of.

Begin learning as much as you can about the needs you find most compelling and about the Christian organizations that minister to those needs. Record what you learn in your journal and share your new knowledge with your vocational study group. Help one another, through prayer and discussion of these urgent areas of human need, to listen for the anguished voice of Jesus. And be ready for the unexpected— the opportunity to plunge headfirst into a ministry of compassionate service.

(3) *Listening for his call in your brokenness and giftedness.* Not only can we hear God call us through the brokenness of others; his call can also come to us through our own brokenness. While many writings on Christian calling emphasize the importance of identifying one's gifts and abilities, virtually nothing has been written on the amazing ways God works through our failures and weaknesses. Yet the Bible is full of surprising ways God acted to turn human failure and defeat into his own glory. We are told he chose the "weak things of the earth to confound the mighty." Somehow God is able to take even our messups, our failures, and our inadequacies and use them to advance his kingdom.

Make a list in your journal of those areas in which you struggle— of your failures and weaknesses, the areas in which you are broken. Wait on God and discuss with your study partners ways in which God can transform each of those areas into a tool for the fabrication of his kingdom . . . and perhaps a vehicle for his calling.

After we focus on brokenness, let's also listen to God call us through our giftedness. Elizabeth O'Connor asserts,

We ask to know the will of God without guessing that His will is written into our very beings. We perceive that will when we discern our gifts. Our obedience and surrender to God are in large part our obedience and surrender to His gifts. This is the message wrapped up in the parable of the talents. Our gifts are on loan. We are responsible for spending them in the world, and we will be held accountable. . . . If we use those [talents] we have, our lives will expand and our capacity will double. A message that sounds throughout the New Testament is here again in the story of the talents: He who loses his life will find it. Cast your bread on the water and it will come back, tenfold.[6]

Undeniably God gave us gifts for a purpose. And those gifts were not given to be squandered aimlessly on increasing the profit margins of a corporation, the bureaucracy of government, or the prestige of a religious organization. He has gifted us to participate with him in the creation of the new. "In every man is the creation story. Since the first day of our beginning, the Spirit has brooded over the formless dark void of our lives, calling us into existence through our gifts until they are developed. And the same Spirit gives us the responsibility of investing them with him in the continuing creation of the world." [7]

Take time in your group to let each member list his or her natural and spiritual gifts as well as the personal heritage out of which those gifts are manifested. Affirm the gifts you see in others in the group. Keep a running list of the gifts that seem to be evident in your life. Also keep a list of major areas of life accomplishment in which you have used your gifts.

In times of solitude, listen for God's voice calling you, out of silence, through your gifts and through your failures into his service. We have absolutely no idea of the amazing ways our Lord might call us through both our brokenness and giftedness to participate in his new creation.

(4) *Listening for his voice in dreams for his Kingdom.* Now open yourselves to dreaming new dreams for your vocation and your future— inviting God's Spirit to invade your imagination. Set aside all your preconceived notions about Christian vocation and service, about your own life situation. God wants to open you up to surprising new ways he could use your life to make a difference in his world. Imagine wholly new ways everything you have written in your journal could be orchestrated together into new vocational opportunities.

Begin with the kingdom. In meditation focus on the present and coming kingdom of God. Picture in your mind the specific ways God's new future of righteousness, justice, peace, reconciliation, wholeness, and love is transforming the suffering, darkness, and injustice of our present age. In your heart and mind, celebrate the inbreaking of God's future. Now picture yourself as being part of the inbreaking of his future in specific new ways.

As you hear him call you through the urgent needs of others, through your own brokenness and giftedness, listen carefully. Imagine fully. Open yourself totally to the Spirit of God as he floods your imaginations with new dreams for your life. Ask yourself this very important question: "How can God most fully use my life and gifts to advance his kingdom in the areas of greatest spiritual, emotional, physical, and economic needs?" (Remember, there are regions of the world congested with servants of the kingdom while others have none. We need distributive justice in Christian service too.)

Collect your dreams as you would so many wildflowers, and enter them into your journal. Capture every detail. Outline creative new ways God might use your giftedness and brokenness to manifest his kingdom in specific areas of human need. Share your dreams, pray over your dreams, and celebrate your dreams with the others in your group. Focus your attention on those dreams that seem most compelling—the ones in which you seem to hear God's call most strongly.

Then, take time to begin researching your dreams. Prayerfully evaluate your present situation to determine if you can follow the vocation of God within the context of your present job and geographical location. Learn which Christian organizations are working in the arena of your interest; research how they are carrying out their service and what they require of those they enlist in their ministry.

At the same time, explore the possibility of creating your own program of kingdom service in conjunction with your church or a Christian organization. Since we will need to dramatically increase our capability for Christian response with declining resources in the eighties, try to imagine creative ways to reduce your needs and find your own independent support if your vocational call is full-time; check into the possibility of "tentmaking." Finally, explore with your group, your family, and your friends the feasibility of your plans and draw up a timetable for a transition toward investing a greater part of your leisure time and working hours in the vocation to which God is calling you.

(5) *Confirming his call through Christian community.* Once God's sense of kingdom call begins to crystallize in your life, it is essential that it be submitted to a group of brothers and sisters for confirmation. The need for such a confirmation has been recognized since the days of the early church, as Richard Foster states:

> Perhaps the most astonishing feature of that incendiary fellowship was their sense of corporate guidance. It was beautifully illustrated in the calling forth of Paul and Barnabas to tramp the length and breadth of the Roman Empire with the good news of the kingdom of God. (Acts 13:1–3). Their call came when a number of people had been together over an extended period of time. It included the use of the disciplines of prayer, fasting, and worship. Having become a prepared people, they perceived the call of God together: 'Set apart for me Barnabas and Saul for the work to which I have called them.' (Acts 13:2). . . . We would be well advised to encourage groups

of people who are willing to fast, pray, and worship together until they
have discerned the mind of the Lord and heard His call.[8]

While you may choose to submit your kingdom call solely to your
study group, I think it might be a good idea to present it to your
larger community of faith for confirmation. However, I have one cau-
tion. I strongly urge you to tie in your life directly with Christians
who share your urgency for the kingdom. If you submit your vocation
for confirmation to a group of people who are simply interested in
maintaining the status quo, they probably won't even understand what
you are talking about, let alone be an instrument for God's corporate
guidance in your life.

Once you have submitted your kingdom dreams to the larger group,
pray with them, worship God, and wait for his guidance. It may take
awhile, but he won't disappoint you. He will confirm his kingdom call
on your life, help you with your fears, and commission you into his
service. We can trust the Holy Spirit to bring a sense of rightness on
the group as we seek him and his will for our lives.

(6) *Listening for his call in lives of service.* Once we have given ourselves fully to his vocation, we will discover the call of God is never
static. Like conversion, it isn't solely an event; rather, it is a dynamic
ongoing process. As we seek first his kingdom in our lives and world
and as we learn to listen to his voice, he will continue to call us. He
may continue to shape our sense of mission in the situation in which
he has placed us, or he may lead us through a series of situations in
which he uses our lives to manifest his new future. In any case, I can
promise you that your life will never be the same again. God will
present you with challenges, opportunities, and not a few frustrations
as you join his adventure.

(7) *Listening for his kingdom call in every dimension of our lives.*
Let's come back to all those particularistic concerns from which usually
begins the quest for God's will. Once we have a clear sense of God's
call on our life, we have the best criterion possible for deciding where
we should work, whom we should marry, and where we should live.
If we genuinely seek his kingdom first, I think the message of Matthew
6:33 is clear: he will provide for our essential needs. He will be with
us in our decisions and in our lives.

That seems to be the model that is most evident throughout the
New Testament: men and women moving out in the world intent on
the mission of Christ seem to be led by God. We never hear them
praying for particularistic guidance or insisting that God let them know
in advance what is going to happen. We see them moving ahead in
their mission confident God will lead them, that he is in their lives

and their decisions. They still made mistakes, and so will we, but if we put God and his agenda first we can know that our God is with us. He is Lord of history and Lord of our personal histories. We can trust him with our lives, our vocations, and our futures.

ORCHESTRATING ALL LIFE AROUND HIS KINGDOM CALL

Seeking First His Kingdom in our Work

No longer will we make decisions about job opportunities singularly or even primarily based on what we want. We have a whole new criterion for decision—what God wants, and how he wants us to be a part of his initiative. For some Christians, vocation and occupation will merge into a single venture. For others, their job will directly complement their vocation but the two will remain separate. Some will find it necessary to actually leave their jobs. Still others may seek a part-time, "tentmaking" job to support their vocation.

For example, in a class I taught at Seattle Pacific I challenged the students to do a research project in which they created a Christian vocation for themselves thirty hours a week in response to an area of compelling human need. I asked them to design an imaginative way they could use their gifts to minister through their church to a specific human need in urban Seattle. "The catch is," I explained, "you don't get an office, a job description, or a salary. Now invent a way you can work twenty hours a week to support your ministry thirty hours a week."

The students came up with some fascinating ways to significantly use their lives to work with delinquents, seniors, and neglected kids while supporting themselves with part-time jobs. As a result of going through this process they discovered they had a much broader array of options than the three or four professions they had been considering in college. They also learned they weren't limited to simply being a functionary in somebody else's shop; they had the ability to create wholly new vocational options for their future. And, perhaps most importantly, they found they could consciously steward their lives for maximum impact for God's kingdom.

Stewardship of one's life is unquestionably the most important area of stewardship. And since most of our waking hours are spent working, our decisions about how we steward our working hours are extremely important. Of course, we do have a responsibility to provide for ourselves and our loved ones. But nowhere in the Bible does it say we have to work forty hours a week to do so! Many in our culture are already simplifying their lifestyles to reduce the number of hours they have to work and to free up a much larger chunk of their time for Christian service. However, even when it proves impossible to reduce work hours or to change jobs, there is an option open to almost all of us. Virtually everyone could give up an evening of TV or a church committee meeting and free two to four hours a week to minister to those in need as part of their ministry calling.

Not only do we need to be more creative in our stewardship of our working hours, we need to be much more creative in discovering where to invest those hours. I am confident God will enable you to discover imaginative new ways you can more fully invest your life in responding to human needs in your community, your state, or perhaps even in another part of the world. Few American Christians seem aware of the myriad ways their talents could be used in Third World countries. Intercristo, The Mennonite Central Committee, and virtually every major denomination have short-term overseas opportunities in construction, business, engineering, health care, education, agriculture, and so on.

Although there are almost limitless opportunities for Christians seeking to serve God, a commitment to seek his kingdom first automatically excludes certain types of occupational options believers feel are often in tension with the agendas of the kingdom.

For example, there is debate today whether Christians can in good conscience work for a large corporation. In a panel discussion printed in *Other Side* magazine, Sandra Boston, a Christian social activist, seriously questioned whether Christians could work their way up in a major corporation without being totally swallowed up in the values of the system. Tony Campolo, a Christian sociologist, was more optimistic; he felt Christians could and should seek to penetrate corporate structures and transform them into "agents of life." [9] My personal conviction is that Christians will never be able to successfully penetrate and effectively change large corporate, governmental, and labor organizations unless they are constantly supported by a group of believers who understand and pray for their difficult calling. Otherwise, I am sure they will be swallowed alive in the cross-currents of culture.

As you discover your vocation and commit your life to his kingdom, you may be faced with extremely tough questions about your occupation. But you will also be confronted with rich new opportunities to create new ways of using your lives to make a difference in the world. The conclusion of this chapter will be devoted to showing how a few people are finding creative new ways to follow their kingdom vocation and integrate it with their options.

Once we have discerned God's vocation for our lives and have some sense of what occupation we are going to pursue, then we have a basis for deciding whether or not to seek additional education. So many people simply go on to school without trying to figure out his calling . . . and sometimes that seems to work. But it seems to me that for those who know their vocation the pathway to their goals should be much easier to see and follow.

The bottom line on the whole issue of vocation and occupation is that as Christians we can and must make occupational decisions and live our working lives in ways that intentionally advance God's kingdom and fulfill his calling. Here too, we need the corporate guidance of Christians with a common vision. But if we put his kingdom first we can be confident he will guide our occupational decisions.

Seeking First His Kingdom in Singleness and Marriage

Your primary decision about God's calling on your life can't help but influence your decision regarding whether or not to marry (if you haven't already made that decision). It is important to recognize that singleness is as much a gift of God as marriage; throughout the history of the church, thousands have heard God calling them into a single life of service. Paul points out that the evident advantage is that single people are less encumbered by the world and freer to work for the kingdom. If you feel God is calling you to singleness in order to be more involved in his ministry calling in your life, I would encourage you to seek confirmation in your small group.

The first question Christians who are contemplating marriage need to ask is, "How compatible are we in our sense of Christian calling?" I know very few Christian couples who seem to be strongly bonded in their sense of Christian calling and vocation, and too many who are mismatched. Tim and Kerry are one couple who are strongly bonded in Christian vocation. They work as a team in their ministry with singles and young adults. They even have a series of hand signals they use when one or the other of them is in front of a group. You can sense they are running stride for stride in their work for the kingdom.

I strongly encourage every couple contemplating marriage to spend at least ten to sixteen sessions with a trained Christian counselor exploring the whole issue of compatibility, particularly as it relates to God's ministry call on their lives. In addition, I am persuaded that every Christian couple needs to be under the care of a small group who not only helps them discover God's ministry call on their individual lives, but also seeks corporate guidance regarding their possible union in Christ. The stakes are simply too high to try to make such life-changing decisions outside of the body of Christ.

For many who are called into marriage, their vocation will include being moms and dads. As their kids grow up, perhaps they will feel called to pray with their group about sharing their parenting vocation with kids no one cares about. In every city in the nation there is a growing shortage of good foster homes for thousands of kids no one wants to adopt because of their handicaps, age, or racial background. Those of us who call ourselves "prolife" have a special responsibility to care for these kids.

If singles, couples, and married people put God's ministry calling on their life first and seek the corporate guidance of the body of Christ, I am confident he will direct their lives and guide their decisions.

Seeking First the Kingdom Geographically

It has been extremely difficult for me to come up with many good examples of Christian laymen who have relocated geographically because of God's call on their lives. Larry and his family are one of the few examples I know. They left a comfortable Wheaton, Illinois, suburb to move into an inner-city community in Chicago near LaSalle Street Church. Their move was of course motivated by God's call on their lives to be more intimately involved with the urban poor.

Unfortunately one of the best examples I know of relocation to act on a sense of calling happened outside of orthodox Christianity. I was sitting on my porch in Seattle one autumn afternoon when three people came up the walk and asked if they could chat with me. They explained that about twenty households had sold businesses in Southern California and farms in rural Oregon to come to Seattle. I pointed out that they had come to the Puget Sound area at positively the worst possible time, because we were in the midst of a serious recession. They said they weren't concerned because they felt they were called to come to Seattle and start a branch of their group "The Local Church." I discovered that I totally disagreed with their theology, but I couldn't help but be impressed with their commitment.

It hasn't even occurred to most Christians that the issue of where we live has anything to do with the kingdom of God. Usually Christians, like their secular counterparts, select a place to live based on affordability, comfort, convenience, good schools, and so on. Once we discern God's kingdom call on our lives, however, all decisions—including where we live—need to be made in light of that primary decision. Again we need the corporate guidance of our group in making decisions about where to live, and we need a sense of openness to God's call on our lives. He can be trusted to guide us.

CREATING BIBLICAL VOCATIONS IN A WORLD OF NEED

Having briefly explored how Christians can find the guidance of God in their life decisions . . . let's look at a few people who have discovered God's exciting vocation for their lives and have found creative ways to orchestrate job, home, and family around their vocation. You will notice that some found their vocation fully compatible with their present occupations, while others found it necessary to make major career changes.

Engineering for the Kingdom

Al has sensed God calling him through his interest in engineering since he was a child. After he got his B.S. in engineering, he had a wide range of job offers to choose from, including designing missiles for Boeing. But he believes strongly that there are no neutral occupations for Christians; the time and creativity we invest in our jobs either improve the human condition or make it worse. So Al turned down the missile job in favor of designing better cardiology equipment to enable doctors to more effectively help heart patients.

Recently, however, God spoke to Al through some kids with cerebral palsy. When he visited an institution for physically disabled children, he learned that many victims of cerebral palsy feel helplessly trapped in bodies that won't move or communicate the way they want them to. All of a sudden, he heard God's call on his life. He realized God wants him to use his engineering skills to create new ways for these kids to get around and communicate with others. He is terribly excited about the new dream God is giving him for working with these kids. He is exploring ways to shift his occupation into his vocation and to work full time at engineering mobility and communications systems for handicapped children.

A Gift of Art, a Vocation of Love

Roger discovered God's call on his life through his gift in art and his deep concern for those in the art community. He works through his sculpture not only to make a statement about his faith, but also to challenge the secular values of contemporary culture. When Roger first started working professionally, he found there was virtually no Christian witness among the professional art community. Many of his friends in this community reflected an alienation and meaninglessness in both their art and their lives. So Roger has focused his professional career as an artist around his concern for his colleagues. In his art, life, and relationships he seeks to communicate the meaning, love, and hope of Jesus that is so central to his own existence.

Vocational Transformation of a Profession

After several years of living compartmentally as a Christian attorney—with his law practice in one compartment and his faith in another—Mark received a new call from God. He felt challenged to view the people he worked with in his profession as more than clients, and so he decided to set aside the first hour of every working day to pray for the people he serves in his legal profession. He held all phone calls and refused all appointments during this period each morning. And he reports that the results are amazing. He finds that he relates with much greater sensitivity to his clients, and is concerned for more than their legal problems. But in addition to noting a change in himself, Mark has seen a number of instances in which God is acting miraculously in the lives of the people he serves.

Speaking out for the Kingdom in a Corporation

A chemist heard God's voice in a different way. He is vice president for research and development in a chemical corporation. He has had a growing awareness that the gospel of Jesus should influence the daily decisions he makes in the production of industrial chemicals. "For years, he built respect among his peers because of his candor about the potential toxic effects of particular chemicals. In the wake of growing concern about chemical spills and health hazards to employees, professional groups of chemists and engineers are asking him to speak, not only about technical breakthroughs, but especially about the ethical responsibility of those with technical knowledge. 'I've always had a basic sense of what was right or wrong,' he says, 'but now I know why it's right or wrong, and nobody will stop me from speaking out.' " [10]

First World Florist, Third World Development Worker

Nearing retirement, Denny Grindal and his wife decided to leave their florist shop and fly to Kenya to see the animals. After touring the large game preserves, they decided to visit a small Presbyterian mission among the Masai tribe, a tribe of tall warriors who live by raising cattle, following their herds from one grazing area to another.

Shortly before Denny and his wife visited the mission, the Kenyan Government had mandated that the Masai people had to give up their nomadic life and stay on a government-assigned reservation. When the Grindals visited the Masai on their reservation they were appalled. The land was barren of grass and water. A drought had killed hundreds of cattle and thousands of Masai were struggling with their very survival.

After meeting Denny, both the tribal leaders and the mission representatives asked him to come back and help them. His response was immediate. "What can I possibly do to help? I am a florist!" So he and his wife returned to the United States and to their florist shop.

But God wouldn't let them forget what they had seen. He called them very clearly through the tragic plight of the Masai. So Denny went to the library and spent several months researching earth-filled dams. Then the Grindals took some money out of savings and returned to Kenya. They met with the tribal leaders and shared their plan; the Masai responded by selling some of their cattle to match the Grindal's money. They worked together to construct the first of a series of huge earth-filled dams. In one night of torrential rain the dam—the size of three football fields—was filled. And they had a celebration.

This couple in responding to the call of God inadvertently created a whole new Christian career for themselves . . . spending six months per year in their florist shop and six months with their new friends in Kenya. In the past ten years of working with the Masai, God has used this couple to build reservoirs, dams, irrigation systems, and permanent housing, as well as start literacy programs, community health projects, preaching missions, and vegetable gardening. They are a beautiful example of the way in which God can use any of our lives to bring real change in our world if we put his kingdom first.

The New Life and the New Vocation of the Galloping Gourmet

The last thing Graham Kerr was concerned about was the kingdom of God. He was at the peak of his television career as the Galloping Gourmet. He was very wealthy. He enjoyed absolutely everything this world had to offer. And he was miserable.

Then one day, as a result of the witness of his newly converted wife, Treena, he dramatically encountered Jesus and his life was totally transformed.

He says that there was no way he could continue his very successful TV career once he had surrendered his life to Jesus. He explains that he had been intentionally cast in the role of one of America's leading hedonists and taste-setters. Everything he used in public, from the cars he drove to the cigarettes he smoked, was provided for him to create the desired image. He says the only thing he ever had to purchase was toilet paper, because that was the only thing he ever used in private.

And so, realizing it was impossible for him to be a model of the self-seeking life and at the same time exemplify the servant life of Jesus, he turned his back on his career and even gave away his fortune.

Graham and Treena have a new career with Youth with a Mission. Their annual breaking even budget is only fourteen thousand dollars—a gigantic step down from the lifestyle to which they had become accustomed. Unquestionably, the most important aspect of the Kerr's new life is their new vocation. God gave Graham a vision of a way in which the waste of the wealthy could bring hope and self-reliance to the lives of the poor. The premise of this program, which Graham calls Project Lord, is that thirty-six Americans who save fifty cents per person per day by cutting back on waste, could support one micro-farm project in Latin America.

Graham and Treena insist they have gained so much more than they ever gave up. Their new life in Christ and the opportunity to be involved in making a difference in the world has brought a profound satisfaction to their life they had never known before.

Dan and Caroline Share a Dual Vocation

Dan and Caroline didn't feel their jobs as teacher and secretary were counter to the aims of the kingdom. But once they understood God's call on their lives, they did feel their jobs were pretty irrelevant, so they decided to change. Their sense of vocation had two dimensions. First they felt called to work with international students, and second, they wanted to be more directly involved in their church.

No sooner had their sense of direction come into focus than their church offered them a half-time position in church administration. Since they lived in a Christian community, they had reduced their lifestyle needs to the point that they could live easily on half an income. Dan and Caroline decided to share the half-time position and work together as a team. That left half their time for working with internationals. They are delighted that they have found a way to be open to divergent and creative ways to use their lives for mission.

Finding God's Quiet Revolution in Mississippi

John Perkins left Mississippi after his brother was brutally killed in an unprovoked racial incident, and he never planned to return. John established a very successful business in southern California; he and his family enjoyed their affluent lifestyle, and he assumed Mississippi was forever a part of his past. Then his life was abruptly changed by accepting Christ, and one of the most remarkable changes in his life was a growing concern for the people back in Mississippi. One day John heard God very clearly instruct him to go back home, to leave his comfortable life in California and start over again in rural Mississippi.

The Perkins family found life in Mendenhall, Mississippi, hard and hungry. But their sense of divine calling enabled them to hang on in a very difficult situation and to start a small church. His ministry grew, and last summer five hundred persons helped John and his family celebrate the twenty-year jubilee of Voice of Calvary Ministries.

John's "quiet revolution" is slowly changing communities throughout Mississippi. Today there is not only a church in Mendenhall where the dream began, but also a health center, recreation center, dayschool, and thrift store. In Jackson, the headquarters for Voice of Calvary is located in a transitional community; the interracial team there models the spirit of reconciliation that is so central to their ministry.

John is committed to finding imaginative ways to work for economic justice for the poor through economic development. He has started a model thrift store in Jackson and his people have been involved in housing restoration for the poor.

In addition Voice of Calvary has started a church in Jackson that is involved in ministries in evangelism, discipleship, and reconciliation. Students come from all over the country to study in the International Study Center and learn how to be Christian activists. They are also starting Christian health clinics in other small communities throughout rural Mississippi. No, John Perkins never planned to return to his hometown in rural Mississippi. But if you could have seen John's face at the celebration of twenty years of Voice of Calvary ministries, you would know that he has never regretted his decision to follow God's call on his life.

Christian Vocation: The Opportunity to Join God in Changing His World

We live in a world of exploding needs in which the most highly trained affluent individuals exchange their gifts in very small enclaves of wealth with others who can afford to pay for the products and services they provide. Most American Christians seem to devote their lives to trying to maintain this consumer party for a few instead of working to bring God's kingdom to the many. Even our distribution of Christian services in the United States and throughout the world needs to be more equitable if we are to reach millions of unreached and needy peoples.

As you listen to hear God's vocation for your life, ask him where he needs you most to teach, to heal, to proclaim, to liberate, to serve the selfless intentions of his kingdom instead of the self-seeking obsessions of this age. If God were really in charge of making the decisions as to where we invested our lives, how do you think he would distribute his servant people in his needy world?

God is quite literally changing the world. Remarkably, he has chosen to act through our lives, our Mustard Seeds. Thomas Merton was right; God does have a kingdom vocation for every Christian. He invites you to join thousands of others in devoting your life to the celebration of turning this world right side up.

For Discussion and Action

1. What is the prevailing attitude toward Christian vocation in many churches? How does this dualistic attitude limit lay involvement in the agendas of the kingdom?
2. Why isn't every job as good as every other job to a Christian committed to the kingdom intentions of God?
3. What is one fairly common pathway that many younger Christians tend to follow in their quest for the will of God? What are some of the problems inherent in trying to find God's will for the private, particular desires of our lives?
4. What is an alternative way to begin the quest for God's will? What should our first question be?
5. What is God's all-encompassing vocation for all Christians, regardless of circumstances?
6. What are the seven steps outlined in this chapter for listening for God's ministry call on your life?
7. How will discovering our ministry calling enable us to more effectively discover God's will in employment, marriage, and location?
8. List: (1) Your understanding of God's intentions for the future and anything that particularly speaks to you out of the Scriptures regarding your calling; (2) The human needs that particularly grip your heart; (3) Your areas of brokenness and giftedness; (4) Your dreams of creative ways all of the above might converge into a new Christian vocation.
9. Share your list and dreams with a group of Christians who share your seriousness for the kingdom, and pray for the guidance of his Holy Spirit.
10. What would be the consequences if even 50 percent of the laypersons in your congregation spent at least one evening a week in ministry to the needs of others?

8.

Seeking First the Future of God through Creative Community

Tim's mouth dropped open in evident surprise as we led him into the dining room. "Happy Birthday in the Fast Lane" was inscribed on the cake right beneath a small model sports car racing down a chocolate road. Tim is the "token pastor" in our small community group from University Presbyterian Church. We have become something of a family to one another in celebrating the high points of one another's lives. When Roger moved into his new art studio, we joined in a time of prayer and dedication. Last week two of the wives joined Sheila for the Bible study in the department store where she works. Next week we are going to spend three days in retreat enjoying one another's children, worshipping God together, and gaining a clearer sense of direction for the seven of us who have committed our lives together to the service of Christ.

That's what brought us together originally—a shared sense of seriousness for the mission of Christ in our world. Our primary motivation was to support one another in our ministries. We do that by helping one another hear God's call, discern how he would use the gifts he has given us, and encourage one another in ministry. In fact, as much as possible we participate in one another's ministries.

For me personally, our group was also an agent of profound healing and love during a time in my life when the bottom completely fell away. After years of being an active but a very independent Christian I discovered I needed community, that I couldn't be the body of Christ alone.

As the members of our community have grown together, we have taken our masks off and discovered we still love each other. I even roped my brothers and sisters into reading this manuscript and helping me get out of the way of what I am trying to say. And they are not the least bit reluctant to straighten me out—in any area of my life.

In our weekly get-togethers, we pray for one another's ministries.

We worship, study the scriptures, plan for the refugee family we are working with, and share very openly where we are in our relationship with God and those around us. We strive to help disciple one another and make ourselves mutually accountable in those areas of lifestyle, attitudes, and service where we believe God is trying to change us. We share transportation, and are available to help one another with financial resources as well. And we thoroughly enjoy just being together—a small part of the body of Christ within a much larger congregation. Quite frankly, I don't know what I would do without the love, support and common purpose I have discovered in a community of shared life.

SPILLING COFFEE AND BALANCING BUDGETS

You see, Christian community is more than just spilling coffee on one another Sunday morning. It isn't simply going to church or participating in endless rounds of committee meetings. And it isn't individuals or "lone ranger" nuclear families showing up when it is convenient. Biblical community is much more than active participation in the institutional church.

Too many of us have allowed the institutional church to become a substitute for organic community. The identity of the church and the meaning of community for many have become hopelessly confused with buildings, budgets, programs, personalities, and—regrettably—even the self-seeking values of American culture. The American church reflects the influence of culture in giving preeminence to the individual over community. This has resulted in a common misperception that participation in community is both peripheral to the mission of the church and optional to the individual believer.

Traditional wisdom in the church dictates when a group of people with needs of some kind appear we set up an institutional program. In planning a futures workshop with a Presbyterian church in the Seattle area, I asked the leaders, "Are the singles, the senior citizens, the single-parent families included in your community?" They responded, "Oh they know they are welcome at our monthly potlucks, and we are setting up a program for singles." "That's not quite what I had in mind. Are they welcomed into your homes . . . in your life together?" It was obvious from their efforts to comfortably reply . . . that I had introduced a new idea.

Unfortunately I believe this is typical of many churches in many denominations. As a result, in a society of growing alienation, fragmentation, and depersonalization the institutional church too often is simply another part of that vast wasteland of loneliness. Small wonder that many of our young find greater love and acceptance in cults than they do in many churches!

But thank God there is a new wind blowing. His Spirit is stirring through the dry bones. "One of the signs of the Spirit's moving in very recent years has been a new concern to discover a biblical picture of the Church," Howard Snyder reports. "There is a growing awareness that many problems in contemporary Christianity trace directly back to the church as essentially static, organizational and institutional." [1]

Christians studying the Scriptures within the traditional church and outside it have begun discovering what it means to be the people of God. "New wine is being poured into old wineskins and they are bursting at the seams. The creation of living, breathing, loving communities of faith at the local church level is the foundation of all other answers." [2]

In this chapter we will explore a biblical definition of Christian community and the characteristics of the church transformed through renewal of community life. We will also examine a broad spectrum of different models for community and suggest some practical ways you can become a part of a community of loving service. It is important to recognize that there is no way we as individual Christians can successfully pursue a lifestyle of celebration and justice or discover God's ministry vocation for our lives on our own. We need brothers and sisters to help us hear, respond, and celebrate God's work in our lives and our world.

COMMUNITY RENEWED, THE CHURCH ALIVE

God's intention from the beginning was to create a people for himself—not an institution, but a community of people who would worship and serve him, a people who would be a foreshadowing of his new future and join him in changing his world.

For those first followers of Jesus, community wasn't optional; it was normative. It was essential to the very life and discipleship of the twelve that they be in community together with Jesus. And the early church met almost exclusively in small household groups that shared worship, life together, and financial resources, and that supported one another in ministry.

Ron Sider says, "the essence of Christian community is unconditional accountability to and unlimited liability for our brothers and sisters in the body of Christ. That means that our time, our money and our very selves are available to our brothers and sisters." He goes on to point out that "that kind of fellowship hardly ever happens in larger churches of one hundred persons or more. It requires small communities of believers like the early Christian house churches. The movement that conquered the Roman Empire was a small network of small house churches." [3]

The history of the church is the history of Christian community from the Franciscans and the Benedictines to the Anabaptist communities in Germany and the Wesleyan Lay Study Groups of England. Over the centuries, much of the renewal of the church has come through small communities, house churches, and movements in which persons are organically linked to one another in common purpose.

The importance of believers participating in community is not only taught in the Scriptures and demonstrated in our Christian past; it is affirmed by many traditions within the church today. "Interestingly, both the Lausanne Covenant and the documents of Vatican II emphasize the same basic concept of the Church: The Church is the community of God's people. . . . This signals a major shift in emphasis in Roman Catholic theology—a change which will likely work as yeast throughout the Catholic world. . . . In describing the Church as 'the community of God's people rather than an institution,' Lausanne endorsed a view of the Church which is both radically biblical and practically important." [4]

But what does it mean to be the "community of God's people?" Perhaps the most meaningful image we can use is this: to be the community of God's people is quite simply to be family. Graham Pulkingham declares, "In every age the church will take an institutional form, but its people—the people of God—must bend every effort toward being a family, in the simplest sense of that word." [5] Christian community then can be defined as what happens when a group of Christians commit their lives together as family, under the lordship of Christ, to seek first his kingdom in a world of growing need. When Jesus said, "Who is my mother or brother, but he who does the will of God?" (see Matt. 12:46–50), he wasn't minimizing the importance of family. He was drawing the family circle much broader, to include not only those who were biologically related, but also those who had become brothers and sisters through the initiative of God. Living in Christian community means being family to the alienated and lonely among us—to the forgotten seniors, the divorced singles, the troubled young. To do this, we don't need more institutional programs or professional staff. We need small groups, "families" where people are known and loved—where they can find healing, discover God's kingdom vocation for their lives, and be empowered to reach out in love to others.

Since participation in community was normative and not optional for the disciples and the early church, it seems reasonable to conclude that as Christ's followers we are still called into community today. It really isn't possible to be a disciple of Jesus alone. We need to be involved not only in the institutional church, but also in small communities where we are known and loved. We need people who have committed their lives to help us discover God's vocational call in our lives and to help us incarnate personally and corporately the right-side-up values of Jesus. We need people to nurture us in our discipleship, to hold us accountable in our growth, and to support us in our ministry for him.

It is my conviction that simply participating in the frenetic activity and programs of the institutional church *cannot* be a substitute for being committed members of a small organic fellowship group. I realize this may be considered an extreme position, but it seems to me that it is fully congruent with the New Testament understanding of what it means to be the community of God. But how can those of us caught up in institutionalism begin to rediscover this kind of community? Where do we begin?

CREATING CHRISTIAN COMMUNITY—OPTIONS AND OPPORTUNITIES

There are a range of different models for those who wish to become seriously involved in Christian community. The first model is to start a small community within the context of an existing institutional church. A number of churches already offer this option to their members. Typically they come together at least once a week.

The Church of the Savior in Washington, D.C., was one of the first churches to pioneer this model. All members of the church must participate in small household groups that have a definite mission focus. Each small group annually signs a covenant which commits them to the disciplines of "daily prayer, daily Bible study, weekly worship and proportionate giving, beginning with a tithe of total gross income. . . . The mission focus of these groups is the liberation of the poor in Washington, D.C. Out of their shared life and celebration they begin to reach out to those in need." [6]

Another model is the formation of small ecumenical groups outside of the institutional church. Participants in such groups continue to participate in their denominational churches while sharing in community with brothers and sisters across denominational lines. These communities don't hold Sunday morning worship or provide the Sacraments; they exist alongside the institutional churches. In groups with names like the Word of God, People of Praise, or The Servants of Light, believers have the opportunity to share in broadly ecumenical communities of faith. In these covenant-based communities, individuals from various denominational backgrounds become committed and accountable to one another in love.

Church-Community is a third option in which the small household group actually becomes a House Church. They conduct weekly Sunday worship, administer the sacraments, and have all the characteristics of a small neighborhood church, except they place much greater emphasis on sharing life and ministry together. Sojourners Fellowship in Washington, D.C., and Reba Place in Evanston, Illinois, are examples of this model. "Church-Communities are also covenant based. They find no problem in being explicit about the . . . requirements for membership. . . . The result is the body as a whole demonstrates many of the ideal characteristics of the kingdom." [7]

The Catholic and Episcopal orders constitute a fourth option for community. In these orders, followers are called into community around the vision of their founder or foundress. The vision essentially becomes a covenant for their common life together. They take vows relating to their common life, which usually include vows of celibacy.

It is possible in any of these models for the individuals not only to enter into a covenant relationship, but to actually live together. Urban and rural Christian communities in which Christians have decided to share all of their lives together are springing up all over the world. By actually becoming family to one another, people who live together in community seem to experience most profoundly what it means to be the people of God.

One of the major benefits of living in a community (as pointed out in chapter six), is that cooperative living releases more resources to be used for the work of the kingdom. For example, the three hundred people who attend Reba Place Church live in extended households and apartments in Evanston within walking distance of one another and their church. About half the people at Reba are freed up to work in the community and in service to the needs of people in Evanston.

Agape Fellowship in Los Angeles is comprised of some forty believers who share an apartment house and a common purse. As a result of the reduced expenses of their life together, they are able to carry on extensive ministries to Asian Americans in the Southern California area.

House of the Gentle Bunyip is a series of residential Christian communities on the outskirts of Melbourne, Australia. Ecumenical in their character and mission-oriented in their focus, they live together with the intention of freeing up as much time as possible to carry out local ministries such as: (1) "Truffle Hunters" outreach programs to street kids, (2) "Billabong" arts and crafts activities, (3) working for the renewal of the inner city, (4) "Monk for a Month" program to provide Christians from institutional churches an opportunity to try living in residential community for a short period without any long-term commitments.

A believer can choose to participate in any one of the four options for community, and either live independently or together with the others in the group. God will direct you into the most appropriate option for you. However, participation in Christian community is *not* optional for those who would follow Jesus. Participation in a living, loving community is a direct expression of the kingdom of God. Howard Snyder declares, "To the extent the church grows and expands throughout the world *and demonstrates true Christian community,* to that extent the kingdom of God has come on earth" (emphasis mine).[8]

As followers of Jesus we are called to seek the kingdom of righteousness, justice, peace, reconciliation, wholeness, and love first in our relationships with those with whom we share community. To the extent that the future intentions of God become evident in our lives together, to that extent we become the presence of the kingdom in society. We need to realize that we are nothing less than an " 'exodus community' pioneering the future of the world." [9]

FINDING A FAMILY

Having discussed the importance of community and reviewed the spectrum of options, we are still left with the question: Where should we begin? Of course, the easiest answer is to plug into an existing small group, in your church or region, whose vision for the kingdom is consistent with yours. If you can't find one in which you clearly sense God's call, then try to find a few other people in your church who seem to have a shared sense of vision and begin a small weekly fellowship group.

If you can't find someone in your congregation with whom you sense a common purpose and bonding, you might consider the ecumenical option. Look for those in other denominations with whom you can begin to participate in a weekly fellowship group that has a shared vision for the kingdom of God.

I would encourage you to go very slowly in moving toward starting a community church or setting up a residential Christian community. For the few that successfully become established, a number simply don't make it.

Personally, it is my conviction that both community churches and residential communities need to have some linkage of support and accountability to a traditional denominational structure. Such a linkage can provide the stability needed for a new community venture. However, in any case, a great deal of prayer, research, and firsthand experience in community life need to precede the inauguration of a new house church or residential community. I know so many Christians who have started an intentional community on the sole basis of good relational chemistry with a few Christian friends. Not until they move onto their acreage or into their shared housing do they begin to explore the purpose for which they have come together. As a result, they often seem to become ingrown, and to reflect the same self-referrent and unstable characteristics of the larger society. Many take a vote every three months and change direction.

FINDING A FOCUS

Frankly, I am much more impressed by the model of the Catholic orders in which people are called together around a central vision. The Franciscans aren't given an opportunity to vote every three months regarding the vision of St. Francis. If an individual can't go along with the direction of the order, he either changes or leaves, but the order remains constant. I think we need more communities like that— groups of Christians with a clear and constant vision of how they are to be a part of the kingdom initiative of God.

In conducting "dream-ins" on creating Christian community, I find people come up with an entirely different vision for community if they are trying to envision an authentic biblical model of shared life than if they merely picture themselves living inside the community. Typically, when they focus on themselves rather than on a shared vision, I hear things like, "The only way my fourteen-year-old will save money is if he can have a dirt bike," to which another dreamer responds, "If your kid gets to have a dirt bike I get to bring my color TV." What results is negotiating to the lowest common denominator, and the sudden sense that suburbia is simply being transplanted to a different location. Without a consistent vision, authentic Christian community is lost.

If we wait upon God, he can be trusted to give us a dream, a vision, a focus for our common life that is consistent with his kingdom intentions for the future. It is important to realize at the onset that, whatever pathway we choose, learning to live in community is going to be hard work, often filled with frustrations, because we are so unlike the one we follow. We also need to realize it will mean surrendering our acquisitive selves to a life of servanthood and our autonomous selves to the guidance of the community. We will learn to live in mutual submission to one another, and we will make ourselves accountable to one another as growing, serving disciples pursuing a common vision.

Too many Christians have entered into communities which tend to focus exclusively on their own needs for healing, fellowship, and love. It is true that life together in community should result in healing, and fellowship and love are crucial elements of sharing life together. But the purpose of getting our needs met and our pain healed is so we can enable others to find healing. E. Stanley Jones has said, "We need to get ourselves off our hands as quickly as possible so we can be of some good to others."

Every group needs to study God's Word and wait before him until they discern what role he expects them to play in the global advance of his kingdom. Some communities may be called to be peacemakers, like Christian communities in Northern Ireland. Others may find their place working righteousness like the brothers and sisters of Voice of Calvary who are evangelizing Jackson State College. Still others may be called to work for justice like the Sojourners Community who live with and work with the poor in Washington, D.C.

Perhaps a vision will be born when a community looks beyond their lives together to God's world. Jean Vanier shows us the urgent panorama: "There are too many people in the world who have no hope. There are too many cries which go unheard. There are too many people dying in loneliness. It is when the members of a community realize that they are not there simply for themselves or their own sanctification, but to welcome the gift of God, to hasten His kingdom and to quench the thirst of parched hearts, that they will truly live community. A community must be a light in a world of darkness, a spring of fresh water in the church for all men." [10]

We hear God's voice in community not only through God's Word and his world, but also through our very lives. In our common life together, we discover both our weaknesses and our gifts, and if we listen to God speaking through both gifts and weaknesses we will hear him call us as a community into life and service. Gordon Cosby of the Church of the Savior insists that if Christians learn to listen to God's call through the gifts of individuals in community, there will be "a revolution in the churches that will bring in a whole new age of the Spirit." [11]

CREATING A COVENANT

All four models of community mentioned earlier in the chapter express their common vision through a covenant statement that lends direction to the community's life together. A new community might find the following questions helpful in drafting a covenant statement:

1. What is our common sense of vision or purpose in relationship to the kingdom intentions of God?
2. What is our commitment to God in worship, celebration, corporate prayer, and study?

3. What is our commitment to one another in developing loving relationships of trust, affirmation, and mutual submission and servanthood?
4. What is our commitment to one another and the kingdom in sharing our dreams, calling out one another's gifts, unbinding one another's lives, encouraging one another's growth and celebrating life together?
5. What is our commitment to economic justice and the kingdom in the ways we steward our resources and the ways we model economic justice through sharing our time, talent, and resources with one another and with the poor?
6. What is our commitment to God and his kingdom in becoming a prophetic community, manifesting the right-side-up values of the new age, and discipling believers in the larger institutional church in those values?
7. What is our commitment to God and his kingdom in becoming accountable to one another in our personal lives in maintaining the discipline of daily meditation, prayer, and study and giving priority to the mission vocation to which God has called us?

Vanier reminds us that those of us who join hands in community "are simply a tiny sign, among thousands of others, that love is possible, that the world is not condemned to a struggle between oppressors and the oppressed, that class and racial warfare is not inevitable. We are a sign that there is hope, because we believe the Father loves us, sends us His Spirit to transform our hearts and leads us from egoism to love, so that we can live everyday life as brothers and sisters." [12]

RENEWING THE CHURCH THROUGH CREATING COMMUNITIES OF WORSHIP, CELEBRATION, INCARNATION, AND SERVANTHOOD

Christian community must begin where our new life in Christ begins—with us in need of re-creation, in need of having our hearts and lives changed. God will use the hard places of shared life to shape us into the kingdom servants he wants us to be. God will use community to profoundly enrich our lives, accelerate our growth, and thrust us into adventures for his kingdom we have never even dreamed of.

But Christian communities can do more than enrich the lives of individuals sharing their lives together. Rediscovering the meaning of community can renew and reform the institutional church as well. If the church is to take seriously the escalating challenges of the future and conscientiously work for the future of God, it must again become comprised of loving communities of shared life and purpose. And community must become a priority in every local church.

I believe the best way for this to happen is for every church to form small "family" groups within the larger context of God's kingdom vision for that body. Already the Spirit of God is flowing through small groups like these all over the country, bursting the dried wineskins of institutionalism. All around I see signs of community that are restoring the church to its biblical role, mission, and vitality. A number of churches are discovering the renewal of their life and mission in the renewal of community life. It is the wave of God's future.

What are the characteristics of the church of Jesus Christ when it is renewed through return to communities of shared life and mission? When the church is indeed the community of God's people, it fulfills its biblical role as a kingdom community of worship, celebration, incarnation and servanthood.

Worship—The Center of Common Life

Even as community is at the very center of what it means to be the church, worship is the very center of the life of community. The adoration and worship of the One who has called us into being is the heart of community. Personally, I believe the Lord's Supper is the very center of worship. "The Eucharist is celebration, the epitome of the communal feast, because in it we relive the mystery of Jesus' gift of His life for us. It is the time of Thanksgiving for the whole community. That is why the priest says after the consecration: 'Grant that we, who are nourished by His body and blood, may be filled with His Holy Spirit and become one body, one Spirit in Christ.' There," Vanier reflects, "we touch the heart and mystery of community." [13]

Every time we celebrate communion together we are not only reenacting the Lord's Supper, we are anticipating the wedding feast we will celebrate in the mountain city of God. Communion is not only the center of our worship, it is the beginning of our celebration of the new age. It is the enactment of our future together within the circle of all God's people.

How we worship, of course, varies according to our denominational tradition, but it is my conviction that believers of all denominations can learn from each other in approaches to worship.

For instance, those of us who are from sermon-centered backgrounds could profit from moving the pulpit over a bit and restoring communion and prayer to the center of our common life. We have so much to learn from the liturgical churches regarding the awesomeness of worshiping the Almighty. David Prior, an Anglican priest, counsels, "Reverence and awe are frequently experienced through silence, and evangelicals particularly need to learn to worship the Lord in the beauty of silence. . . . We need to be awed into silence by the presence of the Lord in our midst." [14]

We can learn other things from other denominations and traditions.

The Quakers have much to teach us using silence in corporate worship to hear the voice of God. They leave their worship format open enough for any member of the body to spontaneously share what God is saying to him or her. In a church I have visited in Seattle, on the other hand, it is a standard joke that if God doesn't get his request in Tuesday morning before the bulletin goes to press, he will not be allowed to participate in the service.

The charismatic and many black churches could let many of us in on the surprising secret that worship is the most exhilarating experience of the human spirit. They could help us let go of our frozen forms and begin worshiping God with our total beings. Not only are the services in these churches more open and spontaneous, the members seem to invest themselves much more fully in the intense and joyous worship of the Lord than many of us are accustomed to doing.

Bruce Larson tells the story of trying to enable a Presbyterian Church back East to free up in worship. Each member of the congregation was presented a helium-filled balloon on a string as they entered. He asked the congregation to let go of their balloons at any point in the service in which they were moved by God. During the opening invocation one or two balloons went up. During the singing a cluster of brightly colored balloons rose together. A couple went up during the choir's anthem and even one or two during the sermon. However, Bruce reports that at the end of the service over a third of those diehard Presbyterians were still tenaciously hanging on to their balloons. They simply wouldn't be moved.

Perhaps most of us hang on a little too tightly to our balloons. The joy has left so many of us; we seem totally unaware that in the resurrection of Jesus the celebration has already begun. A small Anglican church in York, England, was afflicted by this condition. Then came a new pastor whose life had been stirred up by the Spirit of God. His vitality soon infected the small band, and the worship services took on a new life. One day they decided to begin their worship service in the street out in front of their church.

Picture the scene. It is a quiet Sunday morning in the historic, reserved town of York. A small group begins to congregate in front of St. Michael-Le-Belfrey. Suddenly they begin singing and praising God at the top of their lungs; they clap their hands to their joyous songs. They spontaneously begin dancing in front of their church as spectators gather around. They too get caught up in the jubilant spirit of the celebration, and as the celebrants pour, dancing and singing, into their small chapel, spectators join them. This scene has been repeated dozens of times.

Not only is St. Michael's, which was a parish struggling for survival, now thriving and growing; they are sending teams all over Great Britain, working for the renewal of the church through the renewal of worship.

They are teaching congregations to be more joyous and spontaneous in their worship through using drama, pageantry, music, and dance.

The worshipers at St. Michael's have already begun the wedding festival of the Lamb and are having no trouble finding people to join in the jubilation. The renewal of our life together in community will only come as we devote our lives to the worship, praise, and adoration of our God. Let's join our brothers and sisters at St. Michael's in a spontaneous festival of worship in our home groups, our churches, and our residential communities. As we place worship in the center of our common life, we can be sure our Father will renew us, unite us, and use us to change his world.

Celebrating the Transcultural Body of Christ

Jesus' last prayer for us was a prayer for community. He prayed that we would be one even as he is one with his Father. As the first disciples entered into prayer together after the resurrection of Jesus, we are told that they were bonded together in that unity; community flows organically out of our intimate relationship and bonding to the Father.

When the Holy Spirit was poured upon the disciples at Pentecost, they were bonded together as the body of Jesus, and were empowered by God to turn the world right-side-up. When even two or three of them came together, they discovered Christ was present with them in a unique way. The Holy Spirit guided them corporately in discovering their collective mission and their individual vocations. And the Spirit worked powerfully through their lives, gifting them and confirming their words with acts of supernatural healing, deliverance, and love.

Those first communities of love didn't rely on their own initiative, but found themselves swept up in the initiative of God that was changing their world in the name of Jesus. And the God who acted dynamically through them is acting just as dynamically today through communities and churches who devote themselves to his initiative and seek the empowering of his Spirit.

It was no accident that each of the bystanders at Pentecost heard God speaking to them in their own language. That amazing event was a signal that a new society had come into being through the initiative of God, a society that transcended the cultural and national distinctions of the larger human order. There is, in this new community, no such thing as Jew and Greek, slave and freeman, male and female; all are one in Christ Jesus.

In our racist, sexist, elitist, nationalistic society, we are only beginning to understand what it means to be this new community—a transnational body of Jesus. Some Christians in Western Europe have testified that

the more they came to know their brothers and sisters in the Southern
Hemisphere and joined in solidarity with their struggle, the more they
found themselves at odds with the policies of their own governments.
They discovered that often what was good for nations in Western Europe
was destructive to the lives of their brothers and sisters in Christ in
the poorer nations, and they chose to put the body of Christ first.
Wouldn't it be marvelous if all Christians in the United States discovered
a greater bonding with Christians in the Third World than we presently
enjoy with our various political allies? You can be sure such a bonding
with brothers and sisters among the poor would dramatically alter our
political outlooks, too.

In any case, the transnational body of Christ is our family, and we
need to consciously link our lives, churches and communities together
as a witness of the coming transnational community of God. We are
called not to live out some so-called "homogenous principle" that keeps
us in our insulated ghettos of affluence. We are called to model in
our lives, relationships, and communities the reconciling love of God—
his new future for human society.

In 1978, Christians in South Africa held the largest Christian conference in the history of the nation. Thousands of black and white Christians came together in common witness to the reconciling love of God.
By sheer force of numbers, the government was forced to suspend its
apartheid policies and allow Christians to stay in one another's homes
across racial lines. That's what it means to be the reconciled family
of God in a divided world!

Celebrating Our Shared Life

If communities of faith are to renew the institutional church in order
to enable it to respond to the challenges of the future, we need to be
bonded not only in worship and transcultural unity but in shared life
as well. We need to take time to share our dreams and gifts with one
another. Our communities need to help us discover God's vocation
for our lives and to learn how to use our natural and spiritual gifts
to enrich his community and advance his kingdom. We need to take
time to play and work and share with those in our community as a
sign of our common life. We simply need to take time to be family
to one another.

"Moments of wonder" can come from the time we take to be family
together, Vanier states:

These moments of wonder can come on all sorts of occasions—perhaps a
deep warm silence after a brother or sister has shared his or her call, weakness,
or need for prayer; perhaps during a celebration when we are singing, playing

and laughing together. So every community gathering must be carefully prepared, whether it is a liturgy, a meal, a weekend, a sharing or a Christmas
or Easter celebration, each of these can be occasions for wonder. When
something unexpected happens during a celebration—as it often does—we
become conscious of a moment of grace for the community, a passage of
God, a deeper silence; our hearts are touched.[15]

These experiences become the stuff of which the good life of God
is composed. As these experiences help us discover how to live life
more fully together with our Father and our family, we will find it
easier to let go of the cultural notion of the good life that has so capti-
vated our existence. We will find, as we relinquish self-seeking desires,
to be bonded together in family that we will gain much more than
we lose.

Incarnating the New Society of God

Not only are we called to be the family of God celebrating our life
together; we are also called to incarnate his new society in the world
around us, to prophetically challenge the existing order. That means
we are to model together the right-side-up values of Jesus, even when
that means going against the values of the dominant culture. John
Stott couldn't make our responsibility clearer: "He meant His Sermon
on the Mount to be obeyed. Indeed, if the church realistically accepted
His standards and values as here set forth, and lived by them, it would
be the alternative society He always intended it to be, and would offer
to the world an authentic Christian counter-culture." [16]

Jim Wallis makes an amazing assertion. "Proclamation of the gospel,
charismatic gifts, social action, and prophetic witness alone do not finally
offer a real threat to the world as it is, especially when set apart from
a community which incarnates a whole new order. It is the ongoing
life of a community of faith that issues a basic challenge to the world
as it is, and offers a visible and concrete alternative. The church must
be called to be the church, to rebuild the kind of community that
gives substance to the claims of faith." [17] We must become what Sider
calls communities of 'loving defiance.' " [18]

Quite simply, our small communities and the institutional church
are called to prophetically challenge the self-seeking, individualistic,
materialistic values of our secular society. There is absolutely no way
we can authentically speak out against these values when they are so
much a part of lives, our churches, and our Christian organizations.

In fact, one of the primary reasons we need to become a part of
small communities of faith is to enable one another to be liberated
from the values of secular culture. Only in community can those who

love us help us extricate ourselves from the layers of cultural condition-
ing that have paganized our values, and the Spirit of God create within
us the mind and values of Jesus. Only in community can we redefine
our notion of the good life and have the courage to act out our new
convictions. Only in community can we demonstrate in our lives something of the new age of righteousness, justice, reconciliation, peace,
wholeness and love.

What is the process through which the community of God enables
believers individually and collectively to incarnate the values of the
kingdom? The answer quite simply is *discipleship.* "And Jesus came
and said to them, 'All authority in heaven and on earth has been given
to me. Go therefore and make disciples of all nations, baptizing them
in the name of the Father and of the Son and of the Holy Spirit,
teaching them to observe all that I have commanded you; and lo, I
am with you always, to the close of the age' " (Matt. 28:18–20, RSV).

Contrary to what some churches emphasize, discipleship isn't re-
stricted to a spiritual compartment of life. Our commission is to help
our brothers and sisters to observe "all" the teachings of Jesus. That
means we are obligated to teach each other how to turn the other
cheek, go the second mile, love our enemies, visit prisoners, feed the
hungry, clothe the naked, heal the sick, work for peace and justice,
and be servants to all peoples. It means we are obligated to teach one
another how to put his kingdom first by radically reprioritizing our
use of time and resources.

Incarnating the Servant Values of Christ in Organizations that Bear His Name

Recently a Christian educational organization asked me to analyze
the values of their corporation in relation to biblical values. In interview-
ing the staff, I soon became aware that this Christian organization
placed a very high value on bigness, growth, success, and prestige.
During the interviews, two top executives, Jack and Randolph, confessed
that the values of the corporation really reflected their own personal
needs and values. They explained they were driven by personal ambition
and a desire for increasing control and power, although they recognized
these values were in contradiction with the servant values of Jesus.

Unfortunately, I suspect that these Christian executives weren't unusual. It seems fairly evident that many of our Christian churches and
organizations have rather unconsciously adopted the organizational
management and leadership styles of the secular corporate model as
well as the values implicit in those models.

For example, Christian organizations, like their secular counterparts, seem to have an insatiable appetite for growth, bigness, and status. Now, I am not arguing against growth in itself; I see absolutely no merit in organizational stagnation in the body of Christ. But as far as I can tell in my reading of the New Testament, growth was never a conscious goal of the church; it was a consequence. The goals of the early church seemed to have to do with incarnating the kingdom in their lives together, with demonstrating in their service and proclaiming in their words the good news of the gospel.

Often, of course, the truth drew people and growth did occur. But even in the ministry of Jesus, growth was not always the consequence of hearing the truth. We are told that many turned back when they discovered how much it cost to follow him. In other words, when we work for the kingdom, sometimes our churches and organizations will grow, but preaching the truth will cause people to turn away.

Our goal then must be to strive as authentically as possible to incarnate the life and values of Jesus in our life together. The countercultural community of God is to be a leaven that is changing the world without sharing in its lust for power, prestige, and size.

Perhaps nowhere is our preoccupation with power and preeminence in our organizations more evident than in the leadership models we follow. What was Jesus' model of leadership and what did he have to say about the hierarchical leadership model?

Remember Jesus' response when two of his disciples (James and John) expressed their honest desire to be preeminent: "You know that the rulers of the Gentiles lord it over them, and their high officials exercise authority over them. Not so with you. Instead, whoever wants to become great among you must be your servant, and whoever wants to be first must be your slave—just as the Son of Man did not come to be served, but to serve, and give his life as a ransom for many" Matt. 20:25–28, NIV).

Howard Snyder comments,

> Superficially it appears that the problem here is James' and John's desire for a position not legitimately theirs. But Jesus defines the situation more fundamentally: The world's concept of power must not operate within the church. 'Not so with you.' Power in the church is not a question of position or hierarchy or authority. It is a question of function and service. The greatness of a Christian is not according to office, status, degrees or reputation, but according to how he or she functions as a servant.[19]

I know of a few Christian organizations that are struggling to follow this servanthood model of leadership. You don't often find Christian leaders emptying the wastepaper baskets, giving up their prestige, or offering to take a lower salary than those who work for them. You certainly don't find many following the model of Jesus with the twelve and giving away their power so their associates have both the power and ability to do everything the boss can do. And few of us are willing to become a "slave" in all that term implies.

A few groups like Sojourners Fellowship are pioneering this new direction. Jim Wallis, who is the editor of the *Sojourner* magazine the community publishes, is actually taking home a smaller paycheck than the shipping clerk, because the shipping clerk has more mouths to feed. The decision to develop a salary schedule based on need rather than position was based, I am sure, on the premise that "Leadership in servanthood does not have fringe benefits or privileges that others can't enjoy." [20]

The Sojourners Fellowship has also rejected as unbiblical a male-dominated hierarchical leadership model for their community. Much of the present emphasis among evangelicals on male-dominated structures is premised, I believe, on a misunderstanding of the doctrine of headship.

Many Christians have been taught that Paul's teaching on headship is a biblical basis for a male-dominated, authoritarian chain-of-command system. However, a growing number of biblical scholars insist that the word "headship" in the Greek doesn't have anything to do with authority over anyone else—man, woman, or child. It means "life source." Christ is the head of the church because he is its Savior; he "loved the church and gave himself up for her" (Eph. 5:25, RSV). As head he also nurtures her growth (Eph. 4:15–16). This, then, must be the meaning of male headship: self-giving, nurturing love rather than autocratic rule. [21]

Jesus himself never ordered people around or pulled rank. Instead, he invited. He taught. He loved. He nurtured. He served. He trusted the Spirit of God to guide people's behavior. In the New Testament we don't see Jesus ordering his disciples around like a top sergeant. We see him washing their feet.

When we come to understand headship as "life source" instead of authoritarian control, the rug is jerked out from under not only male domination of women, but the whole chain-of-command fiction. I suspect that both the misunderstanding of this doctrine and its extravagant overemphasis has more to do with a male cultural obsession with power and the need to control others than with any other factor.

It strikes me as tragically ironic that a major share of the emphasis on return to authoritarian, hierarchical human control systems is being emphasized by a splinter of the charismatic movement that supposedly believes in control by the Spirit. How can we believe in a priesthood of believers in which God speaks to every individual, and at the same time believe in a hierarchical system in which God speaks through the men at the top to everyone else?

A Servant Community for Others

In the first community, Jesus and the Twelve modeled the values of the new future of God in every dimension of life. All their relationships, including their economic ones, were transformed by the inbreaking of God's future into their midst. They shared a common purse not only among themselves, but with their followers and the poor.

The early church continued to follow the model of economic sharing Jesus had inaugurated with his community. In fact, it was a widespread practice among the early church.[22] "Now the company of those who believed were of one heart and soul, and no one said that any of the things which he possessed was his own, but they had everything in common" (Acts 4:32, RSV).

The reason believers were able to share in this extraordinary way was that their values had been profoundly changed by Christ; they no longer lived for themselves. Their lives were devoted to the service of God, his kingdom, and his world. Through their sharing, they not only modeled the new age of economic justice; they also freed up resources for the work of justice in their own day.

As the church in the late twentieth century is renewed through a rediscovery of community, it has the opportunity to become what it was meant to be: the servant church to the world. From prison we hear Dietrich Bonhoeffer echo the cry for a servant church: "The church is only the church when it exists for others." [23] Being the church for others means, quite simply, that we are to be a church like the one we read about in Acts—our lives, energy, and resources poured outwardly into the needy world that surrounds us.

Given the ways we use our lives, energy, and resources, are we the church for others or the church for ourselves? You will have to answer for your church. But one thing seems eminently clear to me: the church in the United States is amazingly affluent. It is reliably estimated that the total institutional wealth of all churches and religious organizations in the United States is $134.3 billion. $21 billion flows through American Christian organizations annually. "If there is anything about the Christian Church that is clear to religious and non-religious alike," asserts Adam Finnerty, "it is that some nineteen hundred . . . years after the birth of its founder it is a phenomenally wealthy institution. Trying to make it appear otherwise is a little like trying to hide an elephant in a phone booth." He goes on to point out that by becoming a propertied institution, it is inevitably exposed to the danger of becoming conformed to the world and allied to the world's center of power.[24] Tony Campolo has described the church as a gigantic oil refinery with no loading dock because it uses all the oil it produces to keep its own machinery running.

Paul Brandt and Philip Yancey vividly describe what happens in a human body when one cell mutinies and begins drawing life away from the rest of the body, creating a grotesquely healthy tumor. The tumor uses up the resources necessary for the health of the rest of the body in its singleminded preoccupation with its own growth. Are we, the church in the United States, in danger of becoming not only a church for ourselves but also a cancerous tumor in the body of Jesus Christ International? [25] How can we be the church for others when we are using most of our individual and corporate resources on our own growth?

In repentance, let's rediscover what it means to be the servant church for others. Let's look at alternative ways we might use the resources God has entrusted to us to more fully serve others. If we were to return to a network of small house churches on the model of the early church, we would soon discover we don't need most of the buildings we have been erecting for ourselves at incredible expense. At the very least, our churches have the opportunity to become much more imaginative in constructing and utilizing church properties so as to channel as few of our resources as possible away from projects of mission and service to those in need.

East Hill Church in Gresham, Oregon, grew to over forty-five hundred members by 1979. They wanted to construct a building in which the entire congregation could worship together without drawing their members' giving away from the support of their extensive programs of ministry. Their solution? They established a separate corporation to build a self-supporting convention center, which the church uses free.

In some cities, brothers and sisters from different denominations are discovering they can share a common facility. (Some of the most underutilized structures in the United States are church buildings.) I would even go so far as to suggest a moratorium on construction of new facilities until (1) space in existing church structures, community buildings, and homes is fully utilized, (2) assessment of alternate methods of financing new structures (like the East Hill project) is made, and (3) the stewardship of our capital improvement resources in relation to the needs of the Body of Christ International is evaluated.

There are churches that are already discovering the excitement of being the church for others. A pastor of a small Lutheran Church in Washington called the Lutheran Relief Service in New York to inform them that their church would be sending in a check for $100,000. "We decided to borrow the money," he told the astonished chief administrator. "We figure we would be willing to do it for a church addition, so why not for the world's starving people?" [26]

Being the church for others can mean drastically simplifying our institutional lifestyles to free a much greater percentage of our budgets for direct service to those in need. In my work with a broad range of Christian organizations and churches, I have come across very few that couldn't cut fat in the areas of conferences, travel, restaurant expenses, lodging, office furnishings, facilities, and even payroll. We spend outrageous amounts of time in committee meetings and endless conferences. And even though Christian organizations have historically paid lower salaries, they haven't looked very seriously at alternative salary schedules based on need (like Sojourners uses) or extensive utilization of qualified volunteers who essentially pay themselves to minister.

So much of the money we give to projects in evangelism to the unreached and self-help to the poor is consumed in bureaucratic overhead that I am deeply concerned about what may happen if the United States hits a serious economic crunch. If giving to the denominational and other Christian organizations who help the world's poor lessens in times of depression, these organizations may have to use most of the reduced funds that come in just to meet payroll and overhead.

One way to lessen this danger is for all Christian organizations to totally separate their overhead costs from money raised for mission, so that every dollar contributed to mission causes is directly invested in those causes. In other words, overhead costs, including all home-based salaries, should be raised separately from direct mission costs. These overhead costs could be raised from nontraditional sources, such as starting small business ventures and contributing the profits to pay the overhead of Christian organizations. A letter to Christian organizations you support could help encourage them to take this action.

Another way to reduce the possibility of this scenario becoming a reality is to put a moratorium on hiring in our Christian organizations and to spend some front-end resources finding qualified volunteers to fill staff vacancies and new positions. I realize there are problems in working with volunteers. But I am convinced that there are satisfactory compensation systems for rewarding those who volunteer their time and workable contractual systems to insure responsible performance.

It is past time for local churches to change their emphasis from hiring professional staff to challenging and equipping lay people to be the church. One of the major priorities of both the church and small community structures in the eighties and nineties must be the motivating and equipping of the laity to use a much greater part of their lives in service to others.

I would encourage every local church to inventory the collective talent, time, and resources of their congregation, assessing what percentage of the total talent, time and resources of the members and church are actually invested in direct ministry to others. (I realize this might get a bit sensitive, but with care a fairly accurate approximation can be reached.) Then I would suggest the church prayerfully ask God how he would have them redistribute those resources to put his kingdom intentions for the poor, unreached and suffering people first. Ask him to show the congregation a new vision of the role he wants them to play in the adventure of advancing his kingdom. I am confident many congregations will be able to at least match the time and resources they spend on themselves in their service to others.

Since the church exists for others, it is essential that those of us who come together into small community groups ask ourselves how we can use our lives and resources to make the greatest possible kingdom difference in the world. The leadership for dramatically reprioritizing the resources of the church must begin at the grass roots level, with those of us who together commit our lives to seeking his kingdom first. Let's invite the Holy Spirit to flood our imaginations and help us create innovative new ways to more effectively use our lives, our resources, and the underutilized resources of our churches for the service of others.

There are thousands of Christian communities all over the world that are striving to follow the model of sharing and service set by Jesus' community and the early church—to be the church for others. Let me tell you about two of them. Perhaps they will give you some ideas for your own community.

Mission, Ministry and Making a Difference in Missoula

During the social turbulence of the early seventies, a small Covenant Church in Missoula, Montana, made a conscious decision to break out of their ingrown patterns of church life and become a church for the world. In those early days they had an extensive ministry among hippies and the "Jesus People."

In recent years, the church has been broken into twelve house churches, only one of which is residential. In these house churches, brothers and sisters have entered into committed relationships, sharing life and resources with one another. These communities provide pastoral care and discipleship training, and they support one another in their ministries in the community. Two have a common purse, and the others openly share with one another. As a result of their coming together in community and their focus on service, their members are able to share generously of their time and resources in ministry to others in their town. Dan Simmons, the pastor, says, "They have made a conscious decision to become more interdependent and less dependent on the large economic structures of the society."

The Community Covenant Church in Missoula is thoroughly enjoying one another and their opportunities for outreach. Over the last few years, they have been able to free up resources to initiate a drug treatment program, a preschool, a natural food store, a group home for the handicapped, a Christian bookstore, a Christian Street Theater, work on peace and justice issues, and the renewal of other institutional churches. This small church is having a ministry impact on Missoula and surrounding communities that is far greater than one might expect from a church several times their size.[27]

Pioneering and the Potency of Shared Life in Patchwork

The living room is congested with forty adults and kids as the singing begins. It is the Sunday evening celebration of the Patchwork Community in Evanston, Indiana. This community began with three young professional couples and their families.

The one thing these couples all had in common was a sense that their jobs as university professor, minister, kindergarten teacher, and seminary administrator weren't making the kind of difference in the world they really longed for. They wanted to start a community in which they could much more consciously and creatively steward their lives together to have a greater impact on the needs of the poor. They wanted to find ways to live more simply, scaling down their pace and lifestyle to use less of the earth's resources and have more to share with others.

John Doyce, a United Methodist minister in Evanston, and his wife called their friends one day and informed them that they had just purchased a house in the inner city area. The Doyces invited the other two couples to join them in their adventure. After hours of talking and praying, the other two couples decided to go for it. They quit their jobs, pulled up their roots, and moved to Evanston.

From the onset, the three couples agreed (1) to keep their community structure as clean as possible so resources that could be invested in ministry weren't diverted into community maintenance, and (2) to be a joyful community and thoroughly enjoy the venture they were embarking on together.

The two new couples bought homes in the transitional neighborhood near their friends. They took part-time jobs very similar to the full-time jobs they left, leaving a major chunk of their time free for urban ministry. Then they began getting acquainted with their neighbors without any agenda—trying to learn of their concerns. They found that it was an impoverished neighborhood in which there were serious nutritional needs among the elderly and young children. Many families lived in a chronic state of crisis, and there was a high incidence of drug and alcohol abuse and battered women and children.

The house church of these three young couples became not only a place of worship but a strategy center to address the needs of the entire community. The couples drew up a covenant statement for the Patchwork Community that spelled out their common commitment to justice, worship, discipleship and resource sharing. There are three levels of involvement in their community: (1) covenant members who essentially join the founding families in signing the same covenant and devote their life to a specific ministry in the community; (2) partners outside the community who, due to other responsibilities, are unable to sign the covenant but make a pledge to support the ministries of the community; and (3) fellowshiping participants who participate in the worshiping body but make no other commitments. Seventy persons share in one or the other of these levels of participation in Patchwork.

"We have found an amazing potency in our life together," Elaine and Phil Amerson share. "Not many months after we were here, we recognized that our staff was larger than most church or human service agency staffs in the city. We were able to share resources on a project and bring diverse expertise to bear. When we recently posed the question, 'Do you feel you have accomplished more during the last six months working together than you have individually?' there was uniform and joyful acknowledgement of the power of a shared mission.

"In our months here we have seen the establishment of a personal growth center for individual and group counseling; we have worked for the establishment and funding of a nutrition program, canning centers, and a neighborhood gardening project; we have been involved in a number of advocacy efforts for improving housing, legal services and recreational programs; frequently we are asked to preach, teach and hold workshops in churches. . . . We have a vision of a healthy church and powerful people so committed to personal renewal and human reconciliation that abundance is used in behalf of all brothers and sisters who languish in the brokenness of urban life far away from the influence or interest of many churches." [28]

We have the opportunity to join the celebration and the adventure that our brothers and sisters in Missoula, Evanston, and a thousand other communities of faith are enjoying. God has a group of people with which virtually every one of us can begin participating much more completely in the inbreaking of his future. Our common life together will be centered in worship of our God. It will be a living and united celebration of his future, an incarnation of the values of the new age, and a servant community that exists for others and for the kingdom. As we come together in community, the Spirit of God will renew our institutional churches through our renewed life together, until they again become churches for others as he intended them to be.

For Discussion and Action

1. What do many Christians tend to substitute for participation in organic communities of shared life? What is the result?
2. What are the characteristics of community as we see it modeled in Christ's relationship to the Twelve and in the early church?
3. Just what does it mean to be "the community of God's people"? What are the four primary models discussed in this chapter?
4. Why is it important that a group of Christians in community share a common vision or focus? What often happens when a group starts a Christian community without a clear common vision?
5. What role should worship and celebration play in the lives of those who share community?
6. In what ways do the values of the prevailing culture often influence the organizational and leadership models in the church?
7. What are some of the biblical values we are called to incarnate in our countercultural communities, churches, and organizations? What is servant-hood leadership?
8. Attempt to inventory the total monthly amount of time and resources invested in your church, then make the most accurate estimate you can of what percentage of those resources is actually used to directly serve those in need outside the church. Then outline an imaginative way more of that time and those resources could be freed up to directly invest out-wardly in mission.
9. Do you think participating in the kind of community discussed in this chapter would enable you to follow Christ more closely and influence your church to become a church for others? List some specific ways it could help.
10. If you are not in a small group and feel you should be, prayerfully begin looking into locating one or finding one or two other persons who share your kingdom vision to begin one. Set a specific date to begin your search, and ask a Christian friend to hold you accountable for this commitment.

9.

Seeking First the Future of God through Creative Mission to the One-Third World

"Give me five" rang out a tiny voice from beneath mounds of sheets. It was virtually the only English Navie knew. His black eyes danced as he slapped my sixteen-year-old's hand. Navie had lived with his parents, Sem and Souen, at Children's Orthopedic Hospital in Seattle since they had arrived from Cambodia. The United States government had processed their papers with remarkable speed because Navie, who is ten, is suffering from leukemia.

Tim and Kerry, who are members of our small community from University Presbyterian, asked if our group could help sponsor this family (along with a Lutheran Church), since the hospital had offered free treatment for Navie's leukemia. Our response was affirmative, and we helped finish a small apartment in Tim and Kerry's basement for the family.

Navie's leukemia is in remission but he has developed some secondary infections that are threatening his life and putting tremendous strain on his parents. A number of Christians have joined us in a prayer vigil for his healing.

Recently I discovered my son, Clint, had been setting aside his allowance to buy a fishing pole for Navie. And when we took Navie's dad, Sem, fishing, Clint gave him one of his poles. When I asked him why he decided to do that, he responded with a smile, "Didn't someone say if you had two fishing poles you should give one to someone who didn't have any?" I was proud of my son, and only wished we had started years sooner in taking time for others.

THE MISSION OF THE MUSTARD SEED

In so many ways so many of us are already involved in the quiet conspiracy that is turning the world around. Because we control such a large share of the planet's resources and have so much leisure time, we that live in the One-Third World (the nations of the industrialized Northern Hemisphere) have a special opportunity and obligation to participate in God's loving initiative, both in our own nations and in the Two-Thirds World (the less industrialized nations of the Southern Hemisphere).

This chapter will focus on the mission of the church in the One-Third World to those who live with us in the industrialized North—particularly those who live in North America. Then, in the final chapter of this book, we will look at the mission of the church in the Two-Thirds World.

Mission is defined in these two chapters as much more than sending missionaries overseas or doing "home mission" work in the United States. Mission is defined as all that we, the people of God, do to incarnate in our lives, demonstrate in our service, and proclaim in our words the good news that the future of God has arrived. The church is called to be a servant people, a people for others, a Mustard Seed quietly changing the world around us. We are called to work for righteousness, wholeness, love, justice, reconciliation and peace—that's our wholistic mission as the people of God in a world of growing need. We are to labor with God to actually change his world in anticipation of that day when Christ returns and his future comes in its fullness.

In this chapter, we will begin by examining some of the reasons we, the church in the One-Third World, seem to have difficulty being the missioning people God has called us to be. We will examine some ways we can overcome these difficulties. Then we will look at some exciting examples of Christians in the One-Third World who are making a real difference as they seek his kingdom first.

CHRONIC RANDOMNESS, PARALYZING APATHY, AND INSTITUTIONAL EGOCENTRISM

How are we in the churches of the industrialized North responding to our remarkable opportunity to be a missioning people to those around us? Tragically, many seem to be totally ignoring it. Too many Christians in the One-Third World see the church as an institutional agency devoted to simply maintaining society instead of as Christ's living presence decisively changing it.

The only way the church can hope to make a difference in the eighties and nineties is to move mission from the periphery to the very center of our life together. But where do we begin this basic shift of emphasis? We can begin by making mission the integrating center of our life together.

As I have conducted futures workshops in both mainline and evangelical churches during the past six years, I have been astonished at the "chronic randomness" of virtually every church I have worked with. It is the unusual church or Christian organization that has a clear sense of calling—a vision of the specific role God wants them to play in manifesting his kingdom in their community and their world—and that integrates all their activities around that vision. I believe the church is in danger of perishing from a lack of vision. Perhaps even more tragic is the fact that those the church is called to serve are certain to perish if the church doesn't rediscover its vision.

In the vacuum created by the absence of biblical vision the forces of culture are significantly at work shaping the direction, focus and priorities of the church. In a book entitled *A Severe Mercy,* Sheldon Vanauken relates the moving story of his marriage. He describes how they totally abandoned personal selfishness to develop a truly mutual relationship. They described this loving mutuality as "the shining barrier" and devoted their lives to protecting it from all external forces. But the irony was that they didn't really give up selfishness; they simply exchanged individual selfishness for mutual selfishness.[1]

In an age when the church seems to totally lack any sense of compelling vision, I wonder to what extent we have simply substituted institutional selfishness for personal selfishness. To what extent has our purpose been reduced to simply maintaining and protecting our institution from external forces—like so many secular organizations?

The cultural captivity of the church by the values of Western culture has, I am afraid, nurtured its growing apathy towards those in need outside its doors. A bit of graffiti at the University of Washington could with complete appropriateness be painted above the doorways of many of our churches and Christian organizations. In six-foot letters the graffiti reads: "APATHY NOW." And in three-inch letters underneath, someone has written, "who cares?" Who indeed does care . . . about the millions who have never heard the gospel, about the escalating hunger, deprivation, and injustice experienced by the world's poor? Given the total amount we spend in mission to the poor and forgotten in both the Northern and Southern Hemisphere, not very many really seem to care very much.

What we need is a renewed vision of God's expectations for his people in a world of exploding need. We don't have to be satisfied with chronic randomness, institutional selfishness, or paralyzing apathy. We can discover God's intentions for his church today and tomorrow. Our small groups, local churches, denominations, and Christian organizations can recover a compelling vision of how God longs to use his people to change his world.

SEEING VISIONS AND DREAMING DREAMS

How can we recover a sense of collective purpose and common mission? We begin by asking, as we did in chapter five, "What are God's intentions for the human future?" As we search the Scriptures, we begin to grasp the reality that God intends to bring into being a new age of righteousness, justice, peace, reconciliation, wholeness, and love. We begin to glimpse something of the vision God has for the church today.

In other words, we can directly derive our sense of biblical mission today from the intentions of God for tomorrow. He intends nothing less than the total redemption of his people and his world. And if that's what he is up to, then we need to again become a people of courageous visions and transcendent dreams. "The work of the Spirit is the bringing to be of the vision of God. At Pentecost the empowerment of Shalom takes place as the capacitating of persons to 'see visions and dream dreams.' It is the fulfillment of the Old Testament hope that there be a people who will see and serve the future of God." [2]

We have the opportunity "to see and serve the future of God," to dream new dreams of what God would do through us to change his world. Listen for the pieces of the dream that he is giving each member of our groups. Listen for his voice calling through the lives of the desperately needy in our neighborhoods, our nation, and our world. Hear him call us through our collective gifts, brokenness and our own religious heritage.

A widespread and unfortunate tendency among Christians is to content ourselves with little dreams and limited expectations. David Bosch, a South African theologian, points out that because we "know" that not all will accept the gospel, that not all evil, injustice, and exploitation will be corrected, we tell ourselves to be content with partial gains and frequent compromises; and we dare not aim at the stars.

But "As soon as we stop expecting the 'wholesale expectations' the Bible tells us to hope for—that soon do we confess our doubt that Christ is really King—that soon do we begin to assign transformation to the far future, the eschatological wedding feast to the time of the second coming.' But then we can also no longer pray the Lord's Prayer—'Thy kingdom come, thy will be done on *earth* as it is in heaven.' To offer that prayer implies believing Christians make a difference to this world, that things are not to remain the way they are. It implies having a vision of a new society and working for it as though it is attainable. It means in other words, getting involved in God's mission in the world, and calling people to faith in Christ," in order to "share in the mission of transforming the world." [3]

Only God knows the extent to which he can manifest his new age of righteousness, justice, peace, reconciliation, wholeness and love through his people in this troubled age. All he asks us to do is surrender our little contributions—our Mustard Seeds—to the power of his liberating future, and watch what he will do.

Wes Michaelson has caught the dream: "We have the opportunity— the church in the '80's—of being a people of hope. . . . We can provide a model . . . of conscience and of serving and living, which could point all society to a hopeful future. For who better than those called by the God of justice and compassion can demonstrate the job of a whole new way of living, living according to the vision of the kingdom, and living according to the demands and requirements of justice for all people, and increasingly living simply—so that others may simply live." [4]

Jesus calls us out of our institutional randomness, apathy, and egoism to join him in changing the world. He is both our example and the vision of God personified. "Jesus came not only to proclaim the coming of the kingdom, He came also to give Himself for its realization. He came to serve, to heal, to reconcile, to bind up wounds. . . . He is the one who comes alongside of us in our need and in our sorrow. He extends Himself for our sake. He truly dies that we might live and He ministers to us that we might be healed. . . . So it is that the Church announces the coming of the kingdom not only in word, through preaching and proclamation, but more particularly in work, in her ministry of reconciliation, of binding up wounds, of suffering service, of healing. . . . The Lord was the 'man for others', so must the church be 'the community for others.' " [5]

It is time we set aside the fruitless discussion as to whether proclaiming, incarnating or demonstrating the Good News of the Kingdom is most important. In the life and ministry of Jesus no distinction was made between loving words, loving example and loving acts. Unless we first incarnate the good news in communities of loving service we have nothing to say. Unless we act out the good news in works of righteousness, justice, and love our words are empty. Let us acknowledge the breadth of biblical mission and then focus our efforts in those areas of mission to which God particularly calls us.

What a remarkable opportunity! God invites us to join him in a counterinsurgency to forever destroy the works of darkness. We have the opportunity to be both the presence and the agents of his new age, allowing the Lord of history to work through us to bring his new future into being, in anticipation of that day when Jesus returns and his kingdom comes in its fullness.

BEATING THE BLAHS AND CATCHING THE CONTAGION

In spite of this amazing opportunity I run into very few Christians who seem to be very excited about the service of the kingdom. Among those involved in ministry I find a number of folks with terminal blahs, a surprising number who are just plain burned out. Virtually no expression of enthusiasm and precious little celebration accompanies their efforts at ministry. "Faithfulness" is a word I hear tossed around a lot by those in ministry; I think it is a code word which, translated, means, "I will just hang in there and be faithful till Jesus comes but I certainly don't expect anything to happen." Sound familiar?

I have to reach way back into my past to find a good example of someone who was really excited about being involved in the ministry of Christ. Doug was a sophomore at Willamette University when he committed himself to the mission of Jesus in the world. And he prayed a rather presumptuous prayer for a young Christian. He said, "Father, Salem is my Jerusalem, Oregon is my Judea. I commit my life to reach this city and state for Christ and to serve you to the ends of the earth."

When I met Doug he had already been influential in the life of the Dean of Students at Willamette in recommitting his life to Christ, a Mark Hatfield by name (now Senator Mark Hatfield). And Doug had established informal networks of Christians throughout the city of Salem and the State of Oregon. These networks infiltrated every level of life back in the early sixties, enabling participants to share the good news with businessmen, college students, nurses, high schoolers—people in every walk of life. Hundreds of people were being evangelized as the result of the recommitting and vision of one person—Doug Coe.

My strongest memory of that remarkable movement was of people quitting jobs and taking part-time work in order to be involved full time in sharing the good news in their communities. There was no question in their minds; they knew they could make a difference. No blahs, no burnouts, no moping around, or gritting their teeth and being "faithful" for Jesus—they were going to reach the state of Washington and change the world! And they shared Doug's unbridled enthusiasm for the task. Naive? Perhaps. But those who witnessed this movement remember not only the intense enthusiasm but the permanent change in the lives of thousands of people.

I had lunch with Doug a few weeks ago in Washington, D.C. His enthusiasm has not diminished one bit. God is working through his position as the head of an international Christian leadership organization to pull together a network of individuals who are committed to following

Christ in the nation's capital and in strategic leadership centers through-out the world. Doug has been influential in persuading men like Charles Colson to devote their lives to the service of Jesus Christ. And his enthusiasm is still contagious. What a difference God could make through our lives if we allowed him to renew our vision and fire our enthusiasm for the transformation of his world.

SEEKING HIS EMPOWERING PRESENCE
FOR HIS REDEMPTIVE MISSION

But wait a minute. One essential element to realizing the dreams of God is the empowering presence of God in all that we do. It seems to me that many of our churches and our Christian organizations unwit-tingly take God for granted. We seem to rather blithely assume that God is in whatever we decide to do. But it is only when we sense our total inadequacy and seek the empowering presence of God and his spiritual gifts in our lives that we are likely to experience his Spirit working through us to achieve his ends. If we are to make a difference in the world, our lives and words and acts need to be filled with a power that isn't our own. We need to experience God acting supernatur-ally in healing and deliverance while he empowers our programs of social action and evangelism.

But we have been promised that the Holy Spirit will be with us in our mission efforts. One summer I completed an inductive study of the infilling of the Holy Spirit in the book of Acts and I was surprised to discover that every single reference to the outpouring of the Spirit of God was directly related to Christ's mission of changing the world. "But you shall receive power when the Holy Spirit has come upon you; and you shall be my witnesses both in Jerusalem, and in all Judea and Samaria, and even to the remotest part of the earth" (Acts 1:8, NAS).

This is especially important to remember when we are talking about sharing God's love with others. During one of his many speaking tours, the late E. Stanley Jones, missionary and author, was asked by a listener, "How can I love others more?" As I heard the question, my mind immediately filled with possible responses, but I failed to anticipate Jones's reply to this earnest question. He simply instructed the listener to allow God to love him more. He explained, "If you allow God to share the profound unconditional love he has for you, then it is much easier for you to discover he has the same love for others . . . and we can participate with him in his agape love."

BEYOND THE INSTITUTIONALIZATION AND
PROFESSIONALIZATION OF CARE

To meet the escalating human challenges facing us in the last two decades of the twentieth century, the methods of service traditionally relied on by the church in the One-Third World will be called into serious question. We won't begin to have the resources necessary to mount a traditional institutionalized response to those anticipated challenges. We simply won't have bucks to hire all the additional pastors, youth workers, social workers, housing advocates, Young Life workers, and community health specialists we need, or be able to fund traditional institutional programs to get the job done.

But beyond the issue of available resources is the serious question of whether people are best served by the institutionalization and professionalization of care within the larger society and the church. John McKnight points out that regardless of how we expand traditional institutional and professional services to the poor, their problems don't get solved. He suggests, "Consider what would happen in terms of the job structure in the city of Chicago if we didn't have any poor people. How many people in Chicago depend for their work upon the result of racism and poverty? It is a paradox that the people who are the victims of racism and poverty provide a growing proportion of the jobs in a service economy. Their dependency and poverty is the raw material of a service economy." [6]

Are we likely to see major societal change when it is clearly in the interest of the "service economy" to have a permanent underclass of poor people? William Scott in his provocative book *Organizational America* contends that the primary goal of any organization—be it a corporation, a state welfare agency or a church—is self-preservation. If his contention is valid, how can we expect institutions or professional organizations to seriously work for change that could undermine their reason for existence? [7]

A major alternative to the large scale institutionalization of care is the emerging self-help movement. Decentralized, informal networks of self-help projects are springing up all over the One-Third World. These largely voluntary networks are demonstrating low-cost local solutions to many of the most serious problems confronting us today and tomorrow. As we mentioned in chapter three, the church is in an ideal location to catalyze thousands of local self-help projects in community agriculture, preventive health care, self-help housing, alternative technology and voluntary service networks. God is presenting the church with a historic opportunity to become the center of community life again through catalyzing services to replace those cut back by government. By far the most helpful book on the self-help movement is *Helping Ourselves: Local Solutions to Global Problems* by Bruce Stokes of Worldwatch Institute.[8]

To effectively be a missioning people in the One-Third World, the church needs to critically reexamine its longstanding reliance on large-scale institutional or professional solutions to human needs. Let's ask whether our institutional/professional systems are really promoting God's agenda in solving problems and bringing change within the church and the society, or merely perpetuating an expensive service bureaucracy. Christian colleges have for years been unquestioningly preparing Christian young people for involvement in the professional and service industry. Let's critically reexamine whether such involvement will genuinely advance the kingdom of God. Are we really preparing the Christian young to radically change society or simply to fit in and maintain the status quo?

NEEDED: A REVOLUTION OF LAY ACTIVISM

I am not suggesting for a moment that we begin a crusade to dismantle the institutional and professional systems in Western nations. But I am urging that we, the Body of Christ, reclaim a more biblical approach to working for social change. Instead of relying solely on public and private institutional bureaucracies to respond to tomorrow's challenges, let's create forms of local ministry response that flow out of organic Christian communities and activate relatively inexpensive family and community care systems. Let's invite the wealthy private sector, as well as the government, to provide start-up monies and nonfinancial resources to initiate local self-help projects.

And instead of relying on bevies of highly paid professionals to get the job done, let's activate and train our laity to make a difference simply as an expression of their Christian discipleship—without costing the church a cent. Let's staff our churches and Christian organizations with fully qualified lay people who have found some other way to support themselves so that we have more resources freed from overhead to put to work for the kingdom.

Instead of paid professionals working with the poor in the inner cities and commuting back to the suburbs in the evening, let's challenge lay people to relocate and become integral members of communities of need—as an incarnational witness. The Episcopal Urban Bishop's Coalition urges: "We must be willing to choose a new kind of presence in the cities, which calls for less money than for personal involvement in the struggles of the poor. . . . We must decide to be present in the cities wherever the poor are struggling to be free and not just in discreet 'church' programs and operations."

Wesley Frensdorff, reflecting on this challenge, asserts, "For the church to be vital, alive and truly present in the city, it must be owned by the people of the city. It is my conviction that our traditional models of church life (ministry, organization and decision making) are too hierarchical, money dependent, and too centered on the highly educated, professional stipendiary clergy who normally come from the middle and upper classes. It is these models and these dependencies which prevent effective renewal in life ministry and mission." [9] What is true of our mission in the cities is true in every aspect of Christian ministry.

For years many of us have been able to get away with paying others— pastors, social workers, urban youth workers—to do our caring for us. We let ourselves off the hook by explaining that we give money at church, at work, or through our taxes, and that therefore no one should expect us to be involved. In the eighties and nineties that situation has to change. We simply will not have the bucks to pay institutions and professionals "to care" for us. To effectively respond to the incredible challenges of the next two decades, there must be a revolution of lay activism in the compassionate mission of Christ in the world. Bruce Larson accurately observes, "We are most ourselves when we are giving to others." Let's discover our true selves through taking time to give ourselves away.

NEEDED: A RENAISSANCE OF CHRISTIAN CREATIVITY

Not only do we need a revolution of lay involvement, we need a renaissance of Christian creativity. Let's invite the Holy Spirit to flood our imaginations and enable us to create a whole new generation of Christian ministries that are a match for the heroic challenges of tomorrow's world. These creative new ministry forms should be: (1) *Future Responsive,* intentionally responding not only to today's needs but tomorrow's challenges as well; (2) *Kingdom Focused,* consciously designed to carry out the vision God has given a particular community of Christians for advancing his kingdom intentions; (3) *Celebrative,* enthusiastically celebrating the opportunity to participate with God in changing his world; (4) *Community Based,* organically flowing out of communities of shared life instead of totally relying on institutional bureaucracies; (5) *Lay Involved,* significantly increasing voluntary lay involvement and utilizing natural and spiritual gifts instead of relying so fully on a caste of paid Christian professionals; (6) *Incarnational,* compellingly demonstrating small scale, highly replicable, Mustard Seed models intended to achieve real change through incarnational involvement instead of institutional programs; (7) *Imaginative,* creatively imagining wholly new ways to more effectively respond to the enormous needs of tomorrow's society instead of mindlessly doing more of the same; (8) *Creatively Stewarded,* thoughtfully identifying underutilized resources and translating them into positive ministry responses, stewarding all resources to achieve the highest level of kingdom impact while using the least amount of resources necessary, demonstrating how to do more with less; (9) *Self-Reliant,* intentionally striving to enable those who are impacted by the ministry to own their own local programs and self-help projects and become self-reliant as soon as possible; (10) *Ecumenical,* cooperating with Christians of other denominations in common areas of ministry as a witness to our unity in Christ as well as cooperating with both the economic and public sectors when it is consistent with our biblical agenda; (11) *Spirit Empowered,* earnestly seeking the empowering and guidance of the Spirit of God as we seek to labor with him to achieve his intentions for the human future; (12) *Carefully Evaluated,* thoughtfully assessing our effectiveness in acting out the vision of God as we respond to tomorrow's needs.

Generally these principles are followed in the futures workshops I conduct for churches and Christian organizations. They are in essence creativity workshops for planning imaginative responses to a rapidly changing future. In an all-day workshop, we typically spend the morning attempting to anticipate the needs, threats, and opportunities of the next ten years. Then, in the afternoon, we break into small "futures inventions groups" in which we attempt to imagine wholly new ways to be the people of God in a world of growing need. I have been amazed at the creativity I have discovered in every group I have worked with. I am convinced that one of the most underutilized resources in the church today is our creativity. We need to provide opportunities for the laity and the leadership to invite God's Spirit to flood their imaginations, to create a whole new generation of ministry responses to tomorrow's needs.

Let's look at a few examples of some of the creative new ministry expressions that have come out of some of the futures workshops. At John Perkins's Voice of Calvary in Jackson, Mississippi, a new idea for ministry was born. During a futures workshop, one group anticipated that a growing need in Jackson in the eighties was going to be the inability of the urban poor to afford the food in the stores. Given Voice of Calvary's vision of promoting economic justice for the poor, they had a clear sense of biblical mandate in responding to this anticipated need. One of the primary underutilized resources they identified in their area is dormant farmland in Mendenhall, a community thirty-five miles from Jackson.

Their new ministry invention was to organize volunteers to VOC's sister church in Mendenhall to raise fruits and vegetables on the unused land. They planned to truck the produce into Jackson to sell to the urban poor at significantly lower prices than they had to pay in the supermarkets. They expected to show a profit from their venture, and to use that money to start urban farming projects in the poorer areas of Jackson. Last summer they trucked the first crops into Jackson and marketed them at Voice of Calvary's Thriftco Store; the produce sold out almost as soon as it arrived.

In this new ministry, the people in the Voice of Calvary community created an imaginative new way to translate underutilized farmland and volunteer labor in Mendenhall into: (1) low priced, high quality produce for the urban poor; (2) income that can be used to start urban farming projects in Jackson; and (3) ultimately, if they fully implement their idea, an increased level of food self-reliance for the urban poor and therefore more economic justice.

A small rural church in Monroe, Washington, anticipated two areas of need in the eighties for which they were particularly concerned: (1) the projected rise in juvenile crime, and (2) rapidly increasing fuel costs for senior citizens on fixed incomes. They created an innovative ministry in which they secure the services of young men who have been in trouble with the juvenile court. They involve the young men in cutting free wood on public lands and at the same time develop relationships with them; then they take the wood they cut to senior citizens who are on fixed incomes. Through this imaginative ministry, laymen in the church are developing caring relationships with young offenders, and together they are ministering to the needs of seniors in the community at the same time.

After presenting the Western District of Young Life with a forecast of the global needs that are likely to confront us in the future, I broke them into creativity groups. One group came up with a very imaginative idea for responding to the escalating needs of those in the Southern Hemisphere. They proposed that each of the five major districts of Young Life in the United States become linked to a specific region of the Southern Hemisphere; for example, the Western District would be linked to Asia. The group suggested that those in each Young Life district: (1) Promote awareness of human needs in the region of the world they are linked to; (2) Support a specific ministry in a particular country in the region; (3) Send short-term assistance to particular projects. I was delighted to learn recently that the national organization of Young Life has endorsed this creative idea, and that their international director is implementing it.

These are the kinds of imaginative new responses that have been generated in workshops on the future. I am grateful that God's Spirit is inspiring brothers and sisters throughout the "One-Third World" to join his Mustard Seed Conspiracy. They are devoting their lives and resources to seeking first the righteousness, justice, peace, reconciliation, wholeness, and love of God's future in our human present. And they are making a world of difference. Let me share a few of these seeds with you. As you read, it might be a good idea to keep a pencil handy; perhaps God will use these examples to stir your own creativity!

SEEDS OF RIGHTEOUSNESS

God intends to create a society of personal and social righteousness in which the tyranny of selfishness and sin is forever vanquished. Therefore, part of our agenda for mission in the One-Third World means working for righteousness.

Undeniably, one of the most important dimensions of working for righteousness is evangelism—identifying and reaching those who have never heard the good news of the kingdom. Society is most profoundly changed when individuals have their lives transformed by the supernatural power of God. The final statement of the recent Thailand Conference on World Evangelization stressed "the fundamental importance of evangelism and the urgency of the task that is before us." [10]

But there are other important aspects of working for righteousness. In our personal lives and our shared life we are called to incarnate the righteousness of God. We also have a responsibility to become an influence for public righteousness by helping Christians understand the ethical issues of this decade. We must anticipate and biblically respond to such emerging issues as genetic engineering, euthanasia, and subliminal advertising as well as such widely publicized issues as abortion and pornography. And we have a responsibility to call government, corporate, labor, and religious organizations to righteousness as a part of our prophetic mission as well. Let's look at a few seeds of righteousness.

A Transplanted Seed in East Detroit

Church of the Messiah in East Detroit chose to locate in an area noted for its high rates of crime and violence. Instead of starting an institutional program staffed with professionals from the suburbs, they moved their families into the neighborhood. It was their conviction that their witness would flow naturally into the community if they became a people of strong inner life and committed fellowship.

This church has become fully a part of the neighborhood—learning as well as leavening. In addition to being an incarnational witness in the community, they have a special vision of reaching the mentally retarded and mentally ill; these handicapped people comprise nearly one-third of the congregation. The church also recently acquired a twenty-four-unit apartment and renovated it as a center for ministry. The Christians who moved into the apartment building did so with the intention of ministering to other residents as another expression of their incarnational ministry.[11]

A Seed Planted on Mars Hill

Last spring a group of German students from Youth with a Mission were joyously doing traditional folk dances at the foot of Mars Hill in Athens. A crowd began gathering. The students began singing words that reflected their faith in Christ as they continued dancing. Then a few of the German students warmly shared their witness and invited their listeners to talk with them if they were seriously interested in committing their lives to Christ and his kingdom. Over two hundred young people responded. After an extended time of discussion and prayer, members of the Greek Evangelical Church took responsibility for following up these inquirers and bringing them into the fellowship of the church.

A Seed Planted in an Atlanta Penitentiary

The heat and humidity in the prison auditorium in Atlanta was overpowering. Every stitch of clothing on Chuck Colson's body was wet through as he sat quietly on the platform. Over a period of sixteen months, ten men had been viciously murdered in this prison. The prison was a powder keg; perhaps that was the reason the prison officials had decided to let Chuck Colson speak to this very defiant audience. But by the time Chuck arose to speak he felt a strength within him:

"Jesus Christ came into this world for the poor, the sick, the hungry, the homeless, the imprisoned. He is the Prophet of the loser. And all of us assembled here are losers. I am a loser just like every one of you. The miracle is that God's message is specifically for those of us who failed. . . . The message of Jesus Christ is for the imprisoned—for your families, some of them who aren't making it on welfare on the outside. Christ reached out for you who are in prison because He came to take those chains off, to take you out of bondage. He can make you the freest person in the entire world, right here in this lousy place.

"Jesus, the Savior, the Messiah, the Jesus Christ I follow is the One who comes to help the downtrodden and the oppressed and to release them and set them free. This is the Jesus Christ to whom I have committed my life. This is the Jesus Christ to whom I have offered up my dream and said, 'Lord, I want to help these men because I have lived among them. I came to know them, I love them. There is injustice in our society, but we can change it. Yes, God, we can change it. I give my life to it.' "

What happened next can only be explained as an extraordinary outpouring of the Holy Spirit. Men were not only standing throughout the auditorium, they were getting up on their chairs, clapping and shouting. The changes in the faces were awesome. They were warm and smiling. There were tears in the eyes of many where before there had been distrust and hate. . . . Several met Christ that night; we didn't count, but a year later would find nearly 400 men in chapel programs.

A black man, tall and lean with ugly scars on his neck and arms, came up to talk to me but couldn't. He simply leaned his head on my shoulder and cried like a baby. Another, tough-looking white man, a three-day, wiry, black stubble on his cheeks and chin, said, "My whole 39 years were a waste, 20 of them in joints like this. But they were only a preparation for this night. It's all turned around tonight. God bless you." [12]

And Charles Colson's activity in the prisons isn't solely resulting in lives being turned around. He and his colleagues are also working for a more righteous and just prison system as a part of their ministry for Christ.

A Seed Planted in a Persecutor

The words grabbed my heart. I was somehow frightened and uneasy, like a man walking on unfamiliar ground. . . . They haunted me. It was a feeling totally new to me.

Through the days and weeks ahead, those words of Jesus stayed with me. I couldn't shake them, hard as I tried. I wished I had not read them. . . .

Something deep within me, some tiny ember of humanity was still alive somewhere inside me. The life I was leading was not the life that I had wanted to lead. Beating old women was not the kind of life I had dreamed of long ago in my early childhood. My first religion, Communism, I believed in wholeheartedly and gave myself to it without reserve . . . but that belief was gone now, shattered by the realities of life as I had seen them. Nothing satisfactory had replaced the belief I once held.

Sergei Kourdakov had led one hundred fifty raids for the secret police in the U.S.S.R., terrorizing and arresting Russian Christians who met secretly. Gradually he became sickened by the brutality and disillusioned with the practices of the communist state. He gave up his brilliant career with the secret police and chose sea duty to escape what he had been a part of. When his ship was inside Canada's coastal waters he escaped to Canada, but he was unable to escape the haunting words of Jesus or the memory of the vibrant witness of Christians he had persecuted in his homeland.

Once he was settled in Canada, he began attending a Ukrainian church in Toronto. One day during a church service the pastor asked, "Sergei, are you now ready to give your life to God fully and completely?" "Yes," he replied. "As we prayed, something happened in my life—something definite, concrete and positive. . . . Finally, the restlessness, the emptiness, the harshness, and the void in my life had been filled by Jesus Christ. I knew that I, too, was a believer, right alongside . . . the . . . believers I had persecuted! I was one of them!" [13]

A Seed Planted on First Avenue in Seattle

At eleven thirty on a cold, rainy Seattle night you will see kids eight years and up on First Avenue. This is Seattle's Skid Row area—congested with porno parlors, triple theaters, and sleazy bars. The children often wind up in this area because they are either kicked out or run away from their homes. Typically, they are broke, confused, and simply trying to find a way to survive. And they are easy prey to "manipulators" who befriend them, help them out a bit, then offer to teach them how to "make good money" by "turning tricks"—selling their bodies. Fancy sedans cruise First Avenue looking for these pimps and "chicken hawks" and their young proteges; a varied clientele of affluent businessmen, blue collar workers, professionals, unemployed people feeds off this corruption of children. In addition to turning the kids into prostitutes, manipulators train them to roll drunks, shoplift, and peddle drugs. The streets become these children's home; the chicken hawks, pimps, pushers, and "clients" become the adult figures in their lives.

This tragic situation exists in every major city in the United States, and most of the church either is unaware of or has chosen to ignore this growing problem. But when Father Don Erickson discovered the outrageous exploitation of children on First Avenue, he acted. He and some other concerned Christians started a ministry called New Horizons to reach out and help these kids. They help them find emergency food and shelter so they won't become dependent on the manipulators. They try to find Christian foster homes to get the kids out of their destructive environments. They help them find jobs, get them off drugs, work with the courts and social agencies, and provide recreational opportunities, as well as sharing the message of Jesus with them.

One of the unique characteristics of this ministry is that all money donated is used directly to help the children. There are no paid positions—including Don Erickson's. Father Don lives right down on First

Avenue, reaching out to kids through developing loving relationships
with them that provide a way out of the trap in which they find themselves. His ministry is working. Kids are being reached. Their lives
are being transformed by the love of God that they are discovering
in the lives of Christians who care, in homes that are open, and in
relationships that are permanent.

A Seed Planted Down Under

Ten years ago a man named John Smith concluded that outlaw "bikies" in Australia would never be reached by the traditional church.
So he started a Christian Biker's Club called the God Squad. "He
looks and talks like an ancient biblical prophet except he rides a Harley
Davidson 1000 cc motorcycle. He spends a lot of time in pubs, with
drug addicts, bike gangs, and prostitutes. He often attracts enormous
crowds when he speaks, and they listen fascinated for hours," reports
one Christian magazine.[14]

John Smith's efforts to reach outlaw bikies involve a concern not
only for personal righteousness, but for social and public righteousness
as well. He and his supporters have started an organization called Truth
and Liberation Concern which, in addition to working with bike gangs,
is involved in rehabilitation of drug addicts, assistance for the homeless,
and economic development. Smith has become a leading Christian
prophetic voice in Australia for social righteousness and justice.

John Smith explains,

Now, nobody has ever criticized me for helping a poor or needy person.
Nobody does. In fact, the oppressor delights to have people like me around,
because the more somebody else cleans up the mess without the bill being
sent to him, the more he can go on with his exploiting.

But it's when the prophet comes and says, 'thou art the man'—that's
when the crunch comes. Nobody minds you being a champion of the poor;
what they do mind is when the finger is pointed at those who are at the
heart of the unrighteousness that exploits the poverty in men's hearts.
Of course, evangelists have traditionally kept out of that, because evangelism is expensive. . . . The pressure is on financially—to conform to
survive. . . . I've had some pretty blatant emotional tactics used on me
by Christian "respectables." [15]

Having loved the lost and the lonely and the destitute; having sometimes
cared for them, fought for them and spoken for them all over the land,
my prayer is now that God will give me the ability to touch the lives of
the leaders of this nation and the artists and thinkers who so rule the way
people live.[16]

God seems to be answering John's prayer as he labors for righteousness in Australia.

SEEDS OF JUSTICE

God's intention is to create not only a new age of righteousness, but a new age of justice as well. The Scriptures clearly reveal that God intends to create a new society of justice in which all oppression and inequity is ended. The Thailand Consultation on Global Evangelization reiterated, "All God's people should share his concern for justice and reconciliation throughout human society for the liberation of men from every kind of oppression."[17]

The church is only beginning to awaken to the reality that God expects his people to be advocates of justice, committed to ending oppression wherever it is found. And it is still hard for most Christians to realize that a major dimension of the mission of the church is to work for social justice by adopting more responsible lifestyles and becoming advocates of the poor in political and economic arenas. As a biblical people we must join with the poor in their struggle for justice, and this means more than just waiting at the bottom of the cliff with our ambulance service for those pushed off by unjust economic and political structures. We must go to the top of the cliff and struggle to change those unjust structures.

An organization called Evangelicals for Social Action is starting chapters all over the country to work for justice and peace as well as encouraging ministries of righteousness. ESA provides resources on justice education, Christian community planning, biblical lifestyles, and peacemaking. To start a chapter in your community write Ron Sider, President, Evangelicals for Social Action, 300 West Apsley Street, Philadelphia, PA 19144.

Ron Sider writes, "I dream of a time when all the centers of leadership and responsibility in our denominations proclaim with a united voice: 'sisters and brothers, if we are to be faithful to Christ . . . we must confront the terrible reality of systemic injustice'. . . . It is not enough for our relief and development agencies to take some cautious steps toward justice education. . . . 'We must, regardless of the cost, confront our entire constituency with the nature of systemic injustice and our involvement in it.' "[18]

If we are going to follow the One who proclaimed the arrival of a new society of justice for the poor and oppressed, won't we have to join him in working for that society now? Here are some ways a growing number of Christians in the One-Third World are working for social, racial, and economic justice.

Planting a Seed on the South Shore of Chicago

In the fifties, the South Shore of Chicago was an affluent middle-class white community. Rapid growth of surrounding black communities increased demand for housing on South Shore, and the whites fled to other areas, taking most of the businesses with them. The area became 85 percent black. And as so often happens, the South Shore bank dramatically cut back its services and availability of financial resources to the community in 1972.[19] This type of racist bank policy, called "redlining," paralyzes most poorer, predominantly black or Hispanic communities. But it has been justified by banks who claimed they couldn't receive a return on their investment in such neighborhoods.

A Christian urban planner named Stanley Hallett, along with his colleagues at The Center for Urban Affairs at Northwestern University, had a dream for turning the South Side community around by working through the churches and community organizations to achieve economic justice for the people there. Since a year of study pointed to the role of the bank as the most critical factor in urban growth or decline, Stan and those working with him started raising money to buy a bank. In 1973 they acquired the South Shore Bank for $1.3 million. Then they proceeded to get the bank back in touch with the people in the community by holding meetings in church basements and planning neighborhood coffee brunches to learn what dreams people had for their community.

Their plan was to focus on the capacities, not the deficiencies, of the neighborhood. Stan asked, "What is there to work with, what has the capacity to grow, to develop, to achieve? . . . We tried to figure out how we might create a self-sustaining neighborhood development institution. We didn't want one which would draw more and more resources, require more and more subsidies, and make more and more people dependent on next year's grant. We wanted one that would start to generate resources and would have a principle of growth instead of a principle of limitations." [20]

The community elected members to a bank advisory committee, who started planning with the bank how to make the neighborhood of some eighty thousand people work again. The bank took an active role as community developer under its new owners, abandoning all redlining policies: "While the policy of the corporation is to make loans and investments only in situations which it believes offer a reasonable expectation of return to the corporation, it will not attempt to maximize such return at the expense of its primary goal of developing the neighborhood for the benefit of its residents." [21]

Today, Stan Hallet's dream for a renewed South Side is becoming a reality. The bank is financing major rehabilitation projects in the area, and is prospering at the same time. Residents of the South Side are beginning to develop a new pride in their community and are participating in it in a variety of ways. They raise some of their own food in rooftop greenhouses. They have rounded up over one hundred fifty wild dogs that ran in packs and attacked people. They have begun to develop the fabric of a community, and it has become a safer place to live.[22] A study released last year by Richard Taub of the University of Chicago concluded that South Shore was indeed on the rebound. Property values were appreciating, the crime rate was down, median income had increased. Further deterioration was being prevented by active "neighborhood organizations, increasing numbers of middle-class blacks in the community, and renewed commitments to the neighborhood by the South Shore Bank." [23] This Mustard Seed model of an innovative way to achieve economic justice is already being emulated in other communities.

Planting a Seed in Nottingham

"What kind of a society do we want?" asks the Shaftsbury Project in Nottingham, England. "What does it mean to pray God's kingdom come, His will be done on earth?" This evangelical research and educational organization, founded in 1969, takes on the toughest issues— from the just use of the natural resources to racial justice and euthanasia. "The project's aim is to enable Christians, acting upon insights and principles drawn from the Scriptures and with the guidance of the Holy Spirit, to make an informed contribution to the discussion of crucial matters before their nation and the world." [24]

For example, the Shaftsbury Project has one specific study group that is examining the issue of young people and the law in relationship to biblical principles of justice. And it is working to educate Christians on issues of justice and on other social problems, in order that they can make a difference in English society.

Planting a Solar Seed in Springfield, Oregon

A concern for ecological justice is a primary component of the vision God is giving the United Methodist St. Paul Center in Springfield, Oregon. In response to a world of diminishing resources and injustice in the way those resources are distributed the Christians at St. Paul's have drafted a unique covenant based on a growing understanding of their biblical responsibility as affluent American Christians in a world of growing need. Their covenant has three areas of concentration: the society, the church, and the individual family unit.

The church is taking a strong advocacy role in their community and state, promoting energy conservation and the development of alternative forms of energy. They are starting a public education program for publicizing alternative approaches to energy, and creating information booths for community fairs.

St. Paul's Center is one of the first churches in the United States to use solar energy to heat their facility as a demonstration of their commitment to their covenant statement. They are making their experience with solar energy available to other churches.

The families and singles in the church have committed themselves to sharing resources in myriad ways. For example, they have developed a carpooling program for church services and other activities. They are sharing tools and equipment with others in the church. Blood insurance for senior citizens is a part of their program. They have started arts and crafts programs based on recycled materials. Members are educated in how to steward resources more biblically, and many share resources in "extended families," using what they save to reach out to others in ministries of sharing and caring.[25] St. Paul's demonstrates that a local church can make a difference through the more just and compassionate use of finite global resources.

SEEDS OF RECONCILIATION AND PEACE

Undeniably one of the most vivid images of the future of God is the image of a new age of peace and reconciliation in which the instruments of violence are transformed into the implements of peace. In the Beatitudes, the kingdom people of God are admonished to be peacemakers. And yet very few Christians of any tradition, with the exception of the traditional peace churches and a few others, are willing to acknowledge that a major part of the mission of the church is to work for peace and reconciliation. Billy Graham has recently put himself on the line as a leading advocate for nuclear disarmament, declaring, "The present arms race is a terrifying thing and it is almost impossible to overestimate its potential for disaster." [26]

"The time is right for a sweeping reappraisal of the church's teaching on violence. A mountain of nuclear stockpiles on the one hand and an ocean of revolutionary violence on the other converge in our time to make violence the most urgent issue facing this generation. When the books on the human experiment are closed, will the supreme irony of history be that the nation which wrote 'In God We Trust' on its coins destroyed the earth with nuclear weapons it had frantically stockpiled in its frantic quest for security? It is sobering to think that Christians in America, more than any other group, are deciding the answer to that question." [27]

Christians in the United States will have a decisive voice on not only the future of the insane arms race, but also on the forms of institutional violence in which we unwittingly participate and on the growing "us and them" mentality in the United States. Chris Sugden points out what our biblical response must be to all forms of violence, racism, and alienation: "The lifestyle of a kingdom-people is set out in the Sermon on the Mount. They are those who 'make peace'; they are those who love their enemies because God loves His enemies. God loved His enemies by taking the initiative in making peace with them at His own cost. Makers of peace take the initiative in bringing peace." [28] Aren't those who follow Jesus called to be the "makers of peace" and the agents of reconciliation between all peoples?

Our understanding of what the Bible says about God's intentions for the human future should significantly broaden our understanding of what it means to follow Christ and be the missioning church in a world of exploding need. It is time that we discovered that the mission of the church means more than converting individuals to a private faith, promoting church growth, and doing an occasional act of love toward those in need. God calls us clearly through his Word to work for reconciliation and peace in our world too.

Here are some ways Christians in the One-Third World are already working to bring about a future of peace:

Sewing Seeds of Reconciliation between Criminals and Victims

Mennonites in Elkhart, Indiana, have started a community reconciliation program that works in conjunction with the local criminal justice system. It is called VORP—Victim-Offender Reconciliation Program. The idea of the program is to bring the victim of a crime (usually property crimes) together with the offender in a face-to-face encounter to establish reconciliation at a human level and a fair restitution for the crime committed. The idea is to bypass as much as possible the normal court and penal systems, because they tend to be impersonal and ineffective in righting the wrongs that take place in a community, and because they have no interest in working reconciliation between the parties involved.

Thus far, 60 percent of the cases referred to VORP by local judges and the probation department eventually result in successful restitution.

And it is not unusual for a victim-offender friendship to grow out of this more biblically based approach to resolving conflict and reducing crime.

Sowing a Seed Through the World Peace Tax Fund

There are a legion of ways for those committed to waging peace to make their impact felt on larger political systems. Some Christians labor inside the system working on disarmament proposals or lobbying for nuclear nonproliferation treaties. Others refuse to pay war taxes, or they go over the fence at the Trident nuclear submarine base to protest their opposition to the arms race.

Perhaps one of the most innovative proposals is the world peace tax fund bill, which would offer a legal alternative for those who oppose their taxes being used for military expansion. Those who take advantage of this plan would pay their full share of taxes, but they would have a chance to specify that the portion which would have gone to military projects be instead set aside for "peace projects." It is estimated that such a fund might accumulate several billion dollars annually.

One creative way this resource could be used is to fund another legislative initiative, the creation of a National Academy of Peace and Conflict Resolution. Currently the tremendous amount of research on conflict resolution has found very limited application in international negotiating. A Peace Academy could enable us to discover nonlethal ways to resolve international conflicts in an increasingly dangerous world.

In recent years as many as thirty congressmen, including individuals such as Senator Mark Hatfield and Senator Mike Gravel, have supported the World Peace Tax Bill. But so far it has had insufficient public support to pass. In view of Soviet expansionism and the recent decisive national swing to the right, this situation probably will not improve in the near future, unless concerned Christians seriously commit themselves to working for peace.

Sowing Seeds of Reconciliation in Northern and Southern Ireland

Certainly the issue of peacemaking in our world is broader than achieving a disarmament treaty between the United States and the Soviet Union. Our call is to labor for reconciliation between peoples divided by religion, race, economic standing, and traditional animosities.

There are two Christian communities in Ireland committed to the ministry of reconciliation—Corrymeela in the North and Glencree in the South. These two communities share a common focus: "1. They are places where the wounds of history are bitter, open and painful [often the same wounds we can see in our own societies, if in less acute form]. 2. In each case a community of healing is seeking the way of forgiveness and thus preparing the way of peace." [29]

At Corrymeela Christians have already contributed money and work camps to build a coventry house of reconciliation where Catholics and Protestants from divided areas of Belfast come to meet and live together. Glencree, which is located near Dublin, has a similar program. They are bringing Catholic and Protestant young people from the North together in summer work camp experiences. They have also started to bring families together as well.

Obviously the critical situation in Northern Ireland hasn't been solved. But a few Catholic and Protestant Christians are working together as Mustard Seeds of reconciliation, making a real difference in a region of deep pain and open conflict.

SEEDS OF WHOLENESS AND LOVE

God not only intends to create a new society of righteousness, justice, peace and reconciliation, but also one of wholeness and love in which persons and societies brutalized by selfishness and sin are made fully whole. Historically, the church has understood a major part of its mission was to enable individuals and societies to discover healing, wholeness, and the realization of their God-given potential. Since the publication of a book by Carl Henry entitled, *Evangelical Responsibility in Contemporary Theology* [30] in 1957, the evangelical church has slowly begun reestablishing works of wholeness and love as legitimate dimensions of mission. In the last ten years there has been an explosion of evangelical ministries of wholeness and love, from inner city projects to relief and development efforts in the Third World. Christians of all traditions are beginning to work together in addressing urgent physical, economic, and social needs throughout the One-Third World.

Planting a Seed and Selling a Wheelchair in Victoria

Margaret was wheeled into the Charismatic Renewal Center in Victoria, British Columbia. She was suffering from myasthenia gravis, which is progressive deterioration of the nervous system. The doctors had told her that her condition was terminal and they had no way to either arrest or reverse the deterioration of this degenerative killer. But she had heard of the healing ministry at the Center, and decided to give it a try.

During the healing service Margaret wheeled her chair to the front and pushed herself suddenly forward. As she lay face forward on the altar God answered her prayer. Father Dennis Bennett said that her doctors have totally examined her and can only confirm that a miracle has taken place. Margaret has been completely healed from the myasthenia gravis and is leading an active life, including working for wholeness in others. How exciting to know that God is alive and well and is still able to intervene supernaturally to bring spiritual, emotional, and physical healing to those in need.

Planting a Seed in Washington, D.C.

In 1973, a small group from the Church of the Savior decided to do something about the housing shortage in Washington, D.C. Out of that small beginning, Jubilee Housing grew. Today Jubilee Housing is successfully achieving its three objectives: "1. To demonstrate that acceptable inner-city housing could be made available at costs within the budgets of low-income families; 2. To encourage and sustain the participation of tenants in the operation and management of such housing; and 3. To develop a model process from the experience which would be applied by other groups in other communities."

The group from Church of the Savior started by buying two apartment buildings, and worked with the tenants to rehabilitate them. Tenant leadership was trained and took over the management of the apartment houses. In addition, a wide range of social support programs were developed to meet the spiritual, social and economic needs of those in the apartments . . . to encourage personal development and nurture a sense of community.

Jubilee Housing has now franchised their model for other groups to imitate in other cities such as Baltimore and Louisville. They consider replicability of the Jubilee process an essential component of their program.

Planting a Seed in an Urban Wasteland

Luther Place Memorial Church found itself enveloped in the protests, tear gas, and movements of the sixties in Washington, D.C. These outside forces caused the parishioners who stayed with the church to fundamentally reexamine its identity and mission. They discovered God's unique calling for them in the midst of this traumatic transitional period.

The members of Luther Place answered God's call to create an urban hospice, and they have integrated the entire life and mission of the church around this vision.

Painted broadly on the side of Luther Place Church and adjacent block houses are these words, "I was hungry and you fed me, thirsty and you gave me a drink; I was a stranger and you received me in your homes, naked and you clothed me; I was sick and you took care of me, in prison and you visited me" (Matt. 25:35–36, TEV). In a harsh urban environment, these Christians are called to a ministry of hospitality to the rich and the poor, the influential and the powerless, the unbeliever and the faithful. They explain that hospitality is as American as apple pie and as radical as the gospel of Jesus Christ: "To be hospitable is to convert . . . the enemy into a guest. Hospitality is a relationship between host and guest with enough freedom that both can reveal their most precious gifts and bring new life to each other." [31]

Luther Place strives to be a place of homecoming. Every activity is an expression of the church's calling to hospitality, from breaking bread together at the Lord's Table to wide-ranging urban ministries. Those at Luther Place extend welcome, food, and clothing for the needy in their midst. They extend hospitality to Christians who come to Washington, D.C., to lobby for social justice for the poor. And they host interfaith communities at the church itself, and other houses in their vicinity.

PLANTING SEEDS IN THE ONE-THIRD WORLD

There's not space enough in this chapter to tell about the miracles of physical, emotional, and spiritual healing that take place on any given morning at St. Luke's Episcopal in Seattle, or about the imaginative dreams of Art Smith at First Presbyterian in Chicago to empower the poor through teaching them to become self-reliant through such means as solar nurseries, earthworm garbage disposal systems, and systems for processing waste newspaper into home insulation material. One could write an entire book about the Koinonia Community near Americus, Georgia, and the remarkable way they have ministered to the physical and economic needs of people in the name of Jesus.

The fact is that Christians are making a difference in every nook and cranny of the industrialized North. In a legion of ways, they are manifesting the loving kingdom of God to a world of growing need. The tragedy is that so many Christians and so many churches are still silent spectators—standing on the sidelines, quietly living for themselves. Let's join our brothers and sisters all over the One-Third World in the Conspiracy of the Mustard Seed, and rediscover the amazing truth that we live most fully when we give our lives away.

For Discussion and Action

1. Define the word *mission* as used in this and the next chapter. In what ways is this definition broader than what we usually think of as mission?

2. Give three reasons the churches in the industrialized North have trouble being a missioning people to those around us?

3. How do God's intentions for the human future as revealed in his Word relate to the Christian's mission in the world today?

4. What are some alternatives to the professionalization and institutionalization of care for those in need in Western nations? Describe the specific benefits of expanding neighborhood self-help projects?

5. What are some specific ways the laity can be activated to assume a greater share of the responsibility for mission in the eighties and nineties?

6. How can we within the local church discover God's vision for mission and secure his empowering and enthusiasm to act out that vision in our communities and in our world?

7. What are the twelve principles suggested for the creation of new ministries?

8. Anticipate some of the local and national challenges that are likely to confront your church in the next ten years.

9. Create some imaginative new ministries of righteousness, justice, peace, reconciliation, wholeness, and love that respond to the anticipated challenges of the coming decades.

10. List the specific ways your community might be changed if your church renewed its sense of vision for mission and created new ministries to respond to tomorrow's challenges.

10.

Seeking First the Future of God with the Two-Thirds World

The brilliant Haitian sun shone through the large open window as we joined in a large circle. My Haitian brothers firmly clasped my hands as we sang enthusiastically, in English and Creole, "We are one in the Spirit, we are one in the Lord . . ."

I was completely overcome. Even though I had only been an observer, I was profoundly grateful to have been even a little involved in the planning session we had just completed. That week Haitians and Americans, working together, had drafted plans for community health, spiritual renewal, intensive agriculture, and education in a rural Haitian valley—plans that would make a difference in the lives of ten thousand people. Quite honestly, I can't remember a time when I have been happier or more grateful to be alive. I realized in that moment, looking around the circle of glowing faces, that God was acting to bring his new future to Haiti through his church, that we were privileged to be a small part of his initiative.

GOOD NEWS/BAD NEWS

The good news is that all of us in the "One-Third World" have the joyous opportunity to join hands with those in the "Two-Thirds World" (the largely nonindustrialized and poorer nations) in true partnership for the kingdom. The Mustard Seed Conspiracy is already working to turn the whole world right side up.

In Calcutta, for example, God's compassionate love incarnated in Mother Teresa and her sisters is making a redemptive difference not only among the poor and dying, but throughout the entire planet. In Somalia, World Concern, TEAR Fund Holland, and the Salvation Army of England together are manifesting the kingdom of God by working to provide emergency relief for thousands of refugees victimized by war, drought, and famine. In Nicaragua, a Christian doctor named

Gustavo Parajon is working with evangelical Christians to help reconstruct communities devastated by the Somoza regime.

All around the world Christians are working in concert to bring about God's future. The bad news is that serious problems in the international body of Christ are hindering the work of his kingdom. In many instances a lack of vision and misguided methods on the part of the Western church have made it ineffective or even harmful in the cause of global mission.

In this chapter, we will examine both the good news and the bad news of Western mission in the Two-Thirds World. We will look at some of the false assumptions and outdated attitudes that have hampered past mission efforts, and we will explore new directions for mission in which the church North and South can work together in true partnership. Finally, we will look at some specific creative ways the Mustard Seed Conspiracy of righteousness, justice, peace, reconciliation, wholeness, and love is already making a difference in the Two-Thirds World today.

RECOVERING A VISION FOR TRANSGLOBAL MISSION

The mission of the church is global. But many of our churches in the One-Third World, churches that lack a vision even for the human needs of their own immediate communities, seldom give a thought for the work of Christ overseas. Western congregations need to recover a vision of their role in working for the kingdom, and that vision must transcend parochial preoccupations and nationalist self-interest to focus on the transglobal intentions of God.

It is time for those of us who live in enclaves of affluence to learn to hear, see, and touch those in poorer, undeveloped nations who are being destroyed by our personal and institutional lifestyles of indulgence and indifference. We who choose to believe God for the provision of funds to erect multimillion-dollar monuments for the affluent seldom find the same levels of "possibility thinking" for the world's poor and unreached peoples.

But seeds of concern and awareness are beginning to sprout in Western churches! The People's Church in Toronto has a strong vision of the global dimensions of mission. That vision is reflected in the fact that over half of their income goes directly into overseas ministries. I recently heard of a Presbyterian Church in New York State that raises a dollar for overseas ministry for every dollar pledged for the church building fund. My own church, University Presbyterian in Seattle, expresses its strong vision for world mission by sending twenty student volunteers to mission projects in both the Northern and Southern Hemispheres

every year. We support thirty-two missionaries and development workers around the world, and we are preparing a team of twenty people
to go to southern India this fall to work among the poorest of the
poor in self-help projects.

What would happen if the churches of the North were captured by
a transglobal vision of the kingdom intentions of God? How would it
affect our institutional priorities? Our budgets? Our lifestyles? Our careers? When we really put God at the helm of our churches, Christian
organizations, and personal lifestyles, I am sure we are much more
involved with him in the adventure of changing his world.

AMBASSADORS OF TWO GOSPELS AND ADVOCATES OF TWO FUTURES

However, if Christians from the One-Third World are to significantly
increase their involvement with Christians from the Two-Thirds World
in global mission, that involvement will have to be on a whole new
basis. Historically, churches and organizations of the Northern nations
have unilaterally initiated programs of assistance, and this action has
created a relationship in which the donor culture took on the role of
a freely dominating parent and the receptor culture took on the role
of the child.[1] More often than not, this has had the effect of exporting
Western culture along with the gospel of Jesus Christ, and of imposing
that Western culture on cultures ill-equipped to handle it.

Waldron Scott of World Evangelical Fellowship openly confesses,
"We missionaries from the West frequently exhibit an ambition to lead
rather than serve; a drive to dominate rather than develop; a need to
control rather than contribute, to talk rather than listen. An ambience
of arrogance, the smell of superiority envelops us. No wonder then
that Latin Americans cry, 'Missionary go home!', an evangelical leader
in Kenya calls for a five-year moratorium on Western missionaries,
and the principal of a theological seminary in India asserts: 'Relief
agencies and mission boards control the younger churches through the
purse strings. Foreign finances, ideas, and personnel still dominate the
younger churches and stifle their spontaneous growth. . . . so now I
say "the mission of the Church is the greatest enemy of the Gospel." '

"Those of us who signed the Lausanne Covenant in 1974 acknowl-
edged that 'Missions have all too frequently exported with the Gospel
an alien culture. . . . Christ's evangelists must humbly seek to empty
themselves of all but their personal authenticity to become the servants
of others.' "[2]

One African pastor, who had not only received the Gospel but the
Western culture that went with it, was trying to tell his congregation

what heaven was like. Grasping for the right image, he finally blurted out, "It will even be better than the way the missionaries live!"

Unwittingly, we from the West have often become ambassadors for two very different gospels, promoters of two totally divergent futures. From pulpits in the Two-Thirds World we have proclaimed the servant gospel of Jesus and have presented a transcendent picture of the coming future of God. But from our mission compounds we too often have proclaimed through our affluent lifestyles the self-seeking gospel of Western culture.

I suspect that the people in the Two-Thirds World pay more attention to the gospel they see preached in our lives than the gospel they hear spoken from our mouths. In one mission compound I visited, the missionaries have invited the president of the indigenous national church they work with to live in a house in the compound. Instead of the modest two-room thatched homes in which most of his pastors live, he has a spacious concrete-block house like the missionaries—with the same gadgets and the same level of personal affluence. He is modeling the Western lifestyle he has seen preached in the lives of the missionaries. In turn, his pastors are seeking to emulate his lifestyle, and their parishioners too are climbing on the treadmill of upward mobility. The tragedy is that there simply aren't enough resources for everyone in this poor nation to live like Americans. If a few pastors do make it, it will be at great expense to their congregations and programs of ministry, and in contradiction with the servant/leader role the Bible calls us all to fill.

In addition to unconsciously spreading the gospel of Western materialism, we in the One-Third World have also unwittingly propogated a broad spectrum of Western images of God, his world, and human personality, many of which were detrimental to the cultures where they were introduced. For example, Western medical care has often been introduced by the church into the Southern Hemisphere without regard to its cultural impact. In Two-Thirds World cultures, healing is often perceived as intimately involved with the larger spiritual realm. Western medicine, on the other hand, tends to reduce the whole issue of sickness and wellness to physical, biochemical process. Someone has written that the introduction of Western medicine into Two-Thirds World culture by the church and mission boards has done more than any other single force to promote a secularized, naturalized view of the world in developing countries.

Two-Thirds World peoples often seem to have a much more "spiritual" view of the world than do people in Western countries. As a consequence, Christians in the Southern Hemisphere often seem to have a greater sensitivity to the spiritual realm—a greater active dependency on God and a tendency to see the world more wholistically than their Western counterparts.

We Western Christians tend to rely heavily on our own ability and initiative as expressed in program strategies, science and technology, and economic know-how. Once, for example, while I was preparing to write a theology of development for the organization with which I work, I read every evangelical theology of development I could lay my hands on. To my chagrin, I found that there was not a single reference in any of those statements to the role of the Holy Spirit in assisting the world's poor!

In our Western culture we have been programmed to think dualistically of the natural world as nothing but a passive grab bag of resources where we drill our oil, dump our garbage, and set up our campers. Not surprisingly, we also tend to think of persons as nothing but the sum of their organic core and their behavioral surface. In our religious circles we talk about "reaching souls," but we have been conditioned by our economic and political culture to correlate human worth and identity to a person's ability to produce and consume goods and services—to actively participate in a Western notion of the good life.[3] All too often we have exported this dualistic view of human nature to Two-Thirds World nations.

To what extent has the church in the Northern Hemisphere, in its dominant relationship to brothers and sisters in the South, unconsciously imposed Western views of the better future, God, his universe, and human life that have nothing to do with the gospel of Jesus? How can we as Westerners avoid imposing our secular, self-seeking culture on those with whom we work?

Part of the answer is to be found in Stephen Knapp's call to mission that is "at its heart disciplemaking. . . . calling people to new loyalties and out of the world so they can be more effective servants in the world." [4] It seems imperative that anyone who works in another culture first be thoroughly discipled in the servant religion of Jesus—called out of the secular values of Western culture. In addition, he or she must be comprehensively educated to understand and appreciate the culture in which he or she will be working. Appallingly, most missionaries, medical specialists, and development workers have almost no cross-cultural experience or training. It is not surprising, then, that we often enter other people's cultures with an insensitivity that undermines the work of the gospel and the fellowship of the body of Christ.

PARTNERSHIP AND THE COMING OF THE THIRD CHURCH

As we in the One-Third World contemplate mission with our brothers and sisters in the Two-Thirds World, it is important that we realize a new day has dawned. The United States and Western Europe are no longer the sole stewards of global mission. Since the Second World

War, the Spirit of God has quietly been raising up an armada in the Southern Hemisphere. Two-Thirds World Christians are taking decisive leadership in advancing the kingdom throughout the entire world.

"By 1972 there were far more Asian missionaries in various parts of the world than there were European missionaries in the whole of the Third World in 1810 [the year the first American missionary society was organized]. . . . There are at least thirty-four hundred Third World missionaries today, perhaps more. . . . They are deployed by 203 separate agencies in forty-six countries. The leading Third World sending countries according to the number of reported missionaries are Nigeria, India, Brazil, Philippines, Japan, and Mexico in that order. From the city of Madras, India alone an estimated 300 thousand rupees per year are raised for foreign missions." [5]

Here then is the best answer to the problem of paternalism and cultural domination. We need to recognize the maturity the church in the Two-Thirds World has achieved; our brothers and sisters to the South are peers, not children! It is time for us to begin working in true partnership with their organizations, instead of endlessly trying to sustain our own Western organizations overseas. (Many of these organizations seem to be lagging in turning their programs over to indigenous Christian structures. A letter to those you are in contact with, asking them what their timetable for total indigenization is, will alert them to your concern.)

Emilio Castro has asserted, "We have reached the end of the Western missionary era and a new one is beginning which will involve the entire church ministering to the entire world. One characteristic of the new era is that mission will be reciprocal. Western nations will increasingly be receiving assistance from so-called 'mission lands' to minister to those being destroyed in their midst by the side effects of industrialized culture. And of course in the new era global mission will no longer be premised on singularly Western values or a singularly Western understanding of the faith. A rich pluralism of values and viewpoints will characterize this new era of global mission." [6]

In a recent futures workshop, University Congregational Church in Seattle came up with an innovative approach to mission that recognized the contributions to be made by Christians in other cultures. The members of University Congregational proposed first of all to develop a "partnering" relationship with an ethnic church in Seattle. Then, after that relationship was established, the two Seattle churches would develop a similar relationship with a church in Latin America.

In this three-way partnering relationship, the members of each congregation would get to know each other. And then each of the churches would reciprocally minister to one another. The church in Latin America might share a teaching ministry on their perspectives of the gospel and Christian community with the two Seattle churches. The Seattle churches could contribute financial resources to start a community health and nutrition project in partnership with the church in Latin America.

I was delighted to discover that the First Presbyterian Church of Arlington Heights, Illinois, had already established this kind of relationship with the Dominican Evangelical Church in the Dominican Republic. They selected the church in the city of Sanchez to work with most directly. In 1979, twenty-one people were selected from the Arlington Heights church to live with the brothers and sisters in Sanchez for a brief period.

Out of that meeting has come partnership in self-help projects in agriculture, community health, and economic development. It is evident from the reports that the Arlington Heights people have learned more than they ever expected from their new friends in Christ.

This kind of person-to-person fellowship of course carries risks and hazards. But if the relationship is sensitively developed, with extensive cultural preparation and the guidance of a Christian relief and development agency, I am convinced it can be enormously beneficial to the kingdom and to all concerned. Christians in the United States will develop a greater sense of personal responsibility for mission, as well as being able to see their resources at work. And as the people in Arlington Heights Presbyterian and Sanchez Evangelical Church have discovered, they will have a renewed sense of being a part of the international body of Christ—partners in the advance of God's kingdom.

Another creative model of true partnership in mission between North and South is the International Fellowship of Evangelical Students. The members of this fellowship are involved in ministries in evangelism and social action throughout the world. Their executive committee is comprised of twelve members, eight of whom come from the Southern Hemisphere. Their resources are not seen as the property of Christians from the North though a good share comes from that source. They are seen as a resource of the Body of Christ International . . . along with resources of creativity, time and talent contributed by the Third Church. Instead of a Western-based agency using its resources and power to do what it deems best in the South, these Christians work in true partnership in decision-making, policy, finance and mission. This is a model of the future for Western Christian agencies working in the Two-Thirds World.

U.S. POLICY AND THE TWO-THIRDS WORLD

An important but often ignored opportunity for Christians in the United States to participate in global mission partnership directly relates to our economic and foreign policy in the Southern Hemisphere. Individuals have a responsibility to learn the facts and then weigh them carefully in the light of our Christian values, then use any means at our disposal to influence policy makers.

For example, instead of allowing assertions that Nicaragua was overthrown in 1979 because it was on the "Soviet Hit List" to go unchallenged, we can provide a forum for Nicaraguan Christians to tell their own story. Gustavo Parajon, whom I mentioned earlier in this chapter, is head of the evangelical development organization CEPAD in Nicaragua. He has taken time to share with me the situation in his country before and after the revolution.

He told me that under the Somoza regime the people of his country suffered years of systematic oppression, exploitation, and often death. Because Somoza characterized himself as a staunch anticommunist, the U.S. helped finance his oppressive government. The Nicaraguan people had a hundred times more justification for their revolt than the U.S. did in its tax squabble with England. And it is important for us to realize that the Nicaraguan revolution was almost entirely a civil revolt in which there was very little outside influence.

Gustavo explained that there are Marxists involved in the revolution and the new government, but that even the Marxists are strongly opposed to coming under the thumb of any outside government—whether Cuba, the Soviet Union, or the United States. And the new government in Nicaragua is comprised of many non-Marxist leaders, including businessmen, evangelical Christians, and Catholic priests.

"Never in the history of Nicaragua," Gustavo reported, "have our people enjoyed such political freedom. The new regime abolished capital punishment because we didn't want to treat our enemies as we had been treated. There were no firing squads. Today our citizens have greater civil freedoms and more protections for their human rights than they have ever known in their lives. Evangelical and Catholic churches are directly involved with our government in rebuilding our nation. However, if the U.S. and other democratic countries cut their reconstruction assistance to us, it is going to be much harder for us to maintain our independence from Cuba and from others who will offer us money with strings attached."

(I encourage any who question this report on Nicaragua to contact their sister churches in Nicaragua and ask them to report firsthand. The same goes for other strife-torn countries; I am told by believers in Central America that the current unrest also has more to do with years of oppressive political rule and economic exploitation than with outside "influences." A helpful and informative article to read is "Believers Ask Yankees to Remove Cold War Blinders," in *Christianity Today*, March 27, 1981.)

It is the responsibility of the church in the United States to become a voice for our brothers and sisters in the South. We are to be advocates for those who are unable to speak for themselves or make themselves heard over political outcry and rhetoric. Unless we work for justice for the poor in these countries, we can be sure that communists will take advantage of the situation and spread their influence.

(One Christian organization that has become a particularly effective lobbying organization for the poor, the oppressed, and the hungry in the Two-Thirds World is Bread for the World. Anyone who is interested in information on United States policy and the poor can write: Bread for the World, 207 East 16th Street, New York, NY, 10003, or call (212) 260-7000.)

A UNITED CHURCH AND A THEOLOGICAL PLURALISM

In a remarkable overview of the theology of the church in Africa, Latin America, Asia, Northern Europe, and the United States, Vinay Samuel and Chris Sugden convince their readers of the broad pluralism of theologies that exist in evangelical Christianity today. For instance, African theology contains a strong emphasis on the humanizing and liberating aspects of the gospel. Julius Nyerere, an African leader, states, "We say man is created in the image of God. I refuse to imagine a God who is poor, ignorant, superstitious, fearful, oppressed, wretched . . . which is the lot of the majority of those He created in His own image." [7]

The different strands of African theology seem to share a common thread . . . a belief that the gospel is intended to enable individuals to become fully human within the context of African culture. For some African evangelicals, this means a new partnership of the weak and the strong; for some, socialism; for others, political and economic liberation from racism and oppression. Some Africans envision fashioning a uniquely African Christianity; others dream of creating a Third Race of black and white Christians bonded together in common mission of liberation. But all share a strong conviction that the mission of the church must make a real difference in the total lives of people. [8]

The Asian church finds itself an alien community—not only a minority faith, but a minority culture. One unfortunate legacy of Western mission in Asia was the imposition of a Western cultural model of the church. A primary focus of Asian theology today, therefore, is the creation of an authentically Asian church. There is a theological struggle in the Asian church between those, like Choan-Seng Song of China, who don't feel the church will play a major role in God's redemptive plan, and others, like Vinay Samuel of India, who are convinced the church is indispensable to God's plan.

Samuel insists that "The Lordship of God in Christ over nations cannot be experienced or expressed without a community that acknowledges and demonstrates the results of obedience to Jesus as Lord." [9] As a consequence, he concludes, the church in India must examine the culture in India according to biblical values. Christian missions began their work with the poor and disenfranchised but now cater to the elite and wealthy. Samuel and other Indian theologians insist that the church must become an agent of the justice of God, working for real social change among the poor and oppressed.

Latin American theologians have found much of Western theology totally irrelevant to the conditions they see around them. Instead of attempting to answer the inquiry of Western theologians, "Does God exist in a scientific world and how can an individual know him?", they ask a very different question: "What is God's answer for a poor man and a poor community?" Frankly, they don't find our Western answers to this question very helpful. Realistically they have little reason to believe the poor will be helped by a gradual evolution into a constitutional republic; it simply isn't in the cards in most Latin nations. And many economic development programs we have offered as remedies tend to benefit the affluent and powerful elites instead of the poor.

The Latin American Theological Fraternity is a fellowship of evangelical theologians who are wrestling with these tough issues while carrying on a dialogue with liberation theologians. Two members of the LATF, Rene Padilla and Samuel Escobar, presented papers at the Lausanne Congress in 1974 which contributed to the drafting of an important minority report:

We confess that:

We have often been in bondage to a particular culture and sought to spread it in the name of Jesus.

We have not been aware of when we have debased and distorted the Gospel by a contrary value system.

We have been partisan in our condemnation of totalitarianism and violence, and have failed to condemn societal and institutionalized sin, especially that of racism.

We have sometimes so identified ourselves with particular political systems that the gospel has been compromised and the prophetic voice muted.

We have frequently denied the rights and neglected the cries of the underprivileged and those struggling for freedom and justice.[10]

The Latin American Theological Fellowship repudiates the violence advocated by some liberationists as a biblical vehicle to bring justice.

However, they insist that theologians in the United States and Western Europe must give much greater attention to the poor and to the question of how structural evil can be overcome to bring justice and shalom to the oppressed.[11]

In many countries of the Two-Thirds World, theology is moving out into the streets. It is becoming the vocation of the poor as well as the profession of educated elites, and it is attempting to realistically confront the hunger, strife, and human anguish it encounters all around it. We who are the church in the United States and Western Europe have much to learn from our brothers and sisters in Africa, Asia, and Latin America, if we can only set aside our theological paternalism and listen. This amazing pluralism of theological perspectives can add richness and depth to the international body of Christ.

At the same time, Christians North and South can and must be united under the lordship of Christ to carry out his mission in the world. "The world needs to hear and see a united church witnessing and preaching, in word and deed, the liberating message of Jesus Christ, worshiping and serving Him and discipling its peoples on all six continents," Orlando Costas challenges. "Let us, therefore, mobilize all our resources—manpower, finances, talents, imagination, contacts, and opportunities—to meet this open door which the Lord lays open before his church in this hour of history. Let us give ourselves to be a prophetic, priestly, and royal community, in season and out of season. Let us proclaim, teach, and witness to, without reduction or apologies, the whole gospel of the kingdom to the whole man in the whole world. Let us strive for the integral growth of the church to the end that all peoples of the earth might experience God's salvation in Jesus Christ in their struggles for hope and life everlasting, reconciliation and forgiveness, inner brokenness and guilt, solidarity, justice and dignity. Amen." [12]

DREAMING, CREATING, COOPERATING
IN INNOVATIVE MISSION TO TOMORROW'S WORLD

Given the awesome responsibility of global mission confronting the international church of Christ in the final two decades of the twentieth century, how can we in the One-Third World more fully participate in the conspiracy of the kingdom with our brothers and sisters in the Southern Hemisphere? Where does the church in the Northern Hemisphere take hold of the challenge—and what is our share of the responsibility? Where do we begin?

In the first place, in view of the limited time in which we have to respond and the constrained resources with which to work, Christian communities, churches, denominations, mission boards, and relief and development agencies can no longer afford the luxury of working independently of one another—or in competition! We must find ways to collaborate to gain the greatest possible kingdom impact from our limited resources.

After we have committed ourselves to unity in common mission let us consider these steps to increase our effectiveness in global mission in the eighties and nineties:

Anticipating and Assessing Tomorrow's Needs

Instead of simply maintaining existing programs or randomly starting new programs, let's learn first to anticipate those areas where deprivation and human suffering are likely to be the greatest in the future. Let's assess where unreached populations are the largest and growing the most rapidly, and where the smallest amount of resources are being invested by the church to get the job done.

Setting Priorities and Planning Strategy for Tomorrow's Mission

Let's begin collaborating with the church in the South to establish global strategies and priorities as God's Spirit directs us. There is an urgent need for a global mission strategy that is responsive to tomorrow's anticipated needs and is derived from our understanding of the future intentions of God. It is time to set aside our narrow unbiblical views of mission and to find innovative ways to manifest God's future righteousness, justice, peace, reconciliation, wholeness, and love in those sectors of anticipated human crisis.

Dreaming and Listening to Find our Way to Tomorrow's World

Our work in those areas of the world in which the anticipated challenges are greatest demands some fresh approaches. Of first importance is a new level of partnership with larger church organizations of the South and with those specific communities in which we may be invited to participate. Too long have we Westerners tended to assume that we bring God, the Christian faith, civilization, and development with us in our luggage. Let's learn instead to listen to our brothers and sisters in communities of the South . . . and hear God speak through them.

Many Western Christians working for development in Two-Thirds World countries have appropriated the secular approach—asking the "beneficiaries" what their "felt needs" are. If we assume that God was in that community before we arrived, already bringing his future into being, then perhaps we will ask a different question. In the Haiti Project I mentioned earlier, the Haitian codirector asked community leaders, "What are your dreams for the future of your valley .   . your family . . . your children ten years from now?"

Another member of the project staff had already asked the Haitians about their "felt needs," and they had responded that they wanted a road, an irrigation system, a tractor, a bulldozer, etc—purely physical things. But when they started talking about their desired future, suddenly the room was filled with dreams. They envisioned a valley of renewed spiritual life, one in which the majority of people served Christ. They spoke with pride of their Haitian culture, and described those aspects of their way of life they wanted to preserve in the face of modernization. They described a valley in which there were no more hungry kids and in which all children had a chance for an education. And they pictured a community freed from oppression and want. We were struck by the contrast between their "felt needs" and their compelling dreams, and we were struck by our need to more carefully listen to the voice of God in the dreams of our Haitian brothers.

Creating Innovative Ways to Make Today's Dreams Tomorrow's Reality

Mission begins with those who have been entrusted with the dream, those who serve the living God. It begins in communities of faith and spreads as a contagion throughout villages, towns, and cities. It begins in the lives of the insignificant who are empowered by the Significant to change their world. Then, in both the Northern and Southern Hemispheres, the vision of God must find expression in the incarnational presence and innovative ministries of the kingdom. We need a legion of innovative ministries in evangelism, church planting, social justice, reconciliation, education, and economic development flowing from the church if we are to effectively respond to the escalating challenges of the eighties and beyond. Not only must we have God's vision for social change, and his inspiration of creative ways to manifest his kingdom; we must also have his living presence transforming our lives and empowering our service for him.

But making any dream a reality must begin with the people. Paolo Freire understands that. When he enters a new community in Latin America to teach an adult literacy class, he doesn't take any educational materials with him. He develops reading materials out of the themes of the people's oppression—their polluted water systems, their unjust tax structures, their economic exploitation by wealthy landlords. Then, as they learn to read, they also begin to learn that their suffering isn't inevitable. They learn why their children are dying before they reach five years of age, and they begin to learn what they can do to change their plight.

Freire calls this form of education "conscienization," and he intends nothing less than the liberation of both the oppressed and the oppressor from the bondage that is destroying them both. Only as the poor discover their suffering isn't inevitable, that God wills them to be free from oppression and injustice, and only as they discover nonviolent ways to change their society, do they have hope. Churches and mission organizations have found Freire's innovative educational techniques effective in helping bring about social change.[13]

Creating Innovative Ways to Transform Underutilized Resources into the Tools of the Kingdom

As the people of God in the Northern Hemisphere increasingly free up more of their time and resources for the global mission of the church, those resources can and must be translated into positive kingdom change. However, those resources must be used with great care in both the Northern and Southern Hemispheres. A sudden infusion of large numbers of persons or large amounts of money into an impoverished community can often do more harm than good.

A rule of thumb is to introduce the fewest resources necessary to enable churches to begin new ministries in their communities. It is important that ownership and control of these projects be in the hands of those who will benefit from them. In view of escalating needs and limited resources, overseas projects must be designed to become self-reliant as soon as possible. Resources can then be transferred to initiate still other projects for the poor.

Creativity is not only essential in the stewardship of resources drawn from societies of affluence; it is also crucial in using resources within societies of need. A project of the Haitian Evangelical Baptist Church and World Concern illustrates well how an underutilized resource can be transformed into a tool of the kingdom.

Based on a low technology process designed by Dr. Ben Bryant at the University of Washington, a group in Haiti are bonding rice fiber with sulphur and transforming it into a variety of products such as an alternative to the corrugated metal roof, wallboard, and sewer tile. If the project is successful, a cottage industry will be set up by the Haitian Baptist Church and the profits used to finance church planting, literacy and evangelism programs, or community health clinics. With a little imagination Christians working together in the South and North have found a way to transform a throwaway resource into socially beneficial products, jobs for unemployed Haitians, income for depressed communities, opportunity for the local church to become a more active catalyst for social change, and profits which can be used to support Christian ministries to the poor and unreached people in that region.

This is the kind of creativity we must have in the exploding urban corridors and impoverished rural areas of the nations of the South if a vast human tragedy is to be averted. Even the poorest regions of the world have throwaway and underutilized resources that, with a little imagination, can be transformed into the building blocks of God's kingdom. Christians of the North and South need to join hands in imagining wholly new ways to increase food production, health services, economic development, education and evangelism through the more creative and ecologically sound use of all the earth's resources.

MUSTARD SEEDS IN THE TWO-THIRDS WORLD

This chapter began with the declaration that the Mustard Seed Conspiracy is turning the entire world right side up! And that's absolutely true. The exciting news of mission in the Two-Thirds World today is that, one by one, seeds of righteousness, justice, peace and reconciliation, wholeness, and love are being planted. And bit by bit, these Mustard Seeds are changing the world.

SEEDS OF RIGHTEOUSNESS

Of the 4.2 billion people on planet Earth, 3 billion are not Christians. Of this number 2.5 billion are located in 11,300 groups that can only be reached by crosscultural evangelism. To reach these people with the Good News of the kingdom, we must be much more innovative than in the past.[14] There are some exciting examples of crosscultural evangelism that can serve as models for ways we complete the Great Commission:

Planting a Seed with Brass Gongs, Leather Puppets and Javanese Songs

Over 50 percent of those who live in the crowded country of Java are Muslim. In other days the people have been strongly influenced by both Buddhism and Hinduism. Traditional Western approaches to evangelism and church planting in this culture have been singularly ineffective. The East Java Church, the Southern Baptist Mission, and World Vision are involved in formal cooperation in an innovative evangelism program.

They have turned to a cultural solution called Wayang. Wayang is an ancient Javanese art form, a primary form of cultural communication. Essentially in Wayang a set of brass gongs and leather puppets and Javanese songs are used to tell a story—often a Hindu epic. Several persons narrate the story with song, with music from the gongs, and with action from the puppets. Often a Wayang performance can last for hours, and an audience will watch with rapt attention the whole time.

Since Christianity brought Western music, Western musical instruments such as the organ, and Western methods of preaching with it to Java, it has not been viewed by the people as an indigenous faith. And it simply hasn't been accepted in Java as Hinduism, Buddhism, and Islam have been.

Christians have begun using Wayang as a vehicle to share stories from the Scriptures with amazing results. They have discovered that they have an instant audience as soon as they begin presenting Bible stories with gongs, leather puppets and Javanese music. They have even been invited to present their Wayang performances on government TV in Jakarta. Initially, other Christian missionaires resisted this cultural presentation of the gospel, but resistance has died down as public receptivity to the gospel in this new mode has grown.

Planting a Seed with Ablutions, Bare Feet and Segregation

One of the reasons the religion of Jesus has not taken root in Muslim countries is that missionaries have usually insisted on imposing their own culture on the people. Little effort has been made to incorporate cultural practices from Muslim peoples into church customs.

In Bangladesh, three believers have taken a different pathway. Two men from Muslim culture, along with an American Christian named Phil Parshall, have begun churches that operate on the premise, "Whatever the Bible doesn't explicitly forbid, people of a given culture can continue to practice." For example, people take off their shoes before they enter the sanctuary. They participate in ablutions before the service. Men and women sit on different sides of the church.

These churches in Bangladesh have staunchly refused all outside support, in order to maintain their cultural character. And as a consequence of this fundamental cultural integration, they are enjoying a much higher level of cultural acceptance in Bangladesh than Christian churches have previously had. In fact, mission strategists at Fuller Theological Seminary are convinced that only a genuine cultural church will be able to evangelize peoples in Muslim cultures.

Planting a Seed with Roots, Festivals and Healing Services

The poorest of the poor in India are the village migrants, the landless poor who come to the cities in hope of a better life. They are easily exploited, unskilled; their major problem is simply survival. The Pentecostal churches have been particularly effective in reaching these rural migrants because they consciously recreate much of the rural culture in their urban churches. In these churches, migrants find a sense of roots, community life, festivals, dances, and the kind of cultural support they had in their villages. The elders of the Pentecostal churches provide the rural migrants with a substitute for the Village Elder who helped them with decisons and provided counsel. In addition, the Pentecostal churches place high emphasis on prayer meetings and healing services, which the migrants seem to readily accept along with their new faith.[15]

Planting a Seed with a Community of Incarnational Love, Shared Purse and Shared Lives

Ruth and Vishal Mangalwadi are convinced that the most powerful evangelistic proclamation is made not by an individual evangelist or a missionary, but by a community incarnating the message of hope. They have a half-dozen village families living with them in their Christian community in Chhatarpur, India. By having a common purse among three families, they are able to meet all their basic subsistence needs, plus five rupees a month each for spending money.

They insist that all people—high caste or low caste, educated or uneducated—are equally precious in God's eyes, and that therefore resources should be shared on the basis of need. Ruth declares, "It would be sinful to give some privileged people money to waste freely while others of God's children starve. . . .

"The third principle behind community living is loving each other as he loved us. This can only mean giving ourselves for our brothers and sisters. . . . In caste-ridden rural India where untouchability is as rampant today as it ever has been, where the weak still have no dignity, where the poor are denied justice and opportunity, to practice Christian openness of community in the full biblical sense stands out as a powerful testimony to the truth of the gospel and attracts many people.

"Just last Sunday we baptized four Hindus belonging to three different castes—two of these were Brahmin leaders who had been a Sadhu and a Harijan leader. . . . The Brahmin convert had already started eating from the hands of the Harijan convert. If you know anything about untouchability, you will know this act by the Brahmin convert, which is simply the practice of community openness, as a more powerful message than any of us can preach. Because in this act millions of Harijans can see they have as much dignity as a Brahmin. This is community based evangelism." [16]

SEEDS OF JUSTICE

In my contacts with Third World Christians, I have discovered that most of them need no convincing that the pursuit of social justice is a primary part of the biblical mission of the church. In fact, Third World Christians are often much quicker to grasp the biblical demand for justice than are American missionaries who have been programmed to understand faith in purely personal terms. In spite of their reluctance to acknowledge justice as a goal of mission, the justice of God is steadily advancing in the Two-Thirds World.

Nicaraguan Christians frequently sing a song of the God of the poor . . . the God who joins them in their lives and struggle for justice:

"You are the God of the poor—the God human and sincere—The God who sweats in the streets—the God with face bronzed by the sun. And that is why I speak to you as do my people. Because you are the worker God . . . the laborer Christ—the God who works, the Christ who labors— you walk hand in hand with my people."

A Seed Planted in the Backwash of a Tidal Wave

In 1977 a violent tidal wave hit the East Coast of India, killing thousands of people, destroying croplands, and carrying not only many of the dead, but also houses, livestock, and implements away into the deep. In Andhra Pradesh Province virtually nothing was left. EFICOR (Evangelical Fellowship of India Committee on Relief) immediately moved in to help with relief and reconstruction.

EFICOR proclaims the good news to the poor in India: "To poor people Jesus brings the good news that the selfishness of others that keeps them poor can be overcome; that God the King who protects the poor has set up His reign of justice through Jesus, that a new people of God has been created who share God's concern for the poor, that God Himself will provide for their total human needs, and that both now and when Jesus returns, God is at work to fill the hungry with good things. To the rich, the gospel is a challenge to forsake seeking security in their wealth, to repent of oppressing the poor, to share their wealth with the poor, to seek to put into practice the justice of God's kingdom and trust God for their security." [17]

As EFICOR began, with resources donated by Western Christian agencies, to reconstruct sixty villages, the justice they profess as a goal began to be manifested in a very remarkable way. Villagers, many of whom had lost their entire families and all their possessions to the tidal wave, freely gave part of their land to villagers who had none, so that they could all start over again. That's just like the future of God—new beginnings for everyone.[18]

Planting a Seed at Gulf and Western

Gulf and Western is a monolithic American-based multinational corporation that produces an enormous range of products—everything from sugar and auto parts to the *Godfather* movies and the TV program, "Happy Days." But the late seventies were not "happy days" for workers in the Gulf and Western sugar plantations and factories in the Two-Thirds World. There was widespread evidence of exploitation and oppression of workers from the Dominican Republic and Haiti. The workers were actually making less than they made ten years earlier, before an astronomical rise in sugar prices.

One American Christian became very concerned regarding Gulf and Western's corporate policies in the Dominican Republic and decided to do something. Tony Campolo, a Christian sociologist, and ten members of the black church he attends bought eleven shares of Gulf and Western stock and went to the building where the next shareholders meeting was to be held. They didn't picket out front; instead, they entered the meeting and asked to see a corporate executive. They met with a vice president who happened to be an Episcopalian layman, and shared with him what they believed the Bible taught about justice and the treatment of the poor in relationship to the conditions of workers in the Dominican Republic.

Apparently, he was receptive to their concerns. Subsequently a meeting was set up between the executive management of Gulf and Western, the labor leaders who had been attempting to organize sugar workers, and church leaders concerned about the conditions of the workers.

It is important to realize that even one Christian who is concerned for justice for the poor is working with God and can make a much greater difference than he ever imagined. I am sure Tony Campolo is still amazed at the way God used him to speak for those who had no voice. But Christians working together can accomplish even greater results. After two years of lobbying for those who had no advocates in the Third World, the United Church of Christ, the Disciples of Christ and the Passionists won an important victory. They influenced Castle and Cooke, another United States-based corporation, to issue a set of corporate principles that has major implications for poor in all regions where the corporation does business.

Essentially, the statement of principles establishes a responsible labor policy. "The statement commits the company to respect human economic rights, to maintain levels of wages, benefits and working conditions that provide a decent standard of living and to recognize collective bargaining with representatives chosen by the employees." [19]

The struggle is by no means over for economic justice for the poor employed by multinationals in the Southern Hemisphere. However, people of faith have clearly demonstrated that with God it is even possible to see major corporations change to bring justice for the poor.

A Seed Planted in Battlefield in Bangladesh

It all began with a dream—the dream of a Bengali Christian named Paul Muncie. He looked out on the barren battlefield of the Pakistani-Bangladesh war of 1971, and he saw beyond the barrenness and the scarred countryside.

Virtually all the peasants had fled this region. When they returned, their homes and cattle had been destroyed; they had nothing with which to start over. Others had even taken possession of their land and they had to re-buy it.

Paul's was a dream of economic justice. He wanted to see the low-caste peasants begin farmer-controlled cooperatives and gain control over their own lives for the very first time. He envisioned fifty-acre co-ops in which people who had more than one acre would sell to those who had less. The people were open to any proposal that would enable them to farm their land again. They provided the willingness and the World Relief Commission provided the start-up money.

The historic exploitation of the landless poor by the wealthy landowners posed a particularly difficult challenge to Paul's dream of economic justice—since so many of the refugees were landless. Under the existing system they were forced to give 60 percent of their crops to the landowner, keeping only 40 percent. Actually, they wound up giving the landowner an additional 20 percent to pay him back for the input of seed and fertilizer. The sharecroppers could hardly subsist on 20 percent and their children often suffered from malnutrition.

Paul organized the sharecroppers, and the leaders of the organization told the landowners that from now on they would only receive 25 percent of the crops; the sharecroppers would receive 75 percent for their labor or they wouldn't work their lands anymore. The landowners immediately retaliated with angry threats. But when they realized the possible consequences of the boycott the landowners caved in. The shareholders were amazed by their victory. That was the first time they discovered there was power in cooperative action and common purpose.

After the co-ops were established, the people were anxious to begin working the land again. The next hurdle was clearing the land of the high grass that had grown up since the war. Fred Gregory, the World Relief Commission representative to the project, offered to buy every mat the women made from the grass. The land was cleared with amazing speed, and World Relief Commission wound up with fifteen thousand grass mats, which they in turn sold to the United Nations to serve as sleeping mats for refugees in the Bihari camps. They actually made two thousand dollars on the sale, which was invested back in the cooperatives. That was the second time people saw common action work to their benefit.

Farmers bought their seed and fertilizers from their co-ops, and used the profits to buy a low-level lift water pump. The pump enabled every farmer to grow a second crop of high-yield rice. For the third time they discovered the power of cooperative action. Of course, enormous time was spent in teaching farmers how to participate in co-ops. But at the end of three years these farmers were actually going to other regions of Bangladesh and teaching others cooperative farming.

The outcome of this venture even exceeded Paul's dreams for this band of displaced low-caste refugees. They used the money in their co-ops to start schools for their children. They established a community welfare program for people whose relatives had been killed in the war. In 1978 the cooperatives bought four hundred boats and taught hundreds of the landless poor to become fishermen; then they used the rental money from the boats to more than replenish their investment. They also set up a rice milling operation so they could get a larger share of the profit from their crops and avoid giving it over to a middleman. A bus and barge transportation system was added to their self-reliant community.

After the second crop nineteen people from the co-ops ran for the first time in an election for local office, and they all won. The people on the bottom rung of Bangladesh society had for the first time not only achieved a remarkable level of economic justice but an unexpected level of self-reliance and personal dignity—all because a Bengali Christian had a dream and American Christians shared their resources.

SEEDS OF PEACE AND RECONCILIATION

Western missions have been even more reluctant to deal with the biblical message of peacemaking and reconciliation than they have with the cause of justice. Too often we have looked away as those in the Third World have suffered from violence—violence from structures as well as persons, and frequently from structures that we directly and indirectly support. Many Christians are learning that political neutrality in this area is not a possibility. Our silence in the face of the destruction of other human beings makes us accomplices. Fortunately, not all Christians are afraid to stand up to violence . . . or to work for peace.

A Seed Planted in a Farmer's Grave

"Give me your donkey," the Haitian magistrate demanded of the farmer. The farmer drew his animal away. The magistrate shouted his order again as he drew his gun. The farmer stood there in silence as the gun discharged. The magistrate walked home with a new donkey. When the act was discovered he was briefly put in jail, but his wealthy father secured his immediate release. He returned to his duties as magistrate as though nothing had happened.

The community was incensed; however, it had happened before. This time, Christian leaders of this community in northern Haiti decided they were going to put an end to this officially sanctioned violence. At great personal risk to themselves they began organizing the community to advocate the removal of the magistrate.

The entire community came together in a tremendous show of solidarity. They lobbied Haitian officials at the very highest levels of government. The magistrate and his wealthy father began a campaign of intimidation, but it was too late. The people were fed up by years of random violence and oppression by the wealthy in their community, and they took a stand without resorting to violence themselves.

After months of pressure the Haitian Government took unprecedented action and removed the magistrate from office. The community was completely overcome by their amazing victory. Life in this Haitian village is still not perfect, but the community has selected a new Christian magistrate and their stand has brought peace in this important area of their lives.

A Seed Planted Among Native Peoples, Land Claims, and Violence

In Colombia, many have participated in a conscious crusade to push native peoples off their lands through deception, intimidation and violence. Over the years the Indians have been treated as animals. They have been bought and sold as slaves, branded, and slaughtered. Now as land becomes more valuable, many other Colombians are willing to do anything to steal their land. The result has been bitterness and bloodshed.

"On February 7, 1977, the nephew of one of the major [Indian] spokespersons on land ownership in Colombia was assassinated. He had tried to reclaim the land that was given to him through his ancestor." [20]

Entire Indian settlements have been massacred. Not only have the courts been silent; even more tragically, missionaries in Colombia have looked the other way.

A Christian attorney in Colombia is struggling to change this situation. He has become a one-man crusade not only to stamp out violence towards the Indians but also to bring reconciliation between indigenous peoples and the offspring of the European immigrants. He has succeeded in securing full citizenship for native peoples—including protection of their civil rights. He has developed an interface between leaders of native peoples and government. And, belatedly, he has even gotten other Colombian Christians involved in securing peace and justice for native peoples. It is amazing what one believer can accomplish when he decides to seek God's kingdom first in the behalf of others.

SEEDS OF WHOLENESS AND LOVE

Most Christians concede that it is okay for Christians to act in loving ways toward those in need. And a growing number of evangelical Christians seem to feel it is probably within the bounds of acceptable practice to set up agriculture, nutrition, and community health programs to help the poor. In the face of the challenges of the next two decades there is need for a dramatic expansion of our minuscule efforts. Even so, it is important to note a few of the ways in which the love and wholeness of God is making a difference in a world of need today.

Sowing a Seed in a Pleasant Haitian Valley

"Pleasant" is the name of the valley in Southwest Haiti to which community leaders and the Haitian Baptist Church invited World Concern to help them establish a rural health program. From the inception it was decided to establish a health program the people in the valley could afford and control. Therefore, instead of bringing in a doctor or constructing an expensive clinic, another pathway was chosen. Three persons who had been dispensing drugs were identified in the valley.

Members of the project team trained them to diagnose and treat six of the most common illnesses in the valley—malaria, dysentery, worms, etc. The home of each became a rural health clinic out of which they also provided health education. Each of the health providers is trained in a specialty—such as maternal and infant care, family planning, or nutrition—which they use to teach people.

The cost of this system is within the reach of all residents. It is completely self-reliant and is coming under full community control— as a part of the ministry of the Haitian Church in the Plaisance Valley. People who have never seen a health provider during their entire life now have access to basic health care they can afford. It is a small step towards wholeness, but the people are proud of their rural health program, and it has become a model for other communities in Haiti and the Caribbean.

Sowing a Seed in Mainland China

The policeman hid just below the window taking notes on the Christians who were meeting inside in a home in rural China. He had been spying on them for weeks to report them to the government. During that time, he had heard them sing. He had heard them pray. And he had heard them spend hours reading and discussing the Scriptures. One day when he was nearing the end of his vigil he learned he had terminal cancer of the stomach. He was very depressed as he crouched beneath the window. Suddenly he heard them praying for the sick as he had a dozen times before, and he felt strangely drawn.

He got up slowly from his hiding place and walked awkwardly towards the front door of the small cottage. When they came to the door, he told them who he was and what he had been doing. He begged them to pray for him. The small group surrounded him as he knelt and, laying their hands on him, they prayed. God miraculously healed him in response to their prayers. Today the policeman is a member of this small branch of the church in China—a church of tremendous vitality and growth.

Sowing a Seed in Rural Kenya

Shadrack, a tall slender pastor in the Anglican Church in rural Kenya, heard God call him out of the pastorate. The voice said, "You have been using one day for me and six days to farm. I want you to use all your days to serve me." He heard God call him to use all his time to visit the homes and farms of people in his parish. So he started, visiting only Christian homes. Then one non-Christian asked, "Why are you bypassing us?" He visited that family and they became Christians.

Shadrack explained to an international group of Christians, "The Church commissioned me as a rural field worker." He said, "I serve the Lord Jesus Christ by serving people. You see, we come out of a colonial culture where there are masters and workers. . . . It is a good thing to come as a worker . . . so we ask each household, how can I work for you? We were able to work for many households in this area.

"Many children were dying. 'Why?' I asked myself. I see this child die of worms coming out of its nose and mouth. 'Is this child's death the will of God?' I asked. If we succeed in keeping children alive and help people improve their farms, then the rural area will have no vacancy signs. City people will bring their feet there . . . to fresh air, fresh food . . . leave the cities with smoke where people fight among themselves. The country is being changed and happy healthy children are playing . . . and we did it without outside resources. Now the bishops see the need for this type of rural field work. Other projects are starting in agriculture and health. The countryside is blossoming.

"We want to work in cooperation with Christians in other lands. An American made an alternative seed planter. I showed it to my man and asked if he could make a better one. He made a better planter in half the time. . . . If you come I will ask you what you can contribute and we will be partners. If you are a worker . . . you are a servant . . . people like to have servants."

In so many ways, through so many lives of "insignificant" people, so many small Christian communities, and so many modest projects, God is quietly changing his world and bringing his kingdom. The conspiracy of the insignificant Mustard Seed is quite literally transforming the world—even in the face of mounting darkness and suffering. This is an invitation to join brothers and sisters throughout the world in the adventure and a celebration of collaborating with God in changing his world. Only God knows what a difference your insignificant Mustard Seed can make in the conspiracy of his kingdom as we join hands with our brothers and sisters in the Two-Thirds World.

For Discussion and Action

1. In what ways have we in the Western church unwittingly been ambassadors of two gospels and advocates of two different systems of values? In what ways has this been harmful to the people of the Two-Thirds World and to our global Christian witness?

2. In what ways has the church in the Two-Thirds World begun to expand its capacity for mission?

3. Why is it important for us to begin working in genuine partnership with the church in the Two-Thirds World?

4. Why should American Christians seek to influence foreign policy in the Two-Thirds World? What are some ways an individual can bring this about?

5. How can we work together in common mission with the Third Church while learning from one another in our pluralism of biblical theologies?

6. What are the four principles suggested for innovative mission with the people of the South?

7. Assess what percentage of your personal income and church income is invested in direct mission to the poor, forgotten, and unreached peoples in the Third World.

8. Design a strategy through which your church could become more informed of general needs and enter into a partnering relationship with a church in the Southern Hemisphere. Find persons in your church who share your concern for the Two-Thirds World and present your proposal for partnering or other action to your church leadership.

9. List creative new ways you can become an advocate for the poor, forgotten, and unreached in our world through your lifestyle, your community of faith, and your influence with everyone from your friends and your denomination to the United States State Department.

10. As you conclude this book, list the specific ways you hear God inviting you to join the Mustard Seed Conspiracy in your: discipleship, lifestyle, vocation, Christian community, and ministry towards those in need. Share your list this week with Christian friends and ask them to hold you accountable to follow through on God's kingdom call on your life.

Epilogue:

The Beginning of the Conspiracy of the Insignificant

His rough, gnarled hands gently scooped dirt over the seed as the sun warmed the good earth. He walked several more steps, thrust his shepherd's staff into the ground, and planted another seed. Every day he spent all his daylight hours walking the barren hillsides of Provence planting seeds while his sheep grazed.

In 1913 the Provence region in southern France was a desolate area, denuded of trees because of overcutting and overintensive agriculture. Most of the wildlife was gone, water holes had dried up, and most of the inhabitants had given up on the area, too. But not the old shepherd. Every evening in his small cottage he sorted acorns, hazelnuts, and chestnuts for tomorrow's planting.

One day a young man happened on the shepherd and asked, "What in the world are you doing, anyway?" "Well, it is pretty obvious what I am doing: I'm planting trees." "But it will be years before these trees will do you any good!" "Yes, but some day they'll do somebody some good, and they'll help restore this dry land. I may never see it, but perhaps my children will."

Twenty years later the hiker returned to Provence. He was amazed to find the old shepherd still alive and still sorting nuts in his cottage. But he was even more amazed to see the countryside. The entire valley was covered with a beautiful natural forest of all kinds of trees. Life had returned to the barren valley. Wildlife had returned, and the farmers had come back to cultivate the soil again.

A delegation of the Chamber of Deputies from Paris came down to see the miraculous forest. They saw the entire region of Provence restored—its wild life, agriculture, and population. And they honored the man who brought the valley to life again.

The old shepherd had lived to see the seeds he planted transform an entire region. Not everyone may be so fortunate. But we should never underestimate the difference the insignificant can make. A seed or a life, planted in love, can bring surprising change. As you have seen in these pages, God is transforming the world through the conspiracy of the insignificant. In every place, time, and culture he is planting his seeds in this barren earth. And they are bringing new life, new hope, and a new beginning for his people and his world.

What is your Mustard Seed story? How is God acting through your life, Christian community, or church? Would you send us your story? We want to collect as many Mustard Seeds as possible to encourage other Christians throughout the world. Send your stories to: Tom Sine, Community for New Beginnings, P.O. Box 9123, Seattle, WA 98109.

Never has the church had more resources to invest in God's loving conspiracy! Sixty-nine million Americans profess personal faith in Jesus Christ.[1] Sixty-seven percent of Americans today are church members.[2] A recent Gallup study determined 44 percent of the public attend church frequently, and forty-five million Americans fourteen and older described themselves as "highly religious." [3]

What is the collective time, creativity and resources of this vast body of American Christians? What fraction of our time, talent and resources is invested in the work of the church? And what percentage of that resource is actually invested in mission to those in need outside the church—those who will be in even more critical need as we approach the year 2000?

The total amount of time and talent Christians have invested in the church can be estimated only by inference and personal experience. However, according to the 1980 Yearbook of American Churches, forty-two U.S. denominations reported a total contribution of $7,454,316,-525—or a depressingly small amount of $176.37 per member per year. Out of that amount, only 19.9 percent was given out by the church to minister to those in need.[4] In other words, only a tragically minuscule amount of our total resources is invested in mission to those in need outside the church.

What would happen if the sixty-nine million who profess to be Christian or the forty-five million who profess to be "highly religious" made the vast resources of our collective time, talents, homes, churches, Christian organizations, and communication networks fully available for the advancement of the future of God in a world of exploding need? I am convinced God by his power would set this world on its ear again and bring major global change through the reignited church of Jesus Christ.

Remember the first time God turned the world upside down? He did it with a small band of disciples and almost no resources except the power of God. We dare not underestimate what God can do with our small loaves and fishes if we give ourselves without reservation to his world-changing conspiracy. . . .

The point I am trying to make is simply this: We American Christians have seriously underestimated what God could do through his transnational body to change his world. American Christians are the wealthiest Christians in the history of the world and, as a result of an amazing coup by the powers of darkness, undoubtedly the most fatalistic. So many of us no longer believe we can make a difference. But thank God a growing number are joining hands with sisters and brothers all over this world. As we have seen in these pages, God is quietly moving through our lives to change his world. We have absolutely no idea of the difference he could make if we all gave him our lives and talents and resources.

Welcome to the celebration and adventure of the good news that God is redeeming his people and his world. The Mustard Seed Conspiracy begins with you and me. It begins by our learning to pay attention to the signals, anticipate tomorrow's challenges and be moved by others' pain. It begins by our categorically rejecting escapism, gradualism, and the cultural captivity of our faith—by recovering the compelling biblical imagery of the future of God and discovering in that imagery his intentions for today and his hope for tomorrow. It begins with a new, joyous celebration of life, relationships, and vocation, with making ourselves much more available to participate in the loving initiative of God. And it begins with community, incarnating the future of God in the lives of men and women. Finally, it begins with us—the people of God—devoting our lives to the mission of God, seeking righteousness, justice, peace, reconciliation, wholeness, and love in a world of exploding need.

In other words, it begins by realizing that God can use your Mustard Seed and mine to change his world.

Now it's up to us. Let's determine by the grace of Jesus Christ and the power of his Spirit to be individuals, families, Christian communities, and churches for others. Let's give him our broken, selfish lives, our self-serving, random organizations, our culturally conditioned value systems, and in repentance ask him to recreate them into the tools of his kingdom.

Begin by finding one or two other followers who share your seriousness for the kingdom initiative of God. Bond your lives together in desperate prayers and loving relationships. Discover how God wants you to be a part of his conspiracy in discipleship, lifestyle, vocation, and community. Incarnate by his power in your individual lives and your life together the presence of the celebrative future of God. Learn to wait and hear his voice calling you into the world. Then, as he leads you, seek to influence your church and your world for the kingdom.

I believe we are witnessing a widespread movement of believers who are no longer satisfied with a "business as usual" Christianity. They are determined to make a difference in their world, and are much more fully devoting their lives to the mission of the kingdom. West Hills Covenant Church in Portland, Oregon, is an expression of this movement. One hundred sixty to one hundred seventy-five of its members are involved in small home groups. The primary purpose of each group is to help each member become involved in a community of shared commitment and in at least one area of Christian ministry in Portland. They report that 60 percent of their membership have found their ministry vocation and are serving their community. The adventure is renewing their entire church and changing their community.

We have the opportunity to become a part of this movement! We have the opportunity to teach the world to sing and dance—to be Christmas, Easter, and the wedding feast of God, all at the same time, to those around us. We have the opportunity to draw the church much more fully into the Mustard Seed Conspiracy—in anticipation of that day when Christ returns and the celebration breaks out in its fullness.

Let's dare to dream with Christ the "impossible dreams" of what he can do through our Mustard Seeds to change his world as we look forward to that day. Let's constantly remind ourselves that the dream will overcome the darkness. His kingdom will come and his will be done on earth as it is in heaven. In that day he will disarm the principalities and powers of this world and make a public example of them and every knee will bow and every tongue confess that he is Lord . . . and he will reign with his people forever (Col. 2:15).

On August 5, 1898, as Christians stood at the threshold of another new century, Rev. George Hiram Geyer, my great-uncle, preached a sermon on "The Conquering Christ" to a Methodist camp meeting in Lancaster, Ohio. Let me share the conclusion of his message, since we affirm with him that it is only through the power of the risen, conquering Christ that God's conspiracy will win the day:

> Men build their walls against the ocean of God's power, they stand for a season, but the tide rises, the ocean has its way, and they are no more. . . . This is God's world. We need a vision of the Conquering Christ.

> "Of the increase of His government there shall be no end!" There may be apparent lapses. The storm drives great hollows in the smooth surface of the sea and builds high walls of angry water that threaten destruction, but the calm comes again and the sea is smooth. There may appear to our eyes to be lapses—there is no end!

> See the vision today of the conquering Christ. Lose not faith in the prophecy. "He shall not fail nor be discouraged, till He have set judgment [justice] in the earth; and the isles of the sea shall wait for His law." "The kingdoms of this world are to become the kingdoms of our Lord and of His Christ." [5]

As we join together in the Conspiracy of the Mustard Seed, we can be absolutely certain of one thing: as Handel so powerfully proclaimed, "The kindgdoms of this world have become the kingdoms of our Lord and of His Christ; and He shall reign forever and ever, King of Kings and Lord of Lords." As we approach the twenty-first century, our hope is in this conquering Christ and his unshakable kingdom!

Notes

CHAPTER 1

1. Jeremy Rifkin and Ted Howard, *The Emerging Order: God in an Age of Scarcity* (New York: G. P. Putnam's Sons, 1979).
2. Agustin B. Vencer, *1980 Annual Report* (Manila: Philippine Council of Evangelical Churches, 1980), p. 15.

CHAPTER 2

1. D. L. Meadows and D. H. Meadows, *The Limits to Growth: A Report for the Club of Rome's Project on the Predicament of Mankind* (New York: Universe Books, 1972).
2. Mihaljo Mesarovic and Eduard Pestel, *Mankind at the Turning Point* (New York: E. P. Dutton & Co., 1974), p. 1.
3. Robert Heilbroner, *An Inquiry into the Human Prospect* (New York: W. W. Norton & Co., 1975) and William Irwin Thompson, *Darkness and Scattered Light* (Garden City, N.Y.: Doubleday & Co., Anchor Press, 1978).
4. Lynn H. Miller, "UNCLOS: Scrambling for Sea Treasure," *The Humanist*, November/December 1979, pp. 12–13.
5. Heilbroner, *Inquiry into the Human Prospect*, pp. 47–48.
6. Jeremy Rifkin and Ted Howard, *The Emerging Order* (New York: G. P. Putnam's Sons, 1979), pp. 48–49.
7. Alvin Toffler, *The Third Wave* (New York: William Morrow & Co., 1980), p. 345.
8. Michael Parish, "Hoarding Heat to Save the Forest," *Next*, May/June 1980, p. 87.
9. David Hopcraft, "Natures Technology," *Mitchell Award Papers* (The Woodlands, Tex.: Third Biennial Woodlands Conference on Growth Policy, 1979), p. 2.
10. David Pimental et. al., "Land Degradation: Effects on Food and Energy Resources," *Science* 194 (8 October 1976):149.
11. "Is U.S. Paving Over Too Much Farmland?" *U.S. News & World Report*, 2 February 1981, p. 47.
12. Frances Moore Lappe, Joseph Collins, and Gary Fowler, *Food First* (Boston: Houghton Mifflin Co., 1977), p. 262.
13. Beverly Keene, *Export Cropping in Central America*, Background Paper no. 43 (Washington, D.C.: Bread for the World, January 1980), p. 2.
14. Lappe, Collins, and Fowler, *Food First*, p. 186.
15. Selwyn Enzer, Richard Drobnick, and Steven Alter, "Neither Feast nor Famine: World Food 20 Years On," *Food Policy*, February 1978, p. 12.
16. "Dear Mr. Harvey," *World Concern Update*, February 1980, p. 6.
17. Lappe, Collins, and Fowler, *Food First*, p. 6.
18. Michael Harrington, *The Vast Majority: A Journey to the World's Poor* (New York: Simon & Schuster, 1977), pp. 14–15.
19. "Exploitation of Children Documented in World Study," *Christian Science Monitor*, 19 December 1979, p. 15.
20. "Child Exploitation," *Parade*, 25 November 1979, p. 11.
21. Jim Wallis, *Agenda for Biblical People* (New York: Harper & Row Pubs., 1976), p. 85.
22. "His Name Is Niloy," *World Concern Update*, March 1980, p. 11.
23. Barbara Howell, *Women in Development*, Background Paper no. 29 (Washington, D.C.: Bread for the World, November 1978), p. 1.
24. George M. Anderson, "Going Blind in the Third World," *America*, 29 December 1979, p. 428.
25. United States Office of Technology Assessment, *Technology and Population* (Washington, D.C., 21 August 1978), p. 2.
26. "Brandt Sounds the Tocsin," *Time*, February 18, 1980, p. 69.
27. "Nations in Hock, Third World Debt Totalling $500 Billion May Pose Big Dangers," *Wall Street Journal*, 28 January 1981, p. 1.
28. "Global 2000: A Warning," *Agenda*, September 1980, p. 3.
29. Richard J. Barnet, *The Lean Years: Politics in the Age of Scarcity* (New York: Simon & Schuster, 1980), p. 309.
30. "Sidelines," *The Other Side*, February 1981, p. 8.
31. "Study Urges Crop Reform," *Christian Science Monitor*, 2 July 1979, p. 2.
32. Jan Tinbergen, coordinator, *Reshaping the International Order* (New York: E. P. Dutton & Co., 1976), p. 31.

33. "Hemisphere Trends," *America*, January 1979, p. 17.

34. Richard M. Harley, "Success. Cambodia has been saved from a holocaust by one of the greatest international aid efforts in history," *Christian Science Monitor*, 7 January 1981, p. 31.

35. Richard J. Barnet, "Multinationals and Development," in *Growth with Equity*, ed. Mary Evelyn Jegen and Charles K. Wilber (New York: Paulist Press, 1979), p. 149.

36. Tracy Early, "Nothing Has Changed at Nestle," *A. D.*, May 1980, p. 19.

37. Mark Dowie, "The Corporate Crime of the Century," *Mother Jones*, November 1979, pp. 23–25.

38. Herman Nickel, "The Corporation Haters," *Fortune*, 16 June 1980, pp. 132–136.

39. *An Evangelical Agenda: 1984 and Beyond*, ed. Billy Graham Center (Pasadena, Calif.: William Carey Library, 1979), p. 41.

40. Ruth Leger Sivard, *World Military and Social Expenditures*, Background Paper no. 21 (Washington, D.C.: Bread for the World, February 1978).

41. Cees Hamelink, *The Corporate Village* (Rome: IDOC International, 1977), pp. 135–137.

42. Larry Collins and Dominique LaPierre, *Freedom at Midnight* (New York: Simon & Schuster, 1975), p. 233.

43. Gottfried Oosterwal, "Mission in the Year 2000," *Mission Focus* 7, no. 2 (June 1979):27–28.

44. Toffler, *The Third Wave*, p. 345.

45. William Irwin Thompson, *Evil and World Order* (New York: Simon & Schuster, 1975), p. 81.

46. Wallis, *Agenda for Biblical People*, p. 64.

47. Edward C. Pentecost, *Reaching the Unreached: An Introductory Study on Developing an Overall Strategy for World Evangelization* (Pasadena, Calif.: William Carey Library, 1974), p. 5.

48. Waldron Scott, *Bring Forth Justice* (Grand Rapids, Mich.: Wm. B. Eerdmans Publishing Co., 1980), p. 20.

49. Robert McAfee Brown, "Other Eyes, Other Voices," *A. D.*, February 1980, pp. 31–32.

CHAPTER 3

1. Rufus E. Miles, *Awakening from the American Dream: The Social and Political Limits to Growth* (New York: Universe Books, 1977), p. 5.

2. Daniel Yankelovich and Bernard Lefkowitz, "The Public Debate on Growth: Preparing for Resolution," *Mitchell Award Papers* (The Woodlands, Tex.: Third Biennial Woodlands Conference on Growth Policy, 1979), p. 2.

3. Jan Tinbergen, coordinator, *Reshaping the International Order* (New York: E. P. Dutton & Co., 1976), p. 74.

4. "New Rules on Hazardous Waste Will Bring Out 'Shocking' Data," *Seattle Times*, 6 May 1980, p. 5.

5. Tom Sine, "Scenario on 1984" (report prepared for the Division of New Business Research, Weyerhaeuser Corporation, Federal Way, Washington, 1974), pp. 1–5.

6. David F. Salisbury, "Ten Years Later, Environmental Concern Part of U.S. Lifestyle," *Christian Science Monitor*, 22 April 1980, p. 6.

7. U.S. Department of Labor, *Employment and Training Report to the President* (Washington, D.C., 1978), p. 33.

8. Jeremy Rifkin and Ted Howard, *The Emerging Order* (New York: G. P. Putnam's Sons, 1979), p. 84.

9. "The Failure of Conventional Wisdom," *Sojourners*, January 1981, p. 14.

10. Steven R. Weisman, "A Drastic Reagan Program to Avoid 'Day of Reckoning,'" *Seattle Post Intelligencer*, 19 February 1981, p. 1.

11. Colman McCarthy, "Now Dollar and Poor Are Both 'Worthless,'" 4 September 1979.

12. David F. Salisbury, "Reducing High Energy Costs That Rob the Poor," *Christian Science Monitor*, 3 March 1980, p. 10.

13. Clayton Jones, "Sweeping Pension Reform Proposed by Panel," *Christian Science Monitor*, 3 March 1980, p. 3.

14. "Challenges of the '80's," *U.S. News & World Report*, 15 October 1979, p. 46.

15. James D. Williams, ed., *The State of Black America* (New York: National Urban League, 1980), p. 35.

16. "I Feel So Helpless, So Hopeless," *Time*, 16 June 1980, p. 23.

17. Williams, ed., *The State of Black America*, p. 39.

18. "I Feel So Helpless, So Hopeless," p. 23.

19. Mary Ellen Ayres, "Federal Indian Policy and Labor Statistics," *Monthly Labor Review*, U.S. Department of Labor, Bureau of Labor Statistics 101, no. 4 (April 1978):24.

20. Rifkin and Howard, *The Emerging Order*, p. 7.

21. Peter Steinfels, "What Neo-Conservatives Believe," *Social Policy*, May/June 1979, pp. 4–10.

22. Marjorie Jones, "Home: Mother Can't Stay if Aid Ends," *Seattle Times*, 14 February 1981, p. A–11.

23. "In Illinois: Festival of the Fed Up," *Time*, 5 November 1979, pp. 8–11.

24. Milton Friedman, *Free to Choose* (New York: Avon Books, 1980), p. xvi.

25. Harry C. Boyte, "Anatomy of a Citizens' Revolt," *Social Policy*, March/April 1980, p. 26.

26. Vernon Louviere, "How Special Interest Groups Use Their Power," *Nation's Business*, June 1980, p. 38.

27. Tim LaHaye, *Battle for the Mind* (Old Tappan, N.J.: Fleming Revell Co., 1980).

28. Kirkpatrick Sale, "There Is an Alternative: Human Scale," *Next*, May/June 1980, p. 44.

29. R. Buckminster Fuller, *Utopia or Oblivion: Prospect for Humanity* (New York: Bantam Books, 1969).

30. Alvin Toffler, *The Third Wave* (New York: William Morrow & Co., 1980), p. 156.

31. Joel Moses, "The Computer in the Home," *The Computer Age: A Twenty Year View*, ed. Michael L. Dertouzus and Joel Moses (Cambridge, Mass.: M.I.T. Press, 1979), pp. 3–20.

32. Christopher Swan, "People Talk Back to TV," *Christian Science Monitor*, August 1979, p. B12.

33. M. E. Price and J. Wicklein, *Cable T.V.: A Guide for Citizen Action* (Philadelphia: Pilgrim Press, 1972), pp. 17–28.

34. John S. DeMott, "Test-Tube Life: Reg. U.S. Pat. Off.," *Time*, 30 June 1980, p. 52.

35. Ibid.

36. Loren R. Graham, "Concerns about Science and Attempts to Regulate Inquiry," *Limits of Scientific Inquiry*, ed. Gerald Holton and Robert S. Morison (New York: W. W. Norton & Co., 1979), pp. 12–13.

37. Ted Howard and Jeremy Rifkin, *Who Should Play God* (New York: Dell Publishing Co., 1977), pp. 34–35.

38. Michael P. Hamilton, ed., *The New Genetics and the Future of Man* (Grand Rapids, Mich.: Wm. B. Eerdmans Publishing Co., 1972), p. 146.

39. F. M. Esfandiary, *Up-Wingers* (New York: Popular Library, 1973), pp. 177–183.

40. C. S. Lewis, *That Hideous Strength* (New York: Macmillan Publishing Co., 1965).

41. Lane Jennings, "Future Fun: Tomorrow's Sports and Games," *Futurist*, December 1979, pp. 418–429.

42. Charles D. Swann, "The Electronic Church," *A. D.*, October 1979, pp. 17–20

43. Toffler, *The Third Wave.*

CHAPTER 4

1. Donald W. Dayton, *Discovering an Evangelical Heritage* (New York: Harper & Row Pubs., 1976), p. 127.

2. Tom Sine, "Beyond Fatalism," *Radix*, January/February 1980, pp. 15–17.

3. Peter Arnett, "They're Armed and Angry," *Seattle Post Intelligencer*, 2 March 1981, p. A–12.

4. Monte L. Kline and W. P. Strube, Jr., *Eat, Drink and Be Ready* (Fort Worth, Tex.: Harvest Press, 1977), p. 166.

5. Walter Brueggeman, *The Prophetic Imagination* (Philadelphia: Fortress Press, 1978), p. 18.

6. Tom Sine, "Images of the Future in the American Past" (Ph.D. diss., University of Washington, 1978), pp. 236–243.

7. Ibid., pp. 313–331.

8. Merril D. Peterson, *The Jefferson Image in the American Mind* (New York: Oxford University Press, 1962), pp. 3–7.

9. Tom Sine, "Of Parking Places, Pencils and the Pursuit of Pleasure," *The Other Side*, March 1981, pp. 20–22.

10. Spencer Marsh, *God, Man and Archie Bunker* (New York: Bantam Books, 1976), p. 93.

11. Cynthia R. Schaible, "The Gospel of the Good Life," *Eternity*, February 1981, p. 21.

12. Ibid., pp. 21, 26.

13. Richard A. Easterlin, "Does Money Buy Happiness?" *The Public Interest*, Winter 1973, p. 10.

14. Robert Cole, "Our Self-Centered Children—Heirs of the 'Me' Decade," *U.S. News & World Report*, 15 February 1981, p. 80.

15. Erma Bombeck, *The Grass Is Always Greener Over the Septic Tank* (New York: Fawcett Book Group, Crest Books, 1977), pp. 254–255.

16. William Irwin Thompson, *Darkness and Scattered Light* (Garden City, N.Y.: Doubleday & Co., Anchor Press, 1978), p. 67.

17. John White, *The Golden Cow: Materialism in the Twentieth Century Church* (Downers Grove, Ill.: Inter-Varsity Press, 1979), p. 38.

18. Willis W. Harman, *An Incomplete Guide to the Future* (Stanford: Stanford Alumni Association, 1976), p. 25.

19. Daniel Yankelovich and Bernard Lefkowitz, "The Public Debate on Growth Toward Resolution," *Through the Eighties: Thinking Globally, Acting Locally*, ed. Frank Feather (Washington, D.C.: World Future Society, 1980), p. 286.

20. Christopher Lasch, *The Culture of Narcissism: American Life in an Age of Diminishing Expectations* (New York: Warner Books, 1979), pp. 21, 43.

21. Marilyn Ferguson, *The Aquarian Conspiracy* (New York: St. Martin's Press, 1980).

22. Robert J. Ringer, *Restoring the American Dream* (New York: Fawcett Book Group, Crest Books, 1979), p. 316.

23. Ibid.

24. Brueggemann, *The Prophetic Imagination*, p. 11.

25. Ivan Illich, *Deschooling Society* (New York: Harper & Row Pubs., 1971).

26. Peter Marshall and David Manuel, *The Light and the Glory* (Old Tappan, N.J.: Fleming H. Revell Co., 1977).

27. Jim Wallis, *Agenda for Biblical People* (New York: Harper & Row Pubs., 1976).

28. Virginia Stem Owens, *The Total Image: Or Selling Jesus in the Modern Age* (Grand Rapids: Wm. B. Eerdmans Publishing Co., 1980), pp. 25, 55.

29. Wallis, *Agenda for Biblical People*, p. 2.

CHAPTER 5

1. Tom Sine, "A Biblical Theology of Development" (paper prepared for World Concern, Seattle, Washington, 1979), pp. 2–15.

2. Susan Baldauf, "The Mission of the People of God: Coherent Incarnation," (term paper submitted as part of course work at Fuller Theological Seminary, Pasadena, California, October 1979), pp. 1–5.

3. John Bright, *The Kingdom of God* (Nashville: Abingdon Press, 1953), p. 30.

4. Ibid.

5. Ronald J. Sider, *Rich Christians in an Age of Hunger, A Biblical Study* (Downers Grove, Ill.: Inter-Varsity Press, 1977), pp. 62–63.

6. Bright, *The Kingdom of God*, p. 67.

7. Donald B. Kraybill, *The Upside Down Kingdom* (Scottdale, Penn.: Herald Press, 1978), pp. 22–23.

8. John Howard Yoder, *The Politics of Jesus* (Grand Rapids, Mich.: Wm. B. Eerdmans Publishing Co., 1972).

9. Ted Peters, *Futures: Human and Divine* (Atlanta: John Knox Press, 1978), p. 163.

10. Eugene Lemcio, "The Servant as Priest and Advocate" (in-house study done for administration and faculty at Seattle Pacific University, Seattle, Washington, 14 September 1979), p. 3.

11. Carl E. Braaten, *Eschatology and Ethics* (Minneapolis: Augsburg Publishing House, 1974), p. 114.

12. Bright, *The Kingdom of God*, p. 218.

13. Orlando E. Costas, *The Integrity of Mission: The Inner Life and Outreach of the Church* (San Francisco: Harper & Row Pubs., 1979), p. 7.

14. George Eldon Ladd, *The Presence of the Future* (Grand Rapids, Mich.: Wm. B. Eerdmans Publishing Co., 1974), pp. 229–240.

15. Bright, *The Kingdom of God*, p. 221.

16. Peters, *Futures: Human and Divine*, p. 65.

17. John Shea, *Stories of God: An Unauthorized Biography* (Chicago: Thomas More Press, 1978), p. 98.

18. Christopher Sugden, *Social Gospel or No Gospel?* (Nottingham, England: Grove Books, 1977), p. 13.

CHAPTER 6

1. John Alexander, "Why We Must Ignore Jesus," *The Other Side*, October 1977, p. 8.

2. E. Stanley Jones, *The Unshakable Kingdom and the Unchangeable Person* (New York: Abingdon Press, 1972), p. 102.

3. Wallis, *Agenda for Biblical People* (New York: Harper & Row Pubs., 1976), p. 30.

4. Richard Foster, *Celebration of Discipline: The Path to Spiritual Growth* (New York: Harper & Row Pubs., 1978), p. 77.

5. Ibid.

6. Henri Nouwen, "The Desert Counsel to Flee the World," *Sojourners*, June 1980, p. 18.

7. C. S. Lewis, *Out of the Silent Planet* (New York: Macmillan Publishing Co., 1965); *Perelandra* (New York: Macmillan Publishing Co., 1968); *That Hideous Strength* (New York: Macmillan Publishing Co., 1965). Also available as a boxed set (New York: Macmillan Publishing Co., 1975).

8. Foster, *Celebration of Discipline*, p. 25.

9. John V. Taylor, *Enough Is Enough* (Minneapolis, Minn.: Augsburg Publishing House, 1977), p. 41.

10. Jones, *The Unshakable Kingdom*, p. 54.

11. Doris Janzen Longacre, *Living More with Less* (Scottdale, Penn.: Herald Press, 1980), p. 54.

12. Thornton Wilder, *Three Plays: Our Town, The Skin of Our Teeth, The Matchmaker* (New York: Harper & Row Pubs., 1957), p. 100.

13. Frank E. Gaebelein, "Old Testament Foundations for Living More Simply," *Living More Simply*, ed. Ronald J. Sider (Downers Grove, Ill.: Inter-Varsity Press, 1980), p. 27.

14. An Evangelical Commitment to Simple Lifestyle" (report of conference on simple lifestyle sponsored by Unit on Ethics and Society, World Evangelical Fellowship, in London, England, March 1980), pp. 1–2.

15. Foster, *Celebration of Discipline*, p. 75.

16. Ronald J. Sider, *Rich Christians in an Age of Hunger, A Biblical Study* (Downers Grove, Ill.: Inter-Varsity Press, 1978) and Ronald J. Sider, ed., *Living More Simply* (Downers Grove, Ill.: Inter-Varsity Press, 1980).

17. Doris Longacre, *More-With-Less Cookbook* (Scottdale, Penn.: Herald Press, 1976); Frances Moore Lappe, *Diet for a Small Planet*, rev. ed. (New York: Ballantine Books, 1975); Ellen B. Ewald, *Recipes for a Small Planet* (New York: Ballantine Books, 1975).

18. *Alternative Celebrations Catalogue*, 4th ed. (Jackson, Miss.: Alternatives, 1978); Doris Longacre, *Living More With Less* (Scottdale, Penn.: Herald Press, 1980).

CHAPTER 7

1. Barbara Brown Zikmund, "Christian Vocation in Context," *Theology Today*, October 1979, p. 330.

2. John Alexander, "Kingdom World," *The Other Side*, August 1979, p. 12.

3. Elizabeth O'Connor, *Eighth Day of Creation: Gifts and Creativity* (Waco, Tex.: Word Books, 1979), p. 76.

4. M. Blaine Smith, *Knowing God's Will* (Downers Grove, Ill.: Inter-Varsity Press, 1979).

5. John Perkins, *A Quiet Revolution* (Waco, Tex.: Word Books, 1976), pp. 33–34.

6. O'Connor, *Eighth Day of Creation,* p. 15.

7. Ibid., p. 17.

8. Richard Foster, *Celebration of Discipline: The Path to Spiritual Growth* (New York: Harper & Row Pubs., 1978), p. 152.

9. "Crucifixion and the Art of Corporate Compromise," *The Other Side,* August 1979, pp. 16–24.

10. Eileen Frankenberg, "Lay Ministry in Cincinnati," *Theology Today,* October 1979, p. 412.

CHAPTER 8

1. Howard A. Snyder, *Community of the King* (Downers Grove, Ill.: Inter-Varsity Press, 1977), p. 12.

2. Jim Wallis, "Rebuilding the Church," *Sojourners,* January 1980.

3. Ronald J. Sider, *Rich Christians in an Age of Hunger, A Biblical Study* (Downers Grove, Ill.: Inter-Varsity Press, 1977), pp. 193–194.

4. Snyder, *Community of the King,* p. 69.

5. Graham Pulkingham, "The Shape of the Church to Come, Part Four," *Sojourners,* December 1976, p. 11.

6. Elizabeth O'Connor, *Call to Commitment* (New York: Harper & Row Pubs., 1963), p. ix–54.

7. Dave Jackson, *Coming Together* (Minneapolis, Minn.: Bethany Fellowship, 1978), pp. 45–46.

8. Snyder, *Community of the King,* p. 69.

9. Avery Dulles, *Models of the Church* (Garden City, N.Y.: Doubleday & Co., Image Books, 1978), p. 126.

10. Jean Vanier, *Community and Growth: Our Pilgrimage Together* (New York: Paulist Press, 1979), p. 5.

11. Elizabeth O'Connor, *Eighth Day of Creation: Gifts and Creativity* (Waco, Tex.: Word Books, 1979), p. 28.

12. Vanier, *Community and Growth,* p. 199.

13. Ibid., 125.

14. David Prior, *A Vision for the Local Church* (Cape Town, South Africa: Division of Evangelism, Council of Churches, 1976), p. 4.

15. Vanier, *Community and Growth,* p. 106.

16. John R. W. Stott, *Christian Counter-Culture: The Message of the Sermon on the Mount* (Downers Grove, Ill.: Inter-Varsity Press, 1978), p. 10.

17. Jim Wallis, "Rebuilding the Church," *Sojourners,* January 1980, p. 11.

18. Sider, *Rich Christians in an Age of Hunger,* p. 189.

19. Snyder, *Community of the King,* p. 111.

20. Jackson, *Coming Together,* p. 107.

21. Don Williams, *The Apostle Paul and Women in the Church* (Glendale, Calif.: Regal Books, 1979), p. 138.

22. Dulles, *Models of the Church,* pp. 98–100.

23. Ibid., p. 100.

24. Adam Daniel Finnerty, *No More Plastic Jesus* (Maryknoll, N.Y.: Orbis Books, 1977), pp. 143–144, 152.

25. Paul Brandt and Phillip Yancey, "Fat Cells in the Body: Issues of Loyalty," *Christianity Today,* 10 October 1980, pp. 44–45.

26. Finnerty, *No More Plastic Jesus,* p. 173.

27. Sider, *Rich Christians in an Age of Hunger,* pp. 96–98.

28. Joe and Martha Peterson, "On the Road," *Community,* October 1980, pp. 1–4.

CHAPTER 9

1. Sheldon Vanauken, *A Severe Mercy* (New York: Harper & Row Pubs., 1977).

2. Gabriel Fackre, *The Christian Story* (Grand Rapids, Mich.: Wm. B. Eerdmans Publishing Co., 1978), p. 149.

3. David J. Bosch, *Witness to the World: The Christian Mission in Theological Perspective* (London: Marshal, Morgan and Scott, 1980), p. 244.

4. Wes Michaelson, "Shaping Social Welfare Mission and Ministries in the '80's," *Church and Society,* March/April 1979, p. 50.

5. Avery Dulles, *Models of the Church* (Garden City, N.Y.: Doubleday and Co., Image Books, 1978), pp. 98–99.

6. John L. McKnight, *Future of Cities in an Urban Service Economy* (Chicago: Chicago Urban League, 1979), pp. 1–10.

7. William C. Scott and David K. Hart, *Organizational America* (New York: Houghton Mifflin Co., 1979).

8. Bruce Stokes, *Helping Ourselves: Local Solutions to Global Problems* (New York: W. W. Norton & Co., 1981).

9. Wesley Frensdorff, "Theologize but Indigenize Too," *The Witness* 63, no. 6 (June 1980):7.

10. "Pattaya, 1980, The Thailand Consultation on World Evangelization" *On Being* (Victoria, Australia), August 1980, pp. 16–17.

11. Brad Jordan, "Study of Change Within Christian Ministries That Are Serving the Poor" (paper submitted at end of a year-long special study at Seattle Pacific University, Seattle, Washington, 15 June 1979), pp. 24–25.

12. Charles W. Colson, *Life Sentence* (Lincoln, Va.: Chosen Books, 1980), p. 294–299.

13. Sergei Kourdakov, *The Persecutor* (Old Tappan, N.J.: Fleming H. Revell Co., Spire Books, 1973), pp. 219–220, 247–251.

14. "John Smith," *Tell* (Fusion, Australia)10, no. 1 (1980):1.

15. "John Smith," *On Being* 7, no. 2 (March 1980):6–7.

16. "John Smith," *Tell* 10, no. 1 (1980):1.

17. "Pattaya, 1980, The Thailand Consultation," pp. 16–17.

18. Ronald J. Sider, *Christ and Violence* (Scottdale, Penn.: Herald Press, 1979), p. 97.

19. Nathaniel Sheppard, Jr., "Chicago Bank Makes Money on Loans That Aid Deteriorating Neighborhood," *New York Times,* 30 July 1979, p. A10.

20. Stanley J. Hallet, "Critical Urban Trends" (speech given at the 1980 Congress on Urban Ministry in Chicago, Ill., 24–26 April, 1980).

21. Judith Barnard, "Money Matters," *Chicago Magazine,* February 1977.

22. Hallett, "Critical Urban Trends."

23. Gary Washburn, "Bold Parkway Plan Aims to Reclaim South Shore," *Chicago Tribune,* 17 February 1980, p. N14.

24. "The Shaftsbury Project: On Christian Involvement in Society" (brochure distributed by The Shaftsbury Project, Nottingham, England), p. 1.

25. *An Energy Covenant* (Springfield, Or.: St. Paul Center United Methodist Church, 1979–1980), pp. 1–3.

26. Wes Michaelson and Jim Wallis, "A Change of Heart: Billy Graham on the Nuclear Arms Race," *Sojourners,* August 1979, p. 12.

27. John K. Stoner, foreword to Ronald J. Sider, *Christ and Violence* (Scottdale, Penn.: Herald Press, 1979).

28. Christopher Sugden, *Social Gospel or No Gospel* (Nottingham, England: Grove Books, 1977), p. 6.

29. "Action Peace: Projects of Partnership in Healing the Wounds of History" (brochure distributed by Coventry Cathedral, Centre for Social and International Reconciliation, Coventry, England).

30. Carl F. H. Henry, *Evangelical Responsibility in Contemporary Theology* (Grand Rapids, Mich.: Wm. B. Eerdmans Publishing Co., 1957).

31. Henri Nouwen, *Reaching Out* (New York: Doubleday & Co., 1975), p. 64.

CHAPTER 10

1. Vinay Samuel, "Partnership: To Church Credibility in the Third World," mimeographed and distributed privately by Vinay Samuel, 1980.

2. Waldron Scott, *Bring Forth Justice: A Contemporary Perspective on Mission* (Grand Rapids, Mich.: Wm. B. Eerdmans Publishing Co., 1980), pp. 34–35.

3. Tom Sine, "Development, Its Secular Past and Its Uncertain Future," *Evangelical Review of Theology* 4, no. 2 (October 1980): 248–254.

4. Stephen Knapp, "Mission and Modernization: A Preliminary Critical Analysis of Contemporary Understandings of Mission from a 'Radical Evangelical' Perspective," *American Missions in Bicentennial Perspective,* ed. Pierce Beaver (Pasadena, Calif.: William Carey Library, 1977), pp. 164–165.

5. Scott, *Bring Forth Justice,* pp. 37–38.

6. Orlando E. Costas, *The Church and Its Mission: A Shattering Critique from the Third World* (Wheaton, Ill.: Tyndale House Pubs., 1974), pp. 284–285.

7. Vinay Samuel and Christopher Sugden, "An Overview of Literature on Theology of Development" (paper prepared for a conference on Theology of Development sponsored by the Unit on Ethics and Society of the World Evangelical Fellowship, London, England, March 1980), pp. 2–30.

8. Ibid.

9. Ibid.

10. Ibid.

11. Ibid.

12. Costas, *The Church and Its Mission,* p. 313.

13. Paulo Freire, *Pedagogy of the Oppressed* (New York: Herder & Herder, 1970).

14. C. Peter Wagner and Edward R. Dayton, eds., *Unreached Peoples '80* (Elgin, Ill.: David C. Cook Publishing Co., 1980), p. 8.

15. Vinay K. Samuel, *Reaching the Urban Poor* (Bangalore, India: Evangelical Fellowship of India Committee on Relief), p. 1.

16. Ruth Mangawaldi, "Lessons from Life," *Light of Life: Magazine of Christian Growth* (Bombay, India), February 1980, pp. 6–7.

17. Ronald Mathews, *Helping the Poor through Development in the Indian Context* (Bangalore, India: Evangelical Fellowship of India Committee on Relief, 1979).

18. Ibid.

19. Henry J. Frundt, "Corporations and Economic Human Rights" (brief distributed by Interfaith Center on Corporation Responsibility, 1979), p. 30.

20. Alfred P. Torres, "Evangelism or Conquest," *The Other Side*, May 1977, p. 54.

EPILOGUE

1. "The Christianity Today Gallup Poll: An Overview," *Christianity Today*, 21 December 1979, p. 14.

2. "Religious Personality of the Populace," *Christianity Today*, 21 December 1979, p. 16.

3. Ray Ruppert, "New National Study Shows Power of Religious Belief," *Seattle Times*, 31 March 1981.

4. Office of Research, Evaluation, and Planning, National Council of the Churches of Christ in the U.S.A., *American Yearbook of Churches* (Nashville: Abingdon Press, 1980), p. 237.

5. George Hiram Geyer, "The Conquering Christ," *In Memoriam George Hiram Geyer 1868–1900* (Columbus, Ohio: "A Friend," 1901), p. 136.